STUNT

John Baxter

Stunt

The Story of the Great Movie Stunt Men

Doubleday & Company, Inc.
Garden City, New York
1974

For James Broom-Lynne,
who will always land on his feet

Frontispiece picture shows Ben Johnson
in a superb backward horse fall
on Mighty Joe Young (1949)

ISBN: 0-385-06520-5

Library of Congress Catalog Card Number: 73-83614

Copyright © 1973 by John Baxter

First Edition in the United States of America 1974
First published in 1973 in the U.K. by Macdonald and Jane's

Printed in Great Britain

Contents

Acknowledgements

This book rests on the assistance of so many people that it would be impossible to name them all here, but foremost among them are James Broom-Lynne, who set the project in motion, and Richard Johnson, whose idea it was. The extensive research would not have been feasible without the help of the US Department of State, Natalie Henderson and Bob Baker of the American Embassy, London, and Mr J. S. Talbot. I owe a further debt of gratitude to those who provided me with material or helped in other ways, notably – in London – Barrie Pattison, Christopher Lee, Derek Ware, Ben Lyon, Douglas Fairbanks Jnr, Clive Donner, Anthony Sloman, Tristram Cary, Fred Zentner of the Cinema Bookshop, John Kobal, Troy Kennedy Martin, Tony Slide, Leon Boyle, Allen Eyles of *Focus On Film* magazine; in Australia, Ian Klava and the Australian Commonwealth Film Unit; in Washington, the American Film Institute, particularly Sam Kula, and John de Kuiper and Pat Sheehan of the Library of Congress; in Hollywood, Andrew Marton, Yakima Canutt, Carey Loftin, Edward Dmytryk, Hal Needham and Stunts Unlimited, Mrs John P. Fulton and Mrs Mary Lou Fulton, Janaire, Don Siegel, Colin Shindler, Mr and Mrs Forrest J. Ackerman, Joe Bonomo, Allan Dwan, Kirk Allyn, Linda Strawn, Jack Arnold, Kevin Brownlow, Universal Pictures, Cornel Wilde, Marian Nixon, David Chierichetti, Dave Sharpe, Clare Kitson, Mel L. Morse of the American Humane Society and the Humane Society of Marin County. For research facilities I am indebted to the staff of the Academy of Motion Picture Arts and Sciences and the American Film Institute in Hollywood, particularly to Mark Wanamaker of its Stills Archive, and, as all film scholars must be, to the Library, Information Department and Stills Archive of the British Film Institute, London. In addition I would like to thank the Radio Times Hulton Picture Library for permission to reproduce the photographs on pages 12, 13, 15 (top),

64 (top), 121, 122 and 306; likewise the Conway Picture Library for the photographs on pages 190–1 and 282.

Unless otherwise indicated, all the interviews in this book were conducted by myself in London, New York, Washington and Los Angeles between September 1971 and May 1972. Since it is the essence of the book that the people, wherever possible, tell their own story, I have supplemented these with quotations from memoirs or autobiographical articles. Superior numbers in the text refer to sources listed at the end of the book, but because attribution is difficult – obituaries, for instance, often quote the deceased but feel it irreverent to append a footnote giving their source, while the world's film research collections rest on an ocean of ragged clippings, fascinating in content but of clouded ancestry – some are not so annotated. For this I apologize.

I would also like to acknowledge the following sources: *An American Comedy* by Harold Lloyd and Wesley Stout (Longmans Green and Dover Publications), *Hollywood is the Place* by Charles Landery (Dent), *I Am Still Alive* by Dick Grace (Rand McNally), *The Strongman* by Joe Bonomo (Bonomo Studios), *Van Dyke and the Mythical City Hollywood* by Robert C. Cannom (Murray and Gee), *Jungle Performers* by Clyde Beatty and Earl Wilson (Robert Hale and Medill McBride), *The Celluloid Muse* by Charles Higham and Joel Greenberg (Angus and Robertson and Henry Regnery Co.)

John Baxter

1 Hypnotists and Drunken Indians

It is a morning in 1908 on the Pacific coast near Los Angeles, and three men are standing on the rocks at the end of a beach. The two fiddling with a varnished wooden box fitted to a tripod – perhaps a dozen people in California would recognize it as a motion picture camera – are film director Francis Boggs and his cameraman Thomas Persons, who doubles as editor, unit manager and assistant director. They have come from Chicago by train, stopping off to shoot footage of sagebrush and mountains for future films, a trip dictated by their boss, the irascible and ambitious producer William Selig, who has hopes of beating Thomas Edison at this motion picture game. Boggs's *The Count of Monte Cristo* had been all but completed when Selig decided it needed a realistic climax in which the count, escaping from the Château d'If, surfaces into the sunlight of freedom. Sunlight and scenic shores being absent from Lake Michigan, Boggs and Persons have been sent to California, where both are plentiful.

Los Angeles has made a poor impression. Hardly more than a large town of sad two-storey office buildings, it lacks everything Chicago has, including actors. Except for a few recuperating tuberculars, the best Persons has been able to dig up is a hungry hypnotist. As Persons adjusts a wig to cover the man's patent-leather hair, merely making him look more absurd, Boggs wonders if it is possible to sink lower in this already ill-favoured profession. Resignedly, he points out through the surf. 'I want you to swim out to the first line of breakers. When I say "Go", dive under, stay down as long as you can, then surface. Wave your arm in the air when you come up, and turn this way so we can see your face. Right?'

The man looks at Boggs, who is already turning to explain to Persons how he wants the shot to be taken, then at the surf, then at Boggs again. Concentrating on the promised $5, he wades

gingerly into the water and strikes out. They watch his head bob
beyond the line of surf, and Persons starts rhythmically turning
the handle of the camera, murmuring under his breath the 'One
two three *one* two three' of waltz time to keep the speed at a
steady sixteen frames a second. 'Down!' Boggs bawls at the
distant head, which abruptly disappears. They wait. '. . . *One* two
three *one* two three . . .' The head does not reappear. Half a minute
goes by. Still cranking, Persons looks inquiringly at the director.
'D'ya think . . .?' Boggs says nothing, but the flicker of anxiety in
his eyes is eloquent. Persons stops turning. 'Yeah,' he agrees as he
peels off his coat. 'That's a $20 wig.'

The hypnotist survived, and was the cinema's first stunt man.
The story is so typical of those still told about stunters – a life
risked for the combination of glamour and quick profit unique to
the movies, the callous director more concerned with shot than
safety, the shabby prop sustaining an illusion in which nobody is
expected to believe – that an eager historian may well have made
it up. Anecdotes over the years have more often obscured the
truth of the stunt business than illuminated it. Certainly stunt
men, who think mythology absurd, would be contemptuous of

rather than amused by Boggs's hypnotist – an amateur in a field where amateurs have less place than in any other.

Professional stunt men are mainly a phenomenon of the twenties. The hazardous scenes of early films were seldom performed by men with any degree of training; like the hypnotist, they attempted dangerous work for quick profit, with no thought of doing so regularly, or of adopting a professional's caution. Even when Mack Sennett formed his knockabout Keystone studio, the laboratory and university of early stunt technique, his comedians thought of their falls and crashes as part of 'eccentric comedy', and of themselves as performers who just happened to work in a risky part of the business. They would no more call themselves stunt men than an actor who strums the guitar in a play would call himself a professional musician. Stunting as we know it today, in which individuals study the physics of action and use their knowledge to survive, began with early epics like D. W. Griffith's monumental *Intolerance* (1916) whose scenes of Babylon under siege were the most realistic ever attempted. *Intolerance* produced the first legends of stunting, most of them attached, presumably apocryphally, to an Indian named Eagle Eye. Even in 1916 Eagle Eye had a face as creased and worn as an old tobacco pouch, and his efforts as part of 'Griffith's Mankillers', the mob of boxers, thugs and stunt men who defended Babylon's topless towers and whose spirit the director kept up with a stream of martial band music, soon drew even Griffith's admiration. In the midst of a skirmish, some say, a fall was dictated, and Eagle Eye called down his willingness to do it for $3 over his daily $5 fee. The assistant director agreed, Eagle Eye plummetted down to land in the film's sole safety device, a hay cart, only to be whisked away by the frightened horse and not seen for the rest of the day. The hard-drinking old man, Anita Loos claimed, was to do the fall again the next day, but announced that in the intervening twenty-four hours he had been converted to Christianity and signed the pledge. Sober, he explained, he would never do the stunts he had blithely done when intoxicated, and a minister had to be found who would grant a dispensation for one day. Rolling drunk, he toppled off in safety.

Stories like these, of reckless alcoholics who risked their lives daily, obscure the reality of the stunt man's life. Only a handful have been holy fools indifferent to danger, and they have seldom survived even the five years that is a stunt man's average profess-

Left *American stunting in 1915: Harris Gordon and John Lehnberg (falling) stage a chimney-top fight for* The Revenge of the Steeple-Jack

ional life. 'Stunting in the silent days meant walking on tigers' tails,' Kevin Brownlow says,[1] but the good stunt men knew about tigers and avoided them if they could. Those who escaped death, maiming, starvation or boredom in the first five years and went on to create careers for themselves were not daredevils but hard-thinking technicians who squeezed between the apparent danger of their situation and an infinitesimal margin of safety they built into it. In nine months of research I seldom met the handsome, picaresque stunt man of legend. The top stunter was more often a wispy little man in his sixties who, except for the flat-footed walk of the natural athlete and the stiffness of a half-century's sprains and fractures, could be a shop assistant. It is not their bodies that have saved these few top men from injury and death, but their brains.

It goes without saying that their brains are often odd, working to motivations most of us would find alien. There is no single reason why they practise this dangerous profession. It can't be the glory, since the film industry hides their identity and even their existence (even in the seventies, when a film's auditor and still photographer often receive screen credit, the stunt man is rarely

Below and right
Early European
directors used camera
trickery rather than
stunt men: on Le Bon
Ecraseur (1908) *a*
double amputee stood
in for an actor, with
convincing results

mentioned), nor the security or money; for all but the top men the business is absurdly unprofitable. When pressed, they offer reasons for taking up the stunt game – chance, glamour, failure as actors, inability to apply an obscure skill elsewhere – but never any for staying in it. 'Let's face it,' one told me confidentially, 'these people aren't very bright. You have to be bent to knock yourself about year after year for the money we get.' But he had been a stunt man since he was seventeen, and intended to remain one.

It is not with any thought of denigrating the many skilful stunt men of the European and Asian cinema that I have chosen in this book to deal mainly with the Hollywood stunt community, since those I have talked to agree that it is from the American stunt men that most of their techniques have been learned. Eagle Eye and the other Indians who came out of the rodeos in the early days of the century to try movies place the seal of nationality on an essen- tially American trade. Other countries have produced courageous stunt men and women, some of whom are discussed in a later chapter, but stunting belongs to the Hollywood action film, with its blend of fantasy and mechanical dexterity. The cowboy and the Wild West, the log-cabin-to-White-House legend of the presidency, the *Playboy* philosophy are pragmatic myths that give something to aim at and imitate, just as the Hollywood cinema, through publicity and the fan press, presented the stars not as remote luminaries but as heroes or heroines to be emulated. Douglas Fairbanks and Tom Mix proved that the cowboy and the sword-wielding historical hero were nice, ordinary guys, and Hollywood lent all its ability to sustaining the illusion of effortless dexterity.

Just as a complex system of make-up and photography was developed to make all female stars seem flawlessly beautiful – MGM had a so-called 'close-up director' whose job was to sit through every foot of film and ensure that no blemish slipped into a released picture – a sub-industry sprang up to purge the action film of visible discomfort and risk. Its members ranged from actors like Lon Chaney, submerging their personalities to embody the nightmares of mankind just as Fairbanks personified its dreams, through experts in a range of technical skills – process photography, make-up, horse and wild animal training, miniature making, the duplication of every violent effect from the gunshot to crashing a plane in flames – to the stunt men, a group who, though technically and industrially part of this society, remained

*Sources of stunting;
above* twenties
cowboy 'bulldogs' a
calf: below John
Epper, doubling Gary
Cooper, 'bulldogs' a
man in *The
Westerner (1939)*

aloof from it. The tiny Hollywood stunt community, which has hovered between one and two hundred since the First World War, remains isolated by its superstitions, emotional relationships and family ties. Stunt people are often the sons, daughters, husbands and wives of other stunt people, and the growth of teams around a top man, to whom the members pay respect and often a slice of their salary, is one of the field's most striking characteristics. But for all their cliquishness, stunt men are industrially part of the special effects trade, neither madmen nor suicides but technicians in a business to which they contribute an essential skill. Many began as 'property men', making or supplying furniture, weapons, vehicles and other accessories of film-making, and learning in the process how these are reconstructed for use in action films. These men often graduated to become second-unit directors, creating self-contained action sequences – charges, battles – to be slotted into a film later, or stunt coordinators – 'ramrods' in the traditional cowboy slang – who choreograph the brawls and mass horse stunts that are the building blocks of second-unit sequences.

The world's film industries have never acknowledged directly the existence or importance of stunt men, and the suffering and death behind the cinema has always been one of its best-kept secrets. Most accidents in film-making are trivial – by far the biggest cause is slipping on waxed floors – but the carnage is still substantial, and in the past was more so. It is said that more people died in Eisenstein's re-creation of the storming of the Winter Palace in *October* (1927) than were killed in the actual attack, and in the years 1925–30 10,794 people were injured in Californian film productions. Fifty-five of them, mostly stunt men and women, died. In 1929, at the height of the war film boom, sixteen men were killed, including three on Howard Hughes's *Hell's Angels*. Added to this is a record of cruelty to animals, and of wasted materials; cars, planes, buildings. No expense is too great for the authentic thrill of death and disaster, conveyed to a safe, cosy audience.

In the last decade, increasing callousness has destroyed the traditional secrecy. The death of a stunt flier in the thirties was usually hushed up, but when Paul Mantz was killed in 1965 the film *The Flight of the Phoenix* carried a title commemorating the fact. The 1966 award of an Oscar to Yakima Canutt, dean of stunt men, for four decades of anonymous service to the cinema, was a turning-point, and since then stunters have increasingly come into the light, talking about their work and their reasons for doing it, though for many this book provided the first opportunity to discuss their careers. Reactions to the growing interest are varied. Some stunt men reject it entirely. 'Could I talk to you about your days as a stunt man for Douglas Fairbanks?' a scholar asked Richard Talmadge. 'That was my father!' he snapped. Some embark on an endless recital of 'and then I broke' injury anecdotes, and others rail against the trade in a curious self-rejection. A few, usually the most talented, are baffled by sudden outside interest in a calling whose activities and motivations are totally personal. 'Why is it,' Dave Sharpe asked me with genuine puzzlement, 'that people suddenly want to know about stunt men? After all, we've been doing it, some of us, for thirty years.' One can only say to the implied reproach that it is *because* they have done it so well for those three decades that the illusion has rarely been explored, the myth dispelled. Now, with every aspect of the Hollywood cinema made more precious by its imminent dissolution, we can acknowledge the complexity of even this tiny segment, and record the courage, invention, stupidity and death that are its heritage.

2 Sennett's Psychopaths

The following morning I boarded a street car for Edendale, a suburb of Los Angeles. It was an anomalous looking place that could not make up its mind whether to be a humble residential district or a semi-industrial one. It had small lumber yards and junk yards, and abandoned looking small farms on which were built one or two shacky wooden stores that fronted the road. After many inquiries I found myself opposite the studio. It was a dilapidated affair with a green fence around it, 150 feet square. The entrance to it was up a garden path through an old bungalow – the whole place looked just as anomalous as Edendale itself. I stood gazing at it from the opposite side of the road, debating whether to go in or not. It was lunch time and I watched the men and women in their make-up come pouring out of the bungalow. They crossed the road to a small general store and came out eating sandwiches and hot dogs. Some called after each other in loud, raucous voices 'Hey, Hank, come on!' 'Tell Slim to hurry.' . . . Half an hour I stood there, then I decided to go back to the hotel.[2]

The man was Charlie Chaplin, the studio Keystone, and the 'loud, raucous voices' those of Mack Sennett's Keystone Kops. In December 1913 the kops had just made their debut in *The Bangville Police* and Keystone, although its violent comedy style had a national following, was less than two years old. Chaplin returned and within a year became its top comic, only to leave when Sennett, always contemptuous of the star system, refused to raise his salary above $175 a week. Although Keystoners like Slim Summerville and Hank Mann recognized the genius of 'Edgar English' as they derisively called the fastidious Chaplin, they knew, as he did, that he had no place in their piratical society. Most Sennett comedians had been circus clowns or, like Chaplin, vaudeville artists, but of the roughest and least elevated kind. 'Don't fall for this mystique of the circus clown,' one ex-clown stunt man said. 'There are some great clowns in the circus, but for most men it's just the next step up from selling popcorn or mucking out the animals.' Chaplin soon found that even the Fred Karno troupe had more finesse than Keystone.

Sennett took me aside and explained their method of working. 'We have no scenario. We get an idea then follow the natural sequence of events until it leads to a chase, which is the essence of our comedy.' This method was edifying, but personally I hated a chase. It dissipates one's personality . . .[3]

One can visualize the reaction to his remarks in the noisy dressing room – it had been a barn – as ex-prize fighters, acrobats and circus roustabouts made up for the day's stunts and falls. The Keystone gang, like their boss, were hell on philosophy. If they had a *raison d'être*, it was the simple truth on which Sennett based all his work: 'The joke of life is the fall of dignity.'

Sennett's early life – before going on the stage the young Canadian-Irish Michael Sinnott had been a boilermaker – froze him in a posture of truculent contempt for formality and regimentation. In vaudeville and later as a comedian with D. W. Griffith's Biograph two-reeler team between 1908 and 1911, Sennett was notable mainly for his solid physique and delight in destruction. 'Mack knew how, but he didn't know why,' comedy producer Hal Roach said. 'He knew how to do slapstick but he never knew why he did it. It was instinct with Mack.'[4] Perhaps it was because Sennett knocked out Griffith's wife Linda Arvidson while playing a distracted Frenchman in *The Curtain Pole* (1908) where he wove through a quiet community with a new curtain rod, scything down pedestrians and wrecking everything in sight, that the director consistently refused to shoot his scenario about a group of comic policemen; although Biograph made him a director he was stifled by the studio's increasingly stage-bound style. In 1911 he convinced the New York Motion Picture Company, a thin alias adopted by ex-bookies Adam Kessel and Charles Bauman when new Californian betting laws put them out of business, that he could produce and direct a new and popular kind of comedy film, amusing to even the simplest audience.

Sennett's basic team was ex-model Mabel Normand, his leading lady and girlfriend, vaudeville veteran Fred Mace, and a cameraman named Henry Lehrman whose subterfuge to break into Biograph, claiming to have experience in the French cinema, earned him the nickname 'Pathé'. Accepted by Griffith as an extra in one

of his period pictures, he leaped spectacularly from the roof of a
burning building and, when Griffith protested that he had rolled
out of shot, repeated the feat. Sennett marked the short, agile
Austrian as an ideal collaborator. The team grew with Keystone's
popularity. Sennett's first star was Ford Sterling, an ex-circus
clown and tumbler. He was joined by Hank Mann, a steeplejack/
sign-painter who turned acrobat until the Sullivan–Considine
vaudeville chain collapsed, stranding him in Los Angeles. Al St
John, one of the best acrobats in silent comedy, joined the company, along with his uncle Roscoe 'Fatty' Arbuckle, a graduate
from vaudeville 'eccentric comedy'. Later they were joined by
Chester Conklin, Georgie Jesky, Mack Riley, Charlie Avery,
Edgar Kennedy and Bobby Dunn, most of whom came from the
circus. The ranks were further swelled in 1914 when California
banned professional prize fighting and Sennett hired Al McNeil, a
bantamweight who drifted to Keystone as stunt man, along with
racing driver Del Lord. McNeil became Sennett's editor and
assistant, Lord a courageous stunt driver and director. They were
pivots of the Keystone style.

Jesky, Riley, Avery, Kennedy, Summerville, Dunn and Mann

Left *Wagon with
Kops in tow from a
twenties Sennett
comedy (a layer of
sand is the sole safety
precaution)*

made up the original Keystone Kops, with Ford Sterling as their captain. Sennett had thought of the idea as a Biograph assistant director when, sent to outfit a group of policemen, he found another crew had taken the new costumes, leaving only old, baggy uniforms that looked hilarious. Del Lord designed an eight-foot high 'kop wagon', capable of carrying fifteen men, its heavy chassis and special brakes allowing apparently impossible stunts. The wagon, trailing kops like a string of sausages, roared around the suburbs of Los Angeles, weaving with apparent ease among telephone poles or speeding trains – undercranking and McNeil's editing achieved some remarkable effects – or throwing horrific skids, usually at the corner of 8th Street and Figueroa, where a barrel of liquid soap could be spread on the road to improve the effect. Later, more complicated cars were built which fell apart when vital pins were pulled, or emerged from crashes twisted into fantastic shapes. Del Lord relished the Keystone adventures. His first stunt had been to drive a car off a cliff, and shortly afterwards he raced another off the end of Venice pier, a popular Keystone location, at forty miles an hour. His bravado on top of the Detweiler building in downtown Los Angeles so impressed photographer Fred Jackman that he made him his assistant, but even when Lord had become a director he insisted on driving the kop wagon in all its chases.

Sennett ran a tough studio, building a tower office block to keep an eye on all its stages, and sacking writers who proved lazy or argumentative. One he dismissed during the twenties was Frank Capra, who was rehired after he had waited penitently by the studio gates for two days dressed as a tramp. In 1929 *Photoplay* nostalgically recalled what must have been an abrasive working milieu:

Gloria Swanson, never dreaming she would one day become a marquise, lived in a humble dwelling across the street. In private life she was Mrs Wallace Beery. . . . Louise Fazenda was earning $40 a week; some got less. Through the now-sagging gates these famous players used to leave on location trips to Venice or Santa Monica. They sat in the back of the disreputable studio car with Pepper, the cat, Teddy, the Great Dane, and the famous Sennett baby; piled atop all of them were numerous dummies. All the contract players reported at the studios every day whether they were working or not. Scenarios were written on the cuff as the picture progressed.[5]

The Sennett menagerie also included at various times a horse called Butterfly, star of a series of stunt comedies where its rider urged it off sloping roofs or into pools of mud, a variety of dogs, including the piebald Cameo, who could smoke cigars and drink gin, various Great Danes, indispensable as comic props, an elephant, a giraffe, and countless lions, which came to have the same comic connotations to Sennett as policemen. Pathé Lehrman broke away from Keystone in 1914, and in 1917 founded his own Sunshine Comedies whose humour depended almost entirely on lions pursuing terrified Negroes through studio jungles. He created his own animal star, a lion called Old Friday, which appeared regularly, but even Sennett did not care for his colleague's gamy style.

Keystone was a laboratory in which the techniques and terminology of stunt comedy were developed. Falls were 'bumps' or 'Brodies', called after Steve Brodie, who jumped from the Brooklyn Bridge and lived. The comic fall backwards, a Ben Turpin speciality, was known for no logical reason as a '108'. Even today stunt men still call any feat, from comic fall to a multiple car smash, a 'gag'. For weapons, the property men made bricks from felt, or cast bottles from thin plaster of paris and, later, resin. Roscoe Arbuckle is credited with thinking to use a pie, precursor of a later fusillade. (For many years real cream pies were used, but the advent of closed studios made the smell of sour cream impossible to disperse. Shaving foam replaced it.) Set artists became adept in constructing balsa-wood 'breakaway' furniture which disintegrated dramatically but harmlessly on a victim's head, and in building sets which a car could photogenically demolish.

Sennett, though jealous of his comedians and anxious to approve every routine before it was used, allowed his better men a degree of autonomy. Harold Lloyd, briefly at Keystone before his career took off, found the competition nerve-racking.

Once or twice I worked with Fatty Arbuckle, with little success. Arbuckle had the star 'bumpers' of the lot and he led them in person, taking Brodies that shook buildings. I could bump with any of them, but he surrounded himself with a group of regulars who knew his methods so well that they did not need to be told what to do, and weren't, leaving a new man to flounder. As I was on the point of looking elsewhere, they tried me out as an Italian fruit cart vendor. . . . The action called for a motor cycle to rip through my fruit cart and for me to take a comedy fall in the midst of the fruit. . . . The cart was a breakaway, built in two sections. It burst asunder as the motor cycle charged through, the fruit erupted and I leaped into the air and came down on the back of my neck among oranges and bananas to the critical approval of the director. I was one of them.[6]

Keystone had an atmosphere of sardonic sadism, reflecting Sennett's own personality. He loved boxing; he and his stars often acted as seconds at the popular amateur bouts around Los Angeles, and his most constant attendant was his masseur, a Negro ex-wrestler named Abdul Maljan. All the studios at which stunt men worked had practical jokes, but those of Keystone were exceptional. A favourite was to link an electric battery to the staff urinal, and there was generally an electrically wired chair somewhere around. The weekly rise and fall of Sennett's favourite gagman or comedian was watched with interest, and the boss reciprocated with deep suspicion of his staff. On one occasion he hired a man to spy on director Fred Fishbeck, some of whose gags had turned up in the films of a rival studio. While Al McNeil (then an assistant director) was setting a black powder charge under a tree so that it would blow up when a car hit it, the spy, investigating the place some yards away where he had placed the detonator, triggered the charge as McNeil was bending over it. He lost most of his hair and was blind for nine days.

Sennett's autobiography shows something like relish at the risks his actors ran.

Of all the funny men I had on and off the payroll . . . Hank Mann was the toughest. He stayed with me for eight years and worked up to $135 a week, for which he would perform any foolish stunt my psychopaths in the writing room could think up. Once when Hank was working with Arbuckle and Al St John in a sky-line chase sequence (we had a private sky-line along a ridge in the Glendale hills which stood in for sky-scrapers, airplane scenes and cliffhanging frighteners) he was supposed to be yanked out of the driver's seat of a wagon and spread-eagled on the landscape. Al St John was to jerk the pin from the single-tree and the horses were to pull Hank Mann off the wagon. St John had trouble with the pin, sweating and bawling. This delayed the action until the horses had picked up too much speed for such a stunt. When Al did get the pin out, the horses cut loose like runaway ghosts and snatched Mr Mann thirty feet through the air like a kite. . . . (Later) when Wilfred Lucas was directing a chase sequence on top of a three-storey building in downtown Los Angeles, he had seven of the Keystone Kops set to run along the roof forty-five feet above the pavement. Whenever we could,

we arranged safety devices to keep our boys from committing suicide. . . .
For this roof scene we had a protective railing out of camera range around
the roof. Hank Mann ran across the safety railing.[7]

Keystoners took immense punishment in this competitive
system. 'I guess I've bathed in no less than ten tons of very wet
cement,' Snub Pollard recalled. 'I figured up once I have caught
about fourteen thousand pies in my puss, and have been hit by
over six hundred automobiles and two trains. Once I was even
kicked by a giraffe.' Buster Keaton, the most expert of comic
acrobats, was disparaging of the Keystone system. 'Many cops
knew nothing whatever about falling. No one had told them that
both ends of the spine had to be protected when taking a fall. Or
that for one kind of fall you must relax your whole body, for
another you tighten up the muscles of both your back and your
backside. . . .' Even the smallest miscalculations could be dangerous. In 1917 Sennett, visiting the Thomas Ince lot, to which
Keystone was then allied through the Triangle Corporation, saw
Selig actor Nick Cogley, whose 250 pounds and heavy beard had
comic possibilities. He hired Cogley for *Stars and Bars*, a comedy
ending in a chase around the Mecca Bar on the pier at Venice. The
actor was running hard when director George Nichols ordered a
comic turn. Cogley did it, and the abrupt shifting of weight broke
his shin bone in half. A silver bar and twelve screws were needed
to repair it, and Cogley retired into directing. When Sennett,
after the First World War, expanded into both car and air-racing
comedies, Walter Wright took a camera team to Santa Monica
Road Races to get background footage for a film called *Skidding
Hearts*. A car driven by Lewis Jackson, who regularly drove in car
stunts for the serial team of Grace Cunard and Francis Ford, left the
road, killed two onlookers and Jackson, and cut down the trees
where cameraman L. B. Jenkins was sheltering and killed him.
When the cameras were found intact amid splintered tripods,
Sennett ordered the film used, without comment.

Sennett's commercial survival was a Hollywood phenomenon.
He invested lavishly in oil wells, gold mines, a private mountain on
top of which he built his dream villa, and at last in a huge new
studio in the San Fernando Valley. *The Hollywood Kid* (1924), a
comedy set on the lot and using Sennett stars as themselves, shows
how complex his plant had become, incorporating wind machines,
elaborate wiring for electrical effects, plumbing for water gags, a
cyclorama with moving footway for chases, and unlimited lions.

Below *Mack Sennett in* The Hollywood Kid

Appearing as himself, Sennett works on oblivious of the battling comics pouring through his office, and even ignores the lion on his desk until finishing a phone call. Keystone comedy was like its producer, simple, violent and malicious, regarded by contemporary critics and film-makers in rather the same way as critics in the sixties regarded the Three Stooges. But even while Keaton and Lloyd were expanding public consciousness of comedy's subtleties Sennett persisted with remarkable success until profligacy and the Wall Street crash wiped him out. He scraped into sound with some shorts featuring crooner Bing Crosby, and a selection of lion comedies that were, if anything, coarser than those of Pathé Lehrman, but even after selling his new studios to Republic insufficient money remained and he was declared bankrupt in 1933 with liabilities of $5 million. Sennett's contempt for the star system,

and his belief that he could manufacture new stars when needed, worked while comedy was new and its devices unfamiliar, but as the great creators emerged Sennett rashly relinquished his actors to the highest bidder rather than meet their new price. It was Ford Sterling's departure to become his own producer (disastrously) that led to Sennett hiring Chaplin, and he later passed up the chance to hold Arbuckle, Summerville, St John and other featured players who joined the evolving big studios as heads of their own units. Significantly, most of these men promptly eased up on the hectic Keystone schedule, producing longer films with greater care and using stunt men for feats that they themselves were now too old or too cautious to try. The first wave of professional stunters entered movies in this way, and found it impossible to maintain the pace Sennett had set. Bobby Dunn, one of the original Keystone Kops, freelanced with high dives into water but on a comedy in the early twenties failed to notice that a careless technician had thrown a match into the tank. As he hit the water it slashed his face and blinded him in one eye. Richard Talmadge did his first Hollywood stunt on a 1919 Slim Summerville comedy, Dick Grace started in movies as a prop man for Summerville before leaving to stunt for Al St John, and Earl Burgess fell from an aircraft to his death in February 1920 while shooting scenes for Summerville.

Of the comedians who learned their trade with Sennett and then left to form their own units, the most successful, until scandal terminated his career, was Roscoe Arbuckle, whom Joseph Schenck lured away with promises of his own unit and the chance to shine that Sennett never gave his comics. Schenck called Arbuckle's gang the Comique Film Corporation, an oddly genteel name for Hollywood's roughest slapstick studio. The two hundred and eighty-pound Arbuckle, as his brief collaborator Buster Keaton testified, was 'as hard as a brick wall and fast on his feet. No man that size ever took such falls.'

Keaton stayed with Comique from 1917 to 1920, with a gap for war service, and though it took only a few months to see that his future and that of film comedy lay some distance from this violent knockabout, the experience for both Keaton and Arbuckle was an education. One forgets how young these men were. Keystone relied on old stagers like Summerville and Mann, men in their forties who had accumulated enough scars in vaudeville and the circus to cushion them from pain and new ideas. But Arbuckle was only twenty-six when he got his own unit, Keaton twenty-five.

Above *Al St John*

Below *Sennett puddles were always six feet deep: Snub Pollard*

Left *Billy Bevan in a typical Keystone trick car (1925)*

Above right *One of Sennett's comedians, doubling Marie Dressler, is booted off the end of Venice Pier in* Tillie's Punctured Romance (1914)

Below right *Early Sennett stunt clowning on Keystone's private precipice*

They were resilient, receptive, totally without fear. They enjoyed nothing more than the hectic comedy routines and even more violent practical jokes of the two-reel comedy treadmill. Keaton formed a special relationship with Al St John, a wiry acrobat noted for his rooftop stunts and agile leaps. The two men were reckless and indefatigable jokers. In a favourite routine St John leaned out of a fourth-storey window allegedly watching his new car being delivered. He would slip, teeter, disappear, then scream for help as the knuckles of one hand whitened on the window ledge. When Buster leaped to his aid, St John grabbed his friend and pulled him out as well, so that two sets of knuckles now graced the sill. Solicitous friends racing to the window found the men standing on the cornice of the window below, helpless with laughter and oblivious of the drop yawning behind them. (St John was to outlast all but a handful of the great comics. After sound, he returned to vaudeville, and in the fifties began a new career in Westerns as 'Fuzzy' St John or 'Fuzzy Q. Jones', bearded sidekick to a variety of cowboy stars.)

From the outset Arbuckle was baffled by and respectful of his young protégé. Keaton could do anything that Arbuckle could – he even doubled him on falls which producer Lou Anger thought too risky for the big man, proudly framing his $7.50 stunt cheque – and do it with a grace, skill and invention the other envied. A vaudevillian since he could walk, active in his parents' act 'The Three Keatons' as comic foil and eccentric comedian from the age of three, Keaton had long ago learned all there was to know about comedy tumbling. 'Buster' was a nickname given him by Harry Houdini, then an unknown illusionist travelling with the same company as the Keatons and present when, at the age of six months, Joseph Frank Keaton fell downstairs at the theatrical boarding house in which they were staying, and sat there laughing about it. Young Buster's ability to survive was quickly exploited by his father, who sewed a suitcase handle to the back of his overalls and flung him into the wings twice nightly as part of the family act. Buster mastered all the comic falls, including the furious running forward somersault and twist that still retains the name (corrupted to 'Branny') of its inventor, acrobat Fred Borani. By his early twenties, Keaton was exploring the absurdity of fallible man in a world of infallible natural forces which was to be the mainspring of his later independent films.

When Arbuckle left Schenck, Keaton inherited his unit. He

retained little from the Arbuckle days, except gadgets like a car that, at the tug of a wire, collapsed into its component parts; the gag, used in *The Garage* (1919) with Arbuckle, turned up later in *The Three Ages* (Keaton and Eddie Cline, 1923). Such comic gadgets were an obsession – the only greater one was baseball – and he had enlivened summers at his parents' country cottage by booby-trapping the outside lavatory so that, when the chain was pulled, a ·45 cartridge blank exploded under the seat and a fire bell rang overhead (a gag invented in honour of humorist Chic Sale, author of the lavatorial classic *The Specialist*, who was its first victim). The same imagination went into planning *The Electric House*, started in 1921, in which inventor Buster has planned and built a house equipped with every modern convenience. Stunt man Chick Collins, a permanent Keaton staff member (but only, the comedian claimed, because of his baseball ability), offered to double when Buster prepared to step on a moving electric staircase, in case the jerry-built machine went wrong. Keaton refused. As he reached the top of the escalator his shoe caught in the mechanism, his ankle snapped and he fell ten feet to the floor, doing a perfect shoulder roll before fainting from pain. With the star seven weeks in plaster, *The Electric House* was shelved, and Schenck hired Fred Gabourie, Hollywood's best special effects technician, as a permanent Keaton staff member. An inspired practical engineer and stunt director, he was soon to become indispensable.

Without Gabourie, it is doubtful if many of Keaton's most famous stunts would have reached the screen. He engineered the train crash for *The General* (Keaton and Clyde Bruckman, 1926) and received a special credit for it; discovered the old liner that was used in *The Navigator* (Keaton and Donald Crisp, 1924); and designed a landslide of papier-mâché boulders ranging from those the size of grapefruit to eight foot monsters to pursue Buster downhill in *Seven Chances* (Keaton, 1925). For *Sherlock Junior* (Keaton, 1924) he exploited the star's vaudeville background by incorporating some old stage illusions into the film. Parodying John Barrymore's suave Sherlock Holmes, Buster plays a dreamy projectionist who romances himself into the mystery film he is watching, becoming the super-detective who, with the help of his faithful valet Raymond, can escape from any predicament. About to burst in on the robbers, Buster directs Raymond to hold a large flat valise up to the window. A moment later Buster leaps out of the window, throws a somersault and stands up dressed in a floor-

Right *Buster Keaton
and collapsing car in
The Three Ages*

length ladies gown which has been spread out inside the 'break-away' suitcase. (To make sure we appreciate the stunt, the house wall is completely cut away.) Shortly after, trapped in a dead end alley, he sees an old lady selling knicknacks who points encouragingly to her tray. Against all logic he dives straight at it, and disappears. The 'old lady' is just a dress and a pair of shoes covering a trap door in the wall; her head and hands are those of a man lying on a platform on the other side.

For later films, Gabourie and Keaton invented new and more dangerous stunts that exploited Buster's interest in the brute stupidity of matter. Sennett's world stretched or slowed to accommodate his comics; puddles were suddenly six foot deep, car bodies leaped to the upper window of a house on extending mechanisms or were squeezed into strange shapes by a smash. Keaton, by contrast, survived by the merest hair's breadth in a world where natural laws could not be revoked. Trapdoors opened, cannons swivelled, bombs exploded, but at the vital instant Buster always managed to be somewhere else. *Steamboat Bill Jnr* (Charles Reisner, 1927) has the most extraordinary examples of the Gabourie/Keaton technique. Trapped on a steamer paddlewheel, Buster is ducked, lifted and ducked again in an endless cycle, his world in microcosm. Straying into a town that a cyclone is tearing to pieces, he stands bemused in the middle of the street; a house behind him crumples and the entire front wall slams towards him like a two-storey door, but leaves him untouched in the gap left by the window. Keaton loved the gag's bravado, and enjoyed the technical challenge.

First I had them build the framework of this building and make sure that the hinges were all firm and solid. It was a building with a tall V-shaped roof, so that we could make this window up in the roof exceptionally high. An average second-storey window would be about twelve feet, but we're up to eighteen feet. Then you lay this framework down on the ground, and build the window around me. We built the window so that I had a clearance of two inches on each shoulder, and the top missed my head by two inches and the bottom my heels by two inches. We mark that ground out and drive big nails where my two heels are going to be. Then you put that house back up in position while they finish building it. They put the front on, painted it, and made the jagged edge where it tore away from the main building; and then we went in and fixed the interiors so that you're looking at a house that the front has blown off.

Then we put up our wind machines with the big Liberty motors. We had six of them and they are pretty powerful; they could lift a truck right off the road. Now we had to make sure we were getting our foreground and background wind effect, but that no current ever hit the front of that building when it started to fall, because if the wind warps her she's not going to fall where we want her, and I'm standing right out in front. But it's a one-take scene and we got it that way. You don't do these things twice.[8]

Had the wall warped, Keaton would have been killed. Gabourie built the wall solid – it weighed two tons.

On a few films Gabourie's talent was unequal to the sheer volume of the risks Keaton faced. *Our Hospitality* (Keaton and John Blystone, 1923), his parody of a famous Southern feud in which Buster is the love-sick victim pursued by both sides, was shot partly on location at Lake Tahoe and in the Truckee River country, but mostly on the Metro lot. Both locations proved equally risky. For a river shot where Buster rides a sixteen foot log into rapids to rescue his girlfriend (actually his wife, Natalie Talmadge) he allowed her to be doubled but again refused Chick Collins's offer to double himself, relying on Gabourie's assurance that a sixty foot cable with three husky men on the other end would keep the log under control. As Buster paddled into the current he heard the cable part with a soft twang, and was suddenly whisked towards white water. He jumped off, realizing that he was safer in the water where he could swim for it, and found himself chased by the log among the rocks and foam of the rapids. Only chance and a bend in the river saved him from being bulldozed under. The unit prudently returned to Hollywood for the even more hazardous sequence in which Buster, suspended from a rope at the end of a log over a waterfall, rescues Natalie – a dummy this time – even after she has actually gone over the brink.

Left Buster Keaton and paddlewheel: Steamboat Bill Jnr

We had to build that dam. The set was built over a swimming pool, and we actually put up four eight-inch water pipes, with big pumps and motors to run them, to carry the water up from the pool to create our waterfall. That fall was about six inches deep. A couple of times I swung out underneath there and dropped upside down when I caught her. I had to go down to the doctor right there and then. They pumped out my ears and nostrils and drained me, because when a full volume of water like that comes down and hits you and you're upside down – then you really get it.[9]

By contrast *Sherlock Junior*, one of whose highpoints is a comic motor-cycle chase in which Keaton, unaware that the rider has fallen off, weaves through traffic and across a railway line in the path of a train while balanced on the handlebars, was relatively safe. Buster even did the driver's fall while a prop man doubled him riding on the bars. The only accident, and the most serious Keaton ever had, was one about which he knew nothing. Pushed from the top of a train by a water jet, he missed his hold on the rope Gabourie had suspended in the stream and fell heavily. It wasn't until years later that doctors examining him for another reason entirely found that the fall had broken a vertebra in his neck.

Keaton emerged intact from his knockabout comedies mainly because he had sufficient professionalism to calculate his stunts and carry them out with scientific precision. So did Harold Lloyd. Like all silent comedians he took risks, but foresight minimized them, and he achieved wealth and early retirement after some of the riskiest stunts Hollywood had ever seen. In road shows and repertory since he was twelve, Lloyd in 1916 found himself an extra at Universal, working with another bit player named Hal Roach.

Roach surprised me one day by announcing that he had got hold of several thousand dollars with which he intended making pictures of his own. He would be the director and I could be the first brick in his company, at the usual $3 a day.

For their first film Roach chose a Keystone-style comedy based on a comic fall.

A counter-balance device called the Court Flight hauled passengers up and down the short steep grade of Court Street Hill at a penny fare, one car descending on a cable as the other ascends. One of Roach's early inspirations was to have Willie Work [Lloyd's Chaplin-imitation character] roll down this flight between the two tracks. The cameraman stationed himself at the bottom and pointed his lens up the flight. When I had rolled down, with many bruises, and the film was developed, Willie Work was found, inexplicably, to be rolling on a level roadway. We were so green at the business that we didn't know that if you want angle in a picture you first must get angle in your lens. By inclining his camera at the same gradient as that of my descent, the cameraman had flattened it out to a spirit level smoothness. Roach put arnica on my bruises and syrup on my vanity, and we tried it a second time. Now the cameraman stationed himself in a second-storey window across Spring Street at the foot of the flight. His angle was true, but there is more than one dimension to a picture. The scene had been taken at such a distance that Willie Work was a mere blob on the developed negative. We might as well have rolled a dummy down the incline. There was no third time.[10]

In a series of short comedies, first with Roach then independently, Lloyd developed three comic personalities, the third of which, that of a mild-mannered young man in straw boater and horn-rimmed spectacles who achieved the most terrifying stunts with a nervousness that never quite strayed into terror, made him famous. The 'glass character', as he called him, first appeared in *Over the Fence* (1917) and was expanded over two years into a star personality. But Lloyd's career very nearly ended abruptly in 1919, when he was injured in an explosion while posing for publicity pictures. Some fake hand bombs of the black-sphere-and-fuse variety popularly thought to be used by Russian anarchists had been made by the studio prop man for Lloyd and other comedians to use in private stunts of the Uplifters' Club on its country picnics, at which the members put on a show satirizing the news. When one of these, filled with flash powder, smashed an oak table top at the resort of Bear Lake where the picnic was held, the bombs were sent back to the prop man who accidentally mixed them with other fakes which, like most prop bombs, were only fuses attached to empty cases. The publicity man asked Lloyd to light his cigarette from the fuse, but smoke blew across his face, obscuring it. When the fuse disappeared Lloyd lowered his hand; had he not done this the explosion would certainly have killed him. As it was, Lloyd's thumb and forefinger were blown off, one eye damaged so severely that it was thought he would be blinded, and his face painfully lacerated. The studio had a sixteen foot hole blown in its ceiling, and a production man's false teeth were split from side to side. The photographer fainted.

The accident did nothing to dent Lloyd's nerve. He had been billed as 'The Human Rubber Ball' in some of his early comedies on the basis of his acrobatic ability, and now set out to exploit this image in a series of 'thrill comedies'. The first was a one-reel 'glass character' picture called *Look Out Below*.

For it, we built a frame of wooden girders, painted to likeness of steel, two and a half stories high, over the southern portal of the Hill St tunnel, which the city conveniently had bored through the bluff. . . . Neither it nor any of its descendants contained any doubling, double exposure or trick photography. The illusion lay in deceptive camera angles of drop

and height. The second member of the family was a two-reeler called
High and Dizzy, taken on the same scene, but presumably on the ledge of
a completed ten-storey hotel. . . . The third generation was *Never
Weaken*, a three-reel de luxe edition of *Look Out Below*. The thrills came
of my efforts to commit suicide in the belief that Mildred [Davis] had
thrown me down. This time we built our framework of girders on the
roof of the Ville de Paris department store, the owner of which, Bernal
Dyas, is a close friend of Roach. We used the interior of the same store
for the department-store scenes in *Safety Last*, the next thrill picture,
working from closing time until two and three o'clock the next morning.

The success of the thrill idea in one, two and three lengths suggested
trying it at full-program distance. One afternoon in downtown Los
Angeles I stopped to watch Bill Strothers, who called himself the Human
Spider, scale the sheer walls of a high office building. The higher he
climbed the more nervous I grew until, when he came to a difficult ledge
twelve stories up, I had to cut around a corner out of sight of him and
peek back to see if he was over the ledge. If it makes me this jumpy,
what would it do to a picture audience, I asked myself? . . . The plot
gradually worked out this way. I was to be a country boy new to the city.
I get a job clerking in a department store. The pompous floor-walker is
my enemy. I room with Strothers. He innocently makes an enemy of a
policeman. After much comedy business in the store, I sell the manager
on the idea of having a human fly climb the building as an advertising
stunt. When the time comes for Strothers to climb, his enemy, the cop,
is found to be patrolling the beat in front of the store. He gives chase to
Strothers. The store manager impatiently demands to know where my
human fly is. . . . In order to save the situation I reluctantly start to climb
for Strothers, who tells me that he will take my place at the second
storey. But the cop pursues him to the second floor, then to the third and
so on. Meanwhile I have to continue, finally making the entire ascent
myself. . . .[11]

Although the legend has it that Lloyd never used a double,
Richard Talmadge, Harvey Parry and other stunt men replaced
him occasionally, and he later admitted that shooting his thrill
pictures

was very dangerous, but it wasn't as dangerous as it looked. We built
platforms below, which you don't see, and we piled those with mattresses. But we couldn't put railings around the platforms so if you fell on
the mattresses you fell flat on them: they didn't stand any bouncing off
of them. [On one occasion, when a dummy did land on such a platform,
it bounced off into the street.] . . . The first two days I'd go up there; I
had to get conditioned. It took us sometimes well over a month to make

Right *Harold Lloyd*
in Safety Last
(continued overleaf)

one of these sequences, because we could only work between about eleven o'clock and one o'clock, otherwise shadows would come in the street and it wouldn't match the other scenes. But after you were up there a while you felt so sure of yourself you'd go up where there were no platforms at all. . . . We wouldn't have platforms when we made long distances. Then we had wires on us with a harness underneath – we had to do that kind of stuff or the city wouldn't let us do it.[12]

He did, however, suffer the usual sprains, and dislocated his shoulder in the famous scene when, as he grasps the hands of a huge clock for support, the face yawns outwards, leaving him hanging over the street. The clock incident became one of the most famous in film comedy, and when Lloyd visited Chicago to promote *Safety Last* his key publicity stunt was the dedication of a clock on the fifteenth floor of the Wrigley building. A human fly had been hired to double Lloyd, but when the professional refused the job because of a high wind Lloyd was adamant in declining to climb out himself, and made a speech to the crowd instead. The Sennett recklessness had indeed gone for good.

Right *A classic Keystone car routine recreated in Hollywood Cavalcade (1939)*

3 Cliffhangers

If the slapstick comedy, with its circus capers and simple violence, is peculiar to the cinema's first decade, no form more precisely evokes the years of the First World War and the early twenties than the action serial. A natural result of the star system, it fulfilled the promise of Keystone, offering a series of stories about a popular character, linked in a rough continuity to lure audiences back week after week. Episodes of the earliest serials were self-contained, without the 'cliff-hanging' climaxes that were to become essential. Exhibitors called them 'chapter plays', and economically they skated on thin ice. Filming a scripted story was expensive compared with the largely improvised two-reel comedy, and as audiences for action pictures demanded a succession of thrills, costs were forced up by the provision of bigger and riskier stunts. Even so, much was done with little – ten people often making up the entire cast and crew of a serial. William Duncan starred in his serials as well as directing them, always with the same leading lady, Edith Johnson. Francis Ford played the villain in and directed most of those by Grace Cunard, which she usually wrote – Ford's young brother John was often assistant director and stunt man – and John McGowan was both star and director of all the Helen Holmes serials. Ignoring trained actors, serial producers found people with vitality and the proved ability to survive – rodeo riders, acrobats, circus clowns – and built them up into stars. Later, usually with little success, they recruited public figures like escapologist Harry Houdini and boxer Jack Dempsey, around whom an action story could be built.

Stunt men were used promiscuously in the serials, always without credit and often in the face of flat statements from the producers that the star took all his or her own risks. Some, like Yakima Canutt and Dave Sharpe, became minor thirties stars themselves, while others, notably Irving Cummings and Edward

Sutherland, went into directing and production – skills learned early in a field where it was not unknown for the director to pad up and do the stunts his star refused. Some of the most striking figures of the early serials were directors like Woodbridge Strong Van Dyke, known as 'Woody', George B. Seitz and Spencer Gordon Bennett, tough overseers in a business where sensibilities and safety mattered less than getting the film done on time. Seitz could write an entire serial script in a week – he once wrote one in a day – and his personal motto 'Nothing outside me can ever lick me' made him one of the serials' most relentless task-masters, a rigorous craftsman who became MGM's top B-film director in the thirties and forties, best remembered for a succession of *Hardy Family* comedies. Van Dyke also ended up at MGM where his casual good nature persuaded people that the harsh necessities of the serials had been to blame for his reputation. Some of his victims remained sceptical. Bennett stuck to serials throughout his career, and even in the forties was directing them with a rigour many stars remember with discomfort. The brand of the silent serials was not easily expunged.

Chapter plays had been pioneered in Germany, France and England, but the true serial, with its accent on thrills, was an American invention, sparked by the magazine and newspaper fiction of the 1910s. Film producers learned to exploit the vogue; chapter play stories were popular with newspaper readers, and publishers like William Randolph Hearst financed film serials in return for the newspaper rights. Movie serials understandably attracted the writers of newspaper and magazine fiction, some of them from *Cosmopolitan*, another Hearst subsidiary, and Hearst journalism left its mark on the serial forever. His florid exposés of Asian plots, drug dens and general foreign depravity, his adulation of American technological achievement, all found their place, taking the serial some distance from the action film that fathered it. By the end of the First World War, it had developed a unique form. A chapter play cowboy finds a futuristic city under his ranch, a serial queen is pursued by Burmese dacoits through modern New York, her lover boards a train at speed from his motor cycle and is taken off shortly after by a low-flying aircraft: the thrill is everything. This made the serial a dangerous field.

Since most early serials were shot in the East, locations were limited to the rivers and cliffs of the Atlantic coast. Ausable Chasm in upper New York state, a sheer canyon with a boiling river below, was popular, as were sparsely settled Ithaca, Staten Island and the cliffs of the New York Palisades. The serial writers were city men, and dreamed up thrills in an urban setting, often calling for motor-cycle or automobile crashes where stunt men had little opportunity to protect themselves. The gradual move to California, a shifting of interest to outdoor stories and the use of trained cowboys for stunters would change this, but not until after the war. Meanwhile, stunt men and women did their best to find soft spots in the concrete and asphalt of New York.

Edison's 1912 *What Happened to Mary* in six one-reel episodes with Mary Fuller is probably the first serial. Its success demanded a quick sequel, *Who Will Marry Mary?* 'Colonel' William Selig of Chicago, a master of imitation among early producers, promptly put out *The Adventures of Kathryn* in 1913. In each two-reel

Below *Kathryn Williams (with real leopards) in* Captain Kate

episode Kathryn Williams, billed as 'the girl without fear', fought wild beasts from Selig's private zoo. The use of the actresses' real names implied that they took all the risks of their films, and since audiences apparently liked the idea producers sustained the illusion. Even so, by the time Mutual broke in with *Our Mutual Girl* (Jack Noble, 1914), a fifty-two episode serial, the secret of stunt girls was already out. The *New York Times* covered a typical day's shooting with Jean de Kay doubling Mutual's Norma Phillips, who was to be hit by a car.

Miss de Kay was taken to 61st Street and Fifth Avenue early in the morning and instructed by director Jack Noble in the part. A cross was marked on the pavement to point out to both the chauffeur of the racing car and to the actress the spot where the 'accident' was to occur. The racing car was placed about one hundred yards from the spot and timed so that it would hit Miss de Kay at the exact moment she reached the point agreed upon. . . . Four times both actress and chauffeur rehearsed the little drama, Miss de Kay always stepping aside at the critical moment to let the car roar past. Movie patrons want realism nowadays, and although Miss de Kay knew she would be taking a chance, she instructed the chauffeur to put on all the power he could and to trust to her that everything turned out all right. . . . Slowly the girl walked out into the street and the chauffeur raced down the avenue. As he whirled past, Jack Noble the director shouted to him to slow down. Then the 'accident' occurred. Miss de Kay jumped into the air as she was struck and landed full on the mudguard, thus avoiding going under the wheels. The impact cast her off to one side on the sidewalk. Here the director's and her plans went astray. Miss de Kay struck the curb and fell half on the sidewalk and half on the street. Beyond a severe shaking up and some ugly bruises she apparently had sustained no ill-effects of her adventure. On the way back to the studio, however, she pressed her side and complained of a sharp pain. As the car turned into Broadway and 17th Street Miss de Kay fainted and had to be assisted from the limousine into the Mutual studios. A doctor was hastily summoned and after an examination found that the plucky Mutual actress had sustained a broken rib.[13]

The naivety of this and similar stunts surprises modern stunt men, who have developed techniques to cope with such simple risks. Today, Miss de Kay would carry a shopping basket, an armful of parcels or even an umbrella, handbag and gloves which, as the car hit, would be flipped into the air as she did an acrobatic fall, directing the audience's eyes away from the car, which had missed her completely.

The Kalem studio's serial star was Helen Holmes, who had been one of Sennett's Keystone girls and knew the rudiments of cinema survival. A vivacious brunette, Miss Holmes suited the enterprising Kalem, whose speciality was realistic location shooting; for an early Biblical epic it even sent a unit to Palestine. Its owner, George Kleine, had helped form the Motion Picture Patent Company, a monopoly of Edison patent holders that kept early bootleg producers in constant fear of prosecution and, as one of the first companies to move to California, Kalem had almost sole use of the state's sunny landscape. *The Hazards of Helen*, taking its cue from *Our Mutual Girl*, continued almost indefinitely, running to 119 episodes between 1914 and 1916. Most were directed by John McGowan, a young Australian who also played the villain. He married Helen Holmes and, when Kalem refused more money, took her to form the Signal Film Corporation, where she continued making serials for some years. The image of serial heroines as daredevils had more fuel from Miss Holmes. One 1915 fan magazine article recorded breathlessly:

Right Helen Gibson in an early Kalem serial

In *Helen's Sacrifice* she rode a horse over a fifty foot cliff, and leapt from the saddle onto the footplate of a fast-speeding locomotive. In *The Girl at the Throttle* she averted terrible railroad disaster by driving an engine at sixty miles an hour. In *The Stolen Engine* she leapt from the footplate of one engine onto the cab of another travelling in the same direction on a parallel track. In *The Black Diamond Express* she made an exciting dash through the clouds in a monster biplane. In *The Escape on the Limited* she drove a steam railcar at breakneck speed, and in *The Girl Telegrapher's Peril* she leapt from the trestle into the river below.[14]

This is less than the truth. Like most serial stars, Helen Holmes was doubled in all these sequences. Edward Sutherland, later a top director but in 1915 a $15 a week actor on *The Hazards of Helen*, often picked up an extra $5 for single stunts like jumping off a moving train. On the same serial, Gene Perkins, one of the most famous early stunt men, doubled Helen in a sequence where, to escape from a dynamited train, she and the hero grab a rope stretched from a tree to a telephone pole across the track. Both Perkins and stunt man Harold Lloyd (not *the* Lloyd) missed the rope and fell to the ground, Lloyd badly injuring his leg. Sutherland, after suggesting that the cameraman undercrank to speed the action, an old comedy trick, took over from Lloyd, and went through the stunt perfectly – until the explosion blew both him

and Perkins off the rope. This time Sutherland went to hospital. But Helen Holmes's regular double was the girl who replaced her at Kalem when she went to Signal, Helen Gibson.

Bored with life in Cleveland, Ohio, Rose Helen Wenger answered a 1910 advertisement for girls to train as rodeo riders with the 101 Ranch Show. Run by the enterprising Miller brothers from their Ponca City, Oklahoma, ranch, the 101 Show combined rodeo, vaudeville and the travelling show into a popular package. Its stars included footloose cowboys like Tom Mix and Hoot Gibson; Will Rogers did rope tricks. Rose joined the show as a cowgirl, and later married Gibson, its top stunt rider and later a Western film star himself. Always out for profit, the Millers decided to rent the show to the movies in its winter lay-off, and when it moved to Thomas Ince's Californian studio in 1911 (at $2,500 a week) Rose and Hoot went with it to feature in some of Ince's Westerns. Soon Rose Gibson was in demand as a stunt girl, and when McGowan saw her she was immediately signed up as Helen Holmes's full-time double. Rose was game for anything. In *A Girl's Grit* she was to leap from the top of a station to the speeding train. 'The distance between roof and train top was accurately measured and I practised the jump with the train standing still. The train had to be moving on camera for about a quarter of a mile and its accelerating velocity was timed to a second. I was not nervous as the train approached, and leapt without hesitation. I landed right, but the train's motion made me roll towards the end of the car. I caught hold of an air vent and hung on, allowing my body to dangle over the edge to increase the effect on the screen.' When Helen Holmes left, Kalem changed Rose's name and, as Helen Gibson, she took over the serials whose thrills she had provided for some months. She remained a stunt woman and double until her death in 1960, standing in for Louise Fazenda, Marie Dressler, Edna May Oliver and Ethel Barrymore, among others. In 1938, when she was treasurer of the stunt girls' fraternal organization, the chairman of the complaints committee was Helen Holmes.

Among the dozens of tiny East Coast companies fighting to survive around New York, Pathé was one of the poorest. For this reason its manager, Charles Pathé, was enthusiastic when French director Louis Gasnier in 1913 offered a serial package consisting of his own Eclectic Film Company, himself as director (Donald MacKenzie later claimed that he had directed and Gasnier acted

Left. The Perils of Pauline: *Pearl White and Crane Wilbur*

only as producer), an adequate serial story written by magazine journalist Charles W. Goddard and the ambitious George Seitz, and a minor but energetic actress named Pearl White. The story was *The Perils of Pauline*, and even Goddard made no attempt to excuse its triviality. Heiress Pauline, who wants to be a writer, spurns her fiancé and spends a year collecting plots and atmosphere for her books. The indefatigable lover follows, staving off secret societies and Asian masterminds who try to extort her fortune, rescuing her from the results of her reckless quests for material, until she decides to settle down. The first episodes were unexceptional, and Pearl White, little more than an amateur with a history of bit parts in comedies for the Crystal Company and a few years in repertory, was far from a charismatic figure. But *The Perils of Pauline*, released in twenty episodes in 1914, had instant and phenomenal success in both America and Europe. The apparent athleticism of this young blonde girl, her disregard for danger, the nonchalance with which she leaped into the gondolas of balloons or fled from boulders rolled down on her by wild Indians enchanted even sophisticates like Jean Cocteau; he dragged Igor Stravinsky to see some episodes, and wrote plays and poems about an American girl 'more interested in her health than her beauty, who swims, boxes, dances, leaps onto moving trains – all without knowing she is beautiful'.[15] Cocteau had isolated her essential attraction – the sense of the unrehearsed in her movements, an absorption in moving and reacting that seemed totally without artifice.

The real Pearl would have shocked impressionable Parisiennes. Five foot six inches tall, inclined to plumpness (which was accentuated later in her career by heavy drinking), wearing in most of her films rubber reducing bloomers, Pearl's stunts were usually as false as her blonde hair, a wig covering a reddish mop. In 1919, at the height of her career, she wrote an autobiography, *Just Me*, in which she claimed to have run away from her Missouri home to join a circus, and to have lived most of the hazardous events in her films, but since she invented all the details of her family life one must be sceptical about the rest. Spencer Bennett, who began as a stunter in her serials, claims

Pearl insisted on taking chances. We used to plead with her that if she got hurt she would cause a shut-down and put everybody out of a job. On rare occasions she'd admit a scene or sequence called for gymnastic ability which she lacked. Usually, though, we gave in to her rather than lose time arguing.[16]

Serial writer Frank Leon Smith says a man called Rodman Law was kept on the Pathé payroll to double Pearl's co-stars, like Crane Wilbur, her constant suitor, and villain Paul Panzer, but this merely adds to the mystery. Law, whom Smith calls 'the movies' first famous stunt man', was a steeplejack who became famous for his parachute exhibitions before the First World War. In February 1912 he jumped from the arm of the Statue of Liberty, and later from Brooklyn Bridge, a New York skyscraper and eventually, in April 1912, over Marblehead, Massachusetts, from an aeroplane, only the second man in the world to do so. Until war was declared, he travelled around county fairs giving parachute shows, but in 1917 he joined the Signal Corps as a balloonist and slipped out of the limelight. Neither acrobat nor professional double, Law can have had little to do with the White serials, except perhaps to supervise such aerial stunts as the runaway balloon in which Pearl erroneously claimed to have been carried miles during the shooting of the *Perils*.

With rather more evidence, Smith also credits cowboys Eddie Kelly and Dick La Marr with taking some of her risks. Making *The Fatal Ring* the whole company was jailed by a Long Island sheriff and later fined $2 each when a horse from which La Marr, doubling Pearl, had swung into a tree slid down an embankment and was injured, and Smith recalls another instance.

One of the few times I saw her doubled was when she was supposed to work her way along a wire cable strung between two rooftops. With other men in the studio I was called to hold a big carpet under Eddie Kelly, who made the transit in wig and skirts. That carpet, with most of its weight on a picket fence, would have been a poor life net if Eddie had fallen sixty feet.[17]

On her last serial, *Plunder* (1922), Pearl was doubled in a chase sequence by Johnny Stevenson, chauffeur to director George Seitz and an amateur actor anxious to pick up some extra money. The stunt called for Stevenson, in skirt and wig, to leap from the top of a New York bus to the girder of a bridge at the corner of 72nd Street and 3rd Avenue. The use of an amateur in this difficult stunt was typical of the risks taken by serial directors. When the bus-driver failed to keep his speed to the necessary five m.p.h.

PEARL WHITE in "PLUNDER"

Stevenson hit the bridge hard, missed his grip on the dusty metal and, watched by his horrified wife and daughter, who were extras among the bus passengers, fell eighteen feet to the road. He died of cerebral concussion shortly after.

In fairness to Pearl, there is evidence that she often took at least moderate risks. Smith was present when 'a new utility man fixed the rope that suspended her, head down, with her arms bound tightly. The knot slipped, and she fell on her head and shoulders. After that, she insisted that all knots in similar scenes be tied by Charles 'Pitch' Revada, a prop man who also played villain henchmen.' (Revada was one of the team that stayed with Pearl throughout her career. A talented special effects technician, he engineered most of her stunts, designing a mechanical octopus with movable arms for one serial, and for another thoughtfully snipping the teeth of rats with a pair of shears before they were dropped in to struggle with her in the basement of a flooded house.) She ricked her back on *Plunder*, and admitted to other minor injuries; but could any woman, however game, do all the things her friends claimed for Pearl White? Her few public appearances suggest that Pathé preferred the fans to keep their distance, in case the illusion should be shattered. In April 1916 she painted her initials hundreds of feet up a New York building, apparently unseen by anybody, and a year later, just after America entered the war, ascended the Bush Terminal building on a girder (securely roped to a construction worker) to drop flags and leaflets to the crowd below. 'I've done my bit,' she said. 'Now you do yours,' and led thirty men to the nearest recruiting office.

Right *Ruth Roland: The Haunted Valley*

Pearl quickly tired of the serial treadmill. She tried drama, disastrously, and made some inauspicious 1922 stage appearances in Paris and London. The Casino de Paris concocted an elaborate entertainment around her cliff-hanging exploits, which they expected her to duplicate on stage, but when the star explained about stunt men they resourcefully circulated the rumour that a Chinese tong had threatened her life should she appear and the show was cancelled. Back in the USA, she made her last serial, *Plunder*, then returned to Europe, where her lover, Greek financier Ted Cozzika, had bought her the Biarritz Hotel de Paris, once a chateau of the Empress Eugenie. Pearl lived in the imperial boudoir and, turning the other rooms into a casino, slipped into comfortable middle age, overweight and obscurity. She died, of a liver ailment, in 1938.

Even before her retirement into drama the serials had outdistanced Pearl, absorbing her contribution but adding more sophisticated stories, bigger budgets and the 'cliff-hanger' climax. Pathé's new serial queen was Ruth Roland, who so highly regarded herself as an actress that almost every action was doubled while she pestered her directors to include more close-ups of her face. Her regular stand-ins were Gene Perkins and Bob Rose, whose small build made him her ideal double. Even for a man like Rose, who had been a parachute jumper, the Roland serials were dangerous. He saw at least one fatality, when Indian stunter Silvertip mis-timed jumping into a lagoon from a speeding train and hit the bank. The dead man had been wearing a pair of Rose's shoes, which he philosophically retrieved and continued to wear.

Ruth Roland was matched in temperament by Pathé's other serial star, burly Charles 'Hutch' Hutchinson, a minor actor in

Left *Joe Bonomo does
a car-to-plane
transfer on a serial of
the mid-twenties*

repertory who built his athletic ability and skill with motor cycles into a career. Pathé hired him in 1918, with his fiancée Edith Thornton as leading lady, for *Wolves of Kultur*. Hutchinson soon distinguished himself with his reckless stunts, often performed with the hapless Edith. In the first episode of *The Whirlwind* (1920) he leaped a motor cycle over an embankment with her on the pillion. In the resulting crash, half her face was temporarily paralysed. In the same film he crossed a log over Ausable Chasm with her on his back. As they reached the middle, the terrified girl felt him begin to sway. 'Don't worry,' he hissed. 'I have to make it look difficult. Can't disappoint the fans.'

Dubbed 'the Thrill-a-Minute Stunt King' by a grateful Pathé, Hutchinson tried more dangerous stunts, and quickly reached his physical limits. On *Double Adventure* (1921) he broke both wrists in a leap from the upper window of a building into a tree, and the painful fractures took some time to heal. When George Seitz, who had left Pathé to direct and star (unsuccessfully) 'in his own serials, returned to the company and was given *Hurricane Hutch* (1921) to handle, he found that the star's nerve had almost entirely gone. Stunters Joe Cuny and Frank Hagney became permanent

Below *Charles Hutchinson in a jump similar to that on Double Adventure in which he broke both wrists. (This photo reconstruction, usually attributed to The Hurricane, is probably from Double Adventure)*

members of the unit, Hutchinson paying them $5 a stunt. Sketching out the action to Seitz, Hutchinson would say, 'So I get on the window ledge and jump into the street (Let Joe get the $5) and then I jump onto the running board of the car (Let Frank get the $5) . . .' When Hutch refused to swim the rapids of Ausable Chasm with the excuse that the water was not warm enough, Seitz contemptuously swam them, twice. Joe Bonomo came in to do the motorcycle leaps – once a Hutch speciality. On the most spectacular of them, jumping from the wharf to a departing ferry, Bonomo landed safely but skidded on a patch of oil and was thrown

sliding down the wooden deck. Riddled with splinters he watched the cycle disappear overboard. For future stunts of this kind, Bonomo contributed his mite to the growing mountain of technical expertise in the stunt business – a cork on a spool of thread to mark the cycle for divers to recover it. Seitz went on to do *Go Get 'Em Hutch* (1922) and *Speed* (1923) with the star, but accidents and alcohol had impaired his coordination. Spencer Bennett was called in to double for him when he failed in a simple skiing shot on location at Lake Saranac, NJ, and after the failure of *Speed* Pathé decided to ease him out. He was put in *The Fortieth Door* (1924) under Woody Van Dyke, known for his ruthless methods. One of the serial's most ambitious stunts was a leap from a balcony to a chandelier and a swing across the room. Hutch was cautious, but was finally persuaded to do it. As he grabbed the chandelier it tore from the ceiling and he crashed to the floor under it. In agony, he thought he had broken his wrists again, but he had actually dislocated his elbow – backwards.

While Hutchinson was recuperating Van Dyke transferred to Ruth Roland's unit, and made more enemies. *Ruth of the Range* (1923) with Bruce Gordon, and Bob Rose again doubling the star,

Left *Harry Houdini: The Man From Beyond*

had the hero and heroine plunge into a bubbling, poisonous pool. Van Dyke refused the usual sulphur pots and dry ice under the surface to simulate bubbling and had the pool heated with steam from the studio boiler. Both Gordon and Rose fell in and were scalded, but Van Dyke insisted they continue after some brief first aid. After the failure of *Speed* and the other disasters, Pathé dropped Hutchinson's contract. He set up the Hurricane Film Corporation to make *Lightning Hutch* in 1926, but, overweight, rambling and middle-aged, he had lost the last of his appeal, and the serial was a flop. The company, in which his wife and old friends had invested, failed, and Hutchinson disappeared.

Serials continued to attract daredevils and fading matinée idols. After a quick nose restyling, Jack Dempsey featured in *Daredevil Jack* for Pathé in 1920. Jess Willard and Gene Tunney also made a few film appearances, and Harry Houdini too saw a chance to exploit his reputation for invulnerability, a fact that Willard at least resented. In a famous 1918 incident, the boxer turned up at a Los Angeles theatre and publicly accused Houdini of using bribed stooges in his act. Houdini's serials and features, alternating escape tricks with risible love stories – at forty-four, balding, his shortness disguised with elevator shoes, he was no sex symbol – bored audiences, and the star reluctantly added some thrills, in most of which he was doubled by Robert Kennedy, an ex-army flier sporting the rank of lieutenant that stunt pilot Ormer Locklear had made fashionable. Kennedy received even less credit than other stars' doubles. *The Grim Game* (1919) called for Houdini to make a plane-to-plane transfer, but since he claimed to have hurt his wrist Kennedy went up to do it, with director Irvin Willatt shooting from a third camera plane. As the planes converged with Kennedy poised to jump, their wings tangled and both spun towards the ground. Seconds before impact, the pilot managed to wrench them apart, and though both planes were wrecked on landing nobody was killed. When the incident got into the papers, Houdini claimed the stunt as his own, and offered $1,000 to anybody who could prove otherwise. His films continued to fail, and after a break he tried again with an independent serial, *The Master Mystery* (1919), and a feature, *The Man From Beyond* (1921), which mixed escapology – strangling a jailer with his legs while hanging from his wrists in chains, then rifling his pockets and opening a lock with his toes – and dangerous-looking stunts on the Palisades or the rapids above Niagara, where Houdini was clearly not doubled. Even so, the stunts were faked. For the Niagara rescue – shot there in May 1921 – director Burton King built a leather harness sliding on a cable that let Houdini swim through the foaming water with ease.

Scottish actor William Duncan had a long serial career with Vitagraph, in which he claimed 'no doubles, dummies or miniatures' were used. The chunky Duncan was a fine athlete. His claim to have made the first plane-to-train transfer is clearly erroneous – it had been done by Charles Gaemon for Mutual's *Out of the Air* in 1915, if not still earlier by others – but Duncan's spectacular car crashes, executed without any protection, and his high leaps showed courage. He had a lively technical imagination; to achieve a convincing free-for-all, he hid a $5 gold piece in his pocket and told the stunt men it belonged to whoever got it. But some months later this ingenuity was to have its repercussions.

Members of our company travelled to the Santa Cruz Islands, off the coast of California, for the purpose of making scenes, among which was a dive of some eighty feet from a cliff into the ocean. In this particular scene I was diving to escape guards. The guards were supposed to shoot at their victim after he had dived and then leave, assuming that they had killed him. Because of the extremely rough water the boat from which we were shooting the picture rocked so violently that it was impossible to get good close-ups, so we decided to do the close-ups in our studio tank. The idea was to show me sinking in the water, apparently struck by a bullet from the guards' guns, and later swimming under water to escape. Now it is almost impossible for a good swimmer to simulate drowning, as the natural buoyancy of the body tends to make him float. . . . I had an iron ring attached to the cement bottom of our tank, which, by the way, is ten feet deep. A rope was connected to this ring and the other end adjusted in my belt. At one end of the tank men were placed to pull the rope through the ring and draw me down, so that a natural appearance of sinking in the water would ensue. . . . We discovered also that bullets shot from a rifle did not make sufficient splash to be very noticable on the screen. So we secured some heavy iron nuts and stationed men to hurl these as close as they could to my head without hitting me. . . . Action went according to schedule except for one item. Bing! Right on top of my head, one of those iron nuts struck just as the men started pulling me down. Downwards I went, dragged by the ropes attached to the ring at the tank bottom. I was not exactly senseless, but for the life of me I could not imagine why I was down in the water. Finally it came to me that I was attached to a rope. But for what? I could feel it about my legs, at my belt, in my hands when I reached for it. Try as I might I could not think of the reason for that rope. My brain cleared a bit and details of the rope contrivance slowly came back to my mind. I grabbed for the loose end of the slip and seemed to get hold of every portion of it save the loose end. When I did get at the slip knot, the water had swollen it and in my weakened condition I tugged until it seemed my lungs were bursting. At last I managed to free myself and started swimming upward, reached the top black in the face from lack of wind. My band of assistants exclaimed in a chorus, 'Gee, that guy can sure stay under water a long time.'[18]

Irish-born William Desmond was also caught up in the studios' search for personable young actors who could look after themselves, but after being seriously injured in a fifty foot dive on *Perils of the Yukon* (1922) he demanded a double. George Fiske, a stunt man whose speciality was high jumps into water on a horse, was also hurt doing this stunt for Desmond, and the now-busy Joe Bonomo became his regular stunter, while Ray 'Red' Thompson took over Fiske's high horse jump business. (Some sources claim that it was while doubling Desmond that Gene Perkins was killed in a 1925 plane-to-train transfer, but the evidence is confused.)

Many serial stars were, like Desmond, athletic amateurs, but not Eddie Polo. Acrobat, contortionist, tight-rope walker, stunt rider and animal-handler, he was one of the serials' most colourful stars. At various times he claimed to have been born in Italy, a direct descendant of Marco Polo, to have been educated in Vienna and become Europe's youngest circus star; but later he described his true early life, a history of privation, danger and loneliness which many of these circus graduates must have shared, and which makes their arrogance at least understandable.

I was born in the desert in the northern part of California, the youngest member of Polo and Family, circus artists. My four sisters and one brother and father and mother all performed. When I was two years old I started my professional career by appearing in a tiny clown suit. I was gradually taught other stunts, starting with rudimentary kinds of ground tumbling. My father took his show to Italy, and when I was four years old he was hurt in a fall. The show wasn't paying very well, so he distributed his family among a number of other shows. I went to Henry Wolf, small circus proprietor, and did my baby acrobatic stunts with him. The first thrill I have recollection of occurred in Vienna when I was a little over five years old. I made a balloon ascension and a parachute drop with Wolf. I remember I didn't laugh or cry. I just held my breath during that terrifying drop before the parachute opened. When I was six years old I was bound to Wolf to be his apprentice until I was six-teen. He taught me contortion, trap work, wire-walking, horse-back stunts – everything, and not one at a time but all at once. I could put on a whole performance, and sometimes when we had only the wagon show I did, with the clown coming out to entertain the crowd while I changed my costume for the next act.

When I was eleven I ran away. Why not? The work was hard. I got no money, no breakfast even until I had worked around the ring for an hour. I ran away from Hamburg, where we were playing then, and put on little shows of my own in various towns in Germany, France, Italy, Belgium, Turkey and all the Balkan countries. After about four years of that I stowed away in the hold of a cattle boat, and for three days stayed there in the dark with the trampling of hoofs over my head. That's how I got to England. I started saving money then and when I had enough I came to America. I joined the show of Walter Main, then I was with Forepaugh and Sells and then with the Wallace shows. I did an aerial trapeze act in company with Charlie Siegrist, Toto Siegrist and Eddie Silbon. For a number of years I worked in the Barnum and Bailey show 'catching' in an aerial act. I got my teeth knocked out once and my mind knocked out a hundred times when my partner threw too hard. I've been hit that way on the knees so that I'd lose my grip and fall. Of all the falls I've taken, though, the worst was when I was with Wolf. I was ten years old. It was at the Wintergarten, Berlin. I fell sixty feet. Sure, there was a net to catch me, but a man can break his neck falling in a net as well as anywhere. An acrobat knows how to fall; he turns in the air and lands relaxed. I've fallen fifty feet on the bare ground without injury. But in this fall to the net I broke both ankes and it was seven weeks before I worked again.[19]

A circus fall got Polo into movies. He had already done some stunting for 'Bronco Billy' Westerns and 'Slippery Slim' comedies for Aronson's Essanay company, and in 1915 when he was badly hurt during the Barnum and Bailey aerial act Universal offered him a part in a Grace Cunard serial, *The Broken Coin*. Grace Cunard wrote the script, Francis Ford directed and starred, while John Ford had a small role and did stunts. Polo's role, not particularly appropriate for a convalescent, included a plane-to-boat transfer at the harbour in Little Venice, allegedly the first ever filmed, and some lively fights. After a few episodes Polo, perhaps under-standably for a man with his instinct for self-preservation, dis-carded the character make-up dictated by Ford, on the grounds that his fans wouldn't recognize him, and demanded a better role. It was the first of Polo's many disputes with producers, but since his egotism was mixed with a reckless skill, few cared to argue with him. A self-appointed expert on every aspect of stunting, he appeared at the 1915 San Diego Panama-Californian Exposition and, to challenge the claim of cautious army fliers that high parachute jumps were unsafe, made a 4,280 foot jump himself. (Shortly afterwards, he rode a horse off a fifty foot cliff into a lake; Polo survived but the horse was killed.) From a man with such genius for publicity, Universal were prepared to endure a great deal, and even though it was necessary to write him out of *Peg o' the Ring* in 1916 for refusing yet again to obey Francis Ford, he remained a top

serial star.

The pace soon began to wear him down. 'The movies,' he wrote, after reminiscing about his dangerous life in the circus. '*That's where you get hurt.*' In 1918 on *The Bull's Eye* he was trampled by a horse and badly injured. A lion used in another serial slashed his arm. Of grappling with two stunt men on *The Vanishing Dagger* (1920) before making a forty foot fall into a lake, he said, 'I felt fond enough of those extras to have gone on hugging them all day.' Gene Perkins increasingly took over his more risky falls before his early death. Polo's personality finally wore Carl Laemmle out, and the actor formed his own Star Serial Corporation to make the independent *Captain Kidd* (1922). Released when the boom was flagging, it flopped, and although Polo continued in films until 1930, a poor voice ended hopes of a feature career. Apart from a guest appearance in the Deanna Durbin musical *Hard to Handle* in 1943 he was not seen again.

Serials survived until television, never regaining the old vitality. In a feature-based industry they were not sufficiently lucrative to justify more than tiny budgets, but became, as well as a dumping ground for athletes or cowboys who lacked acting ability but not daring, a useful training ground for action filmmakers. While one director handled dialogue scenes, another was out in Griffith Park with a gang of stunt men doing the fights, falls and chases. B. Reeves Eason, Otto Brower and Yakima Canutt, later famous for their second-unit direction on major features, learned the trade here. Like the two-reel comedy, serials were a laboratory of action film technique. Some of their devices are still in use: slowing the camera (usually to eighteen frames a second for sound, the famous 'Western Eighteen') to pep up a chase (swordplay goes best at twenty frames, and a fight at twenty-two); the mechanics of the horse fall and the picture fight, of jumps and breakaways, the idea of building sets slightly smaller to exaggerate an actor's height, and the use of the 14·2 hand 'quarter horse', faster and more agile than the sixteen hand riding hack and thus safer for stunt falls: all these were serial innovations. The stage was set for better action films, in which the stunt man had an important part.

4 Tom (Mix) and Doug (Fairbanks)

Film producers of the twenties quickly found that while the thriving vaudeville circuits were an inexhaustible reservoir of comedians, no corresponding source existed for action heroes who could give physical expression to the myths of the cowboy and frontiersman – dull, undramatic men romanticized by popular literature. Films were still made in the East. California and the West, with their rodeo riders, were too remote for most companies, who did their best with Broadway actors. The first stars of frontier films had only the vaguest knowledge of the real West. 'Bronco Billy' Anderson who cranked out 376 films between 1909 and 1914 from a private train which chugged through the West, stopping at a likely town where he recruited a supporting cast from the locals, chose one of the six basic plots on which all his films were based, and shot his film before moving on, was actually a Chicago businessman named Max Aronson whose only experience of a horse when he entered films had been posing on one for a magazine cover. Even by the end of his career he was only moderately adept and local cowboys or ex-circus riders like Eddie Polo doubled him in riding scenes. Dustin Farnum, hired by Cecil B. DeMille to star in *The Squaw Man* (1913), Hollywood's first Western, had come no closer to the West than a supporting role in the original play, but despite this both he and his brothers William and Franklyn became famous as action stars. William S. Hart also belonged to the stage. He had played Mesalla in the famous Broadway *Ben-Hur*, Armand in *Camille* and a variety of dramatic roles unrelated to the West of which he became the most famous early resident. All these actors resourcefully imitated seasoned frontiersmen, lecturing on the significance of Western dress – Hart was very strict, justifying each buckle and flap with a meticulousness that convinced all his fans – and hiding the fact that real cowboys doubled the few risky scenes required of them.

Above *Tom Mix and Tony*

Below *Tony visits Mix while the latter recovers from an appendix operation*

Hart, Anderson and the Farnums remained respected Westerners throughout their careers, but as they reached the peak of their popularity in the autumn of American innocence just before the First World War, a less cautious breed of screen hero was emerging. Vitagraph had begun hiring real cowboys to advise on its Westerns and perform the stunts; for years Fred and Robert Burns were fixtures in the old Santa Monica mansion which was Vitagraph's first West Coast studio, producing a weekly one-reel Western, and cow hands learned that a winter in Los Angeles could bring in almost as much from movie riding as they earned all summer at rodeos.

They were basically stunt men, propping up an Eastern actor who could hardly sit his horse, but it was inevitable that this noisy group, probably the last generation of real cowboys, would eventually throw up its own star. Writing for *Photoplay* in 1922, Terry Ramsaye gave a glowing picture of his discovery.

In the early summer of 1910 Colonel Selig sent a camera crew into Oklahoma to make pictures of frontier life. . . . A whole constellation of star cowboys was rounded up to perform for the camera their feats of skill and daring. While the cowpunchers circled and wheeled and galloped and jumped their bucking mounts for the camera, a United States marshal sat lazily with one leg over the saddle horn, watching the proceedings with an interested eye. From time to time he nimbly rolled a cigarette in a bit of corn husk, Mexican fashion. His air of indifference would have indicated that he thought very little of the cowboys' performance. . . . 'Is this a private round-up or can I get in?' 'If you've got any speed, help yourself to the excitement,' the cameraman replied. . . . There was action aplenty. Then, just by way of topping it off, he roped and bulldogged a steer in a close-up in a matter of sixteen seconds. In July, Selig released *Ranch Life in the Great Southwest* and Tom Mix was started on his way to fame.[20]

If this story of Mix's movie debut seems too smooth, his official biography reads even more like a Western novelette. Born in a log cabin in El Paso, Texas, son of a Southern colonel and a half-Indian mother, he enlisted in the Spanish–American War, became a courier for Theodore Roosevelt's Rough Riders and watched the charge up San Juan Hill. A sniper's bullet went through both cheeks, damaging the roof of his mouth, but he later fought in both the Philippines Insurrection and the Boxer Rebellion, where he was wounded in the battle of Tien-Tsin when a shell smashed the artillery wagon he was helping to push; splinters lacerated his

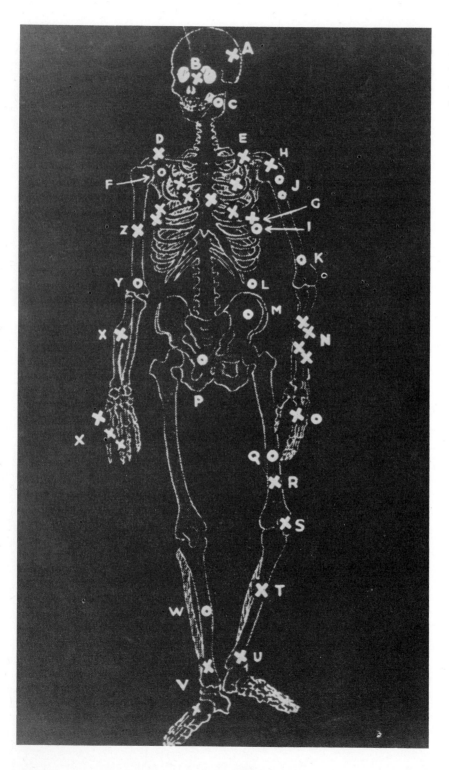

Left *Tom Mix's
alleged injuries: the
crosses indicate
breaks, the circles
bullet-holes*

scalp and broke his nose. He took a job breaking horses for the British Army in the Boer War, and was present (as a non-combatant, the studios hastened to stress) at the relief of Ladysmith. Back in the USA he drifted into law enforcement, first with the Texas Rangers, later as sheriff of Chioto, Oklahoma, and deputy marshal for the East Division of Oklahoma before taking up ranching. In 1932, *Motion Picture Classic* magazine published Mix's grim medical history, listing twenty-six major injuries (helpfully indicated on a Stetsoned skeleton) including a neat hole through the pelvis, allegedly contributed by one of the murderous Shont brothers – he promptly killed him – whom Mix arrested for rustling, and conscientiously noting that

Scars from twenty-two knife wounds are not indicated, nor is it possible to show on the diagram the hole four inches square and many inches deep that was blown in Mix's back by a dynamite explosion. There are also scars from fourteen buckshot in his left arm.[21]

People who knew Mix are sceptical about these colourful stories. Yakima Canutt, who first met Mix in 1923 while still a rodeo rider, remembers him as 'a man with a lot of good principles, but the awfullest liar in the world'. He once enthralled visitors to the studio with a story of his lawman days, rich in colour, courage and carnage. 'When the people had left I said "Tom, you kinda handle the truth a little bit reckless, don't you?" He said "What the hell. Look, they want to be entertained, so you tell them a story. I told them a story out of one of my pictures. That's showmanship."' Mix was really born in Mix Run, Pennsylvania, the son of a lumberman. A wild boy, he left school in the fourth grade after a gun with which he and a friend were playing went off and hit him in the leg. Except for an incident in 1925 when Mix was shot in his Hollywood home (allegedly by a burglar but actually by his wife) it is unlikely that he ever felt another bullet. He may have been in Cuba with Roosevelt, and he did later produce a group portrait of a military unit with him prominent in the front row, which he claimed to be the company he served with in China, but the rest of his military career, like his law enforcement stories, is probably an invention. By 1908, aged twenty-seven, he was an experienced rodeo rider, taking out the Champion Steer Thrower award at Seattle in 1909, and shortly afterwards joining the 101 Ranch Show, initially as a livestock foreman but later as one of its travelling team. In 1909 he was champion at rodeos in Prescott,

Arizona, and Canon City, Colorado, one of a successful troupe that included Hoot Gibson and Will Rogers. Knowing that the Miller brothers were considering offers from California film companies to employ the show in its winter layoff, Mix was intrigued when, calling to collect a prize cheque from the offices of the Cheyenne 'Frontier Week' rodeo, the committee chairman showed him a cable from William Selig in Chicago asking if he knew a cowboy willing to do stunts for a film on Western life. Mix promptly offered his own ranch and services, and after the success of *Ranch Life in the Great Southwest* Selig signed up Mix as the company's 'technical consultant'.

As Mix soon discovered, the 'technical consultant' was there to take risks for Selig's better paid serial and action stars; his title quickly changed to 'safety man'. Today the safety man stands just out of camera range to catch horses, manipulate wires or help the working stunt man in case of trouble, but Mix's duties went beyond this. He stunted for all Selig's stars – a photograph shows him wrestling with a python on one early drama – and went on location with serial units. Shooting *Lost in the Jungle* (F. J. Grandon) near Jacksonville, Florida, in 1914, he supervised a stunt in which serial heroine Kathryn Williams was to be menaced by a leopard as she cowered between two logs. The leopard had been trained to eat chickens, one of which was tethered beyond the logs just out of camera range, and while the animal-handler confidently expected his cat to leap in that direction, Mix stood by with a Winchester. Just as the cameras began turning and the leopard was released, a breeze feathered Miss Williams's hair and the animal, confused, jumped on her instead, digging its claws into her scalp. A shot was impossible, so Mix grabbed the leopard's tail and dragged it off. Selig, seeing the new man's potential, was ready to make Mix a star, but this was prevented by a running feud with the Miller brothers, who had also had plans for Mix. In 1910 they charged him with breach of contract and, when he seemed disinclined to answer this charge, added to it one of theft, technically 'embezzlement', of a horse, which they claimed Mix borrowed without permission to ride in a rodeo; he had broken his leg and in the resulting mêlée the horse, said the Millers, disappeared. (Since Mix later claimed to have acquired his highly intelligent horse Tony in 1909 or 1910 for $5, one can't help associating the two facts.) Mix was released pending a decision that was never given. Selig promptly placed Mix under contract – the Miller case dragged on

*Right Tom Mix as
clown . . . and
professional*

until 1937, when Mix settled out of court for $50,000 – and be-tween 1911 and 1916, first as stunter then as a featured player, Mix made seventy Westerns for the studio in which he broke and rode wild horses, performed countless transfers from horses to trains, wrestled wild animals and toppled wagons. Each of his legs was broken four times, and he also fractured ribs, ankles and hands; but his popularity soared.

When Ramsaye wrote his highly coloured story of Mix's dis-covery (no doubt retailed by Mix himself) he was merely telling the readers of *Photoplay* what they wanted to hear. Mix, by then William Fox's top star with a weekly salary of $17,000 and a vast international following, was, he assured them, the American dream made flesh – no actor but a cowboy who relived on film the events of a dangerous life. Hart's severity and stoicism had implied he could fight, ride and kill like the mythical Westerners, but since his films lacked obvious stunts the issue was never tested. Mix ended this convention. Although his incorruptible cowboy, slow to anger but tireless in revenge, echoed Hart's, indisputable evidence of his physical force and dexterity was there on the screen in stories that showed him battling gunmen, riding wild horses, toppling from cliffs, recklessly leaping into space, and later doing wild stunts with aircraft and automobiles. He set the pace of action film-making in the post-war period; actors died in exploits no real Western bandit or lawman would have con-sidered for a moment, and which Mix achieved only at the cost of injuries that would have killed any normal man. But Mix was not normal. His own summing up of his approach to film stunts suggests a phlegmatic acceptance of opposition and a contempt for his physical limits.

I never go back in doing any stunt. I go forward constantly. That is because the human body is so constructed that muscles and bone protect the front of the body. Man was made to advance. No matter what pro-fession he may choose, his success is measured by the rapidity with which he advances. I figured it out when I started to do my stunts before the camera, and it has saved my life many times. Always advance, keep your head and you can do any trick you want to do. You must keep your nerve too, or you will hesitate – and he who hesitates is lost.[22]

By the end of his life – he retired in 1935 and died in a 1940 car crash, aged sixty – this philosophy (a nonsensical one physically, since stunt men always prefer to take blows on the well-padded buttocks and back) had left his body a mass of scars, the bones of his arm and shoulder blades held together with surgical wire, his joints crippled with arthritis.

At Fox, Mix expanded the personality developed in his Selig films. Dressed in flamboyant clothes – seeing Yakima Canutt's fancy two-tone shirts when they met in 1923, he promptly had forty made up and started a fashion – and riding his 'wonder horses' Tony and Old Blue, the former credited with almost human intelligence and the ability to understand fifty words, he showed unfailing good humour, chivalry and contempt for reward in a series of successful features that built Fox into a major studio. On film, Mix never drank, smoked or showed disrespect for a woman. His nondescript history was obscured by fanciful press releases (as was the fact that Tony was actually three or four horses, the now ageing 'star' being reserved for close-up tricks like his ability to untie knots with his teeth: sheltered from hard work, Tony lived to thirty-four). Mix succumbed totally to his publicity, sporting a huge car with a saddle on its bonnet and 'TM' monograms on its side. He wore $500 panama sombreros with crowns of an almost ludicrous height – $1,000 a year was spent just on

copies of his hat for admirers – and exaggerated cowboy clothes, including a horsehair belt whose buckle, inlaid with his initials in diamonds, was engraved 'Tom Mix, America's Champion Cowboy'. His personal powerboat was named *Miss Mixit*, his second daughter Thomasina. When he formed the TM Bar Ranch to rent horses and Western gear to the studios, he had the trade mark painted on the roof of his house and was widely publicized in a photograph showing him, allegedly in his living room, surrounded by Western incunabala. His mansion was one of Hollywood's most luxurious, with a huge pool around which an almost continuous party seemed to be in progress, and a fountain in the foyer that played multi-coloured jets of water.

Mix, for all the publicity, remained tough. His films were shot on location, and although a chuck wagon provided reasonable meals, such trips, usually to the village of Palm Springs, were an ordeal. Mix still insisted on doing his own stunts but doubles were provided for the female stars. Marian Nixon worked with him on *The Last of the Duanes* and *Riders of the Purple Sage* (both Lynn Reynolds, 1924). 'I remember one scene where we're riding along a road. I'm sitting back of someone who is running off with me. They had the front legs of the horse wired, so as they pull the wires on the front legs of the horse to throw him, Tom rode in and just picked me up off the back of this saddle and put me on his knee and away we went. I was young and eager and I did everything to please. They had a double for me there – a girl named Crete Sipple – but I was young and anxious to make good. You got more credit for it and could be photographed better if you were doing it yourself rather than have a stunt woman.'

Although this had always been Mix's philosophy, he was slowing down. In 1925 – he was forty-five – he again broke his arm when a coach overturned, pinning him under it. In 1926 a similar accident fractured his knee; he wore a brace on that leg for many years. Reluctantly he brought doubles onto his team, including trick rider Buck Jones, later a star in his own right, but Mix resented the necessity and all were sworn to silence. Sound finally ended Mix's career: a flat Midwestern voice clashed with the physical image he put forward. He spent three seasons with the Sells-Flato circus and starred in some B-films. His last was a 1935 serial, *The Miracle Rider* (Armand Schaefer, B. Reeves Eason), and in the final humiliation a penny-pinching Mascot company, able to afford his salary for only a few days, used him for close-ups and dialogue scenes, calling in Cliff Lyons, a graduate of the *Ben Hur* chariot race and countless Westerns, for the stunts that made up most of the story. Lyons found Mix, even at the end of his career, an awesome figure. 'He was a helluva engineer,' he said. 'He rode superbly. He figured out stunts scientifically, and broke every bone in his body doing them.' It was this stoicism in the face of danger that impressed everybody who worked with Mix. There has probably never been another actor with less concern for his own comfort. Mix once complained to director Lambert Hillyer of a bad toothache, but since one of his foibles was a distrust of doctors there seemed no alternative but to endure it. Missing him shortly afterwards, Hillyer went to his tent, and found him trying to pull out the tooth with pliers. 'Mix had guts, and to spare,' Hillyer recalled respectfully.

The career and phenomenal popularity of Douglas Fairbanks followed naturally from the fashion for outdoor adventure Mix and the serial stars created. Fairbanks refurbished it for the twenties, identifying his films with the expansive policies of his hero, Teddy Roosevelt, whose wary pacifism and doctrine of 'preparedness' he lived by. His personal philosophy was an almost childish optimism, and an adulation of physical fitness expressed in simplistic slogans, mostly expansions of *mens sana in corpore sano*. 'One of the best things in this little old world is enthusiasm,' he said in one of the inspirational books ghosted by his secretary Kenneth Davenport. 'To be successful you must be happy; to be happy you must be enthusiastic; to be enthusiastic you must be healthy; and to be healthy you must keep mind and body healthy.' His early films for Triangle, whose backer, Harry Aitken, had hired the young actor on a buying trip to Broadway, after admiring leaps he did over a bench for newsreel cameramen, were Westerns made under the grumpy supervision of D. W. Griffith. Griffith thought Fairbanks a brainless clown fit only for Mack Sennett slapstick, but the actor quickly saw his *métier* and, when the ailing Triangle was unwilling to exploit it, left to form a company that would. Here Fairbanks's original business thinking ended. Although an active partner in the United Artists organization which he founded with Chaplin, Griffith and Mary Pickford in 1919 to distribute their work and that of other independent film-makers, he left management to the shrewd Miss Pickford, whom he later married, and to businessmen like B. P. Schulberg, mastermind of the UA deal. His energy was reserved for the massive action spectaculars with which he enchanted America through the twenties, and when sound ended the fashion he declined to a slightly pathetic ex-idol pursuing beautiful women around Europe. He died at fifty-six in 1939, his tanned body apparently untouched by age but actually so muscle-bound that the blood could barely circulate. He had not so much died, some friends thought, as run down.

Even on Broadway before the First World War, Fairbanks was famous for his athletic ability, disrupting rehearsals by walking upstairs on his hands, or offering to leap twelve feet from a balcony when a more conventional descent seemed insufficiently dashing. Joining Triangle, he attacked film-making with a frightening zest. Compact, dark, he had the resilience and bounce of a

Below *Douglas Fairbanks:* The Three Musketeers

Right *Still agile, Fairbanks jumps a fence in New Zealand while making* Around the World In Eighty Minutes (1931), *watched by Victor Fleming*

rubber ball, while a permanent grin neutralized the broadness of his stage acting style. In *The Habit of Happiness* (Allan Dwan, 1916) he fought five of the toughest extras to be found in the studio's 'bull pen'; his hands and face were so battered that shooting stopped until the swellings went down. *The Half Breed* (Dwan, 1916) cost him eyelashes and hair when the forest fire from which he rescued actor Sam de Grasse ran out of control, and in *Manhattan Madness* (Dwan, 1916) a stage pistol went off in his face, blinding him for three weeks. Fairbanks accepted the discomforts and risks without complaint.

As his independent productions made him famous, Fairbanks's life assumed some of the quality of his films. Like many actors he surrounded himself with an *équipe*. Anita Loos, then a young scenarist with Triangle whom Fairbanks took with him when he left, along with her husband, director John Emerson, recalled them vividly.

Prominent in Doug's retinue were two prize-fighters, Spike Robinson and Bull Montana, who drew salaries for sparring with the boss. Spike behaved with the ponderous dignity of an ex-champ, but Bull Montana was as gentle as a lamb. He had cauliflower ears, a cauliflower nose and also a cauliflower brain which supplied the troupe with low comedy that was almost Shakespearean. Another important member of our group was Doug's valet, Buddy, a bright young man of sepia colour who took a large part in all our fun . . .[23]

Bull Montana – real name Luigi Mantegna – was hired initially as a bodyguard for Fairbanks, but went on to a minor career in his and other films, culminating in a role as the Missing Link in *The Lost World* (1925). His enormous car and tomato-red shirts – bizarrely echoing Fairbanks's love of silk shirts and of a perfume called 'Ciro's Surrender' which he often wore – made him a Hollywood character. Less prominent were Kenneth Davenport, secretary and friend, John Pitcairn, his personal make-up man, and brothers Robert and John Fairbanks. John became the company's business manager, and Robert, an engineer, planned many of the stunts for Doug's later big-budget films that were to make him famous.

Fairbanks's work often shows timing worthy of the great comedians; Harold Lloyd gave a likely reason: 'Chaplin, Laurel and Hardy, Fatty Arbuckle; we all used to gather, a great many of us, over at Doug Fairbanks's dressing room at United Artists. He had a steam room there. We all used to go in there and take steam.'[24] (By contrast, Fairbanks hated central heating, and his house, 'Pickfair', was reputedly the most uncomfortably cold in California.) He also operated a full-sized gym, where he worked out with Robinson, Montana, sword expert Fred Cavens or other visiting athletes while the gang watched from the sidelines, or planned elaborate practical jokes on one another. A chair wired to give electric shocks was a fixture of all Fairbanks bungalows, as it had been at Keystone.

Doug enjoyed the company of tough men; some of their masculinity rubbed off. On *The Black Pirate* (Al Parker, 1926) he had a team of ex-boxers, sparring partners, bouncers and thugs for his crew. After shooting, they retired to his bungalow and wrecked furniture, the star and each other in violent bouts of an indoor tennis Fairbanks had invented and which, logically, he called 'Doug'. He entertained with equal verve, luring friends on roundabout dawn treks at the end of which they would find themselves back in the grounds of Pickfair being served breakfast from a chuck wagon to the adenoidal serenading of a cowboy trio. He also earned a reputation for sexual athleticism. 'That Fairbanks!' Sam Goldwyn is reputed to have said. 'He spends every minute of the day making love.' 'Impossible,' his friends countered. 'He must do something in between times.' 'I guess he practises,' Goldwyn said.

Since doubles were common by the time Fairbanks became famous, his insistence up to 1920 on doing most of his own stunts is puzzling. Part of the reason was sheer high spirits. 'He was by nature very athletic,' Douglas Fairbanks Jnr said, 'and enjoyed doing stunts just for the fun of it, off stage. If he saw a gate, rather than go through the gate he'd hop over it. If he saw a desk, he'd rather vault over the desk than walk round it.' There was also an element of bravado, and he enjoyed challenging the film crew to risk injury with him, as proof of his greater virility. Making *The Man from Painted Post* (1917) on location at the Grand Canyon, he suddenly jumped from the canyon edge across a sheer drop to the table-sized peak of a pinnacle some feet out from the cliff. Eileen Percy, his leading lady, screamed and director Joseph Henabery was speechless. When Fairbanks leaped back, scenarist and fellow-conspirator Tom Geraghty said, 'Now try it with Henabery on your shoulders like you did with me last night.' Fairbanks squatted obligingly, but Henabery declined, to the derision of the whole crew. Fairbanks finally met his match in two technicians as rough and tumble as he was, director Allan Dwan and Victor Fleming, who drove a cab before becoming a cameraman and was one of the most adventurous of early film-makers. He challenged them to join him on the roof of the train in which they were going on location for *A Modern Musketeer* in 1918. Passengers were startled a few minutes later by three faces peering from outside the windows.

Minor injuries in such escapades, combined with his growing popularity and the impossibility of getting insurance cover, led Fairbanks to revise the form of his films. Audiences wanted more than mere dexterity, and Robert Fairbanks designed elaborate tricks that kept the mixture fresh. Doug learned the use of bull-whip, bolas and the rudiments at least of swordsmanship. For *Robin Hood* (Allan Dwan, 1922) and *The Thief of Baghdad* (Raoul Walsh, 1924), Fairbanks's two most successful films, Robert, helped in the case of *Robin Hood* by Dwan, who had been an engineer, designed sets which attributed to Fairbanks an almost superhuman skill. To allow him to slip with impossible ease down a huge curtain in *Robin Hood*, a slide was hidden in the drapery, and furniture was precisely built to suit the length of his reach and jump. In *The Black Pirate* where, swinging to the face of a

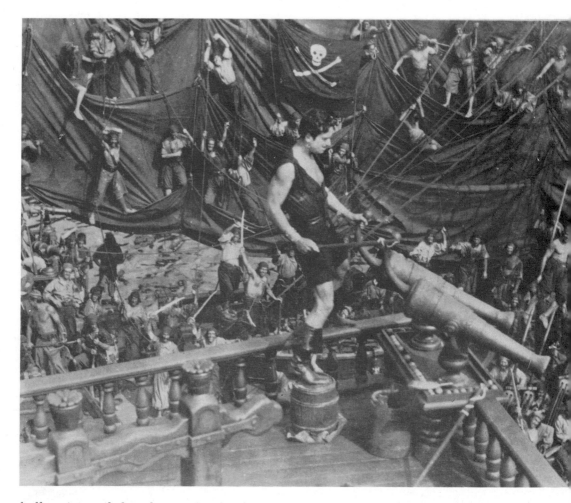

balloning sail, he plunges his knife into it and slides gracefully to the deck, his fall slowed by its friction, both the knife and Fairbanks's torso were supported by piano wire, almost invisible and immensely strong, though inclined to break if even slightly kinked. In *The Thief of Baghdad*, weeks were spent planning single stunts. His son said, 'They wouldn't just walk out one morning and say "Let's do this" or "Let's do that." Sets would be designed and the idea of a stunt sketched out on paper ahead of time, and he would rehearse it as carefully as, say, Fred Astaire would rehearse, then choreograph a dance routine. For example, in *The Thief of Baghdad* he had an idea of jumping into a huge pot or vase, about eight feet tall, then bouncing out of one into another, then another. He began first with a series of trampolines without anything around them at all. Then, little by little, he had barriers

The athlete triumphant: Fairbanks in (above) The Black Pirate *and* (right) The Thief of Baghdad

put up so he was jumping higher from one trampoline to another. Then higher and higher. Then he enclosed the trampolines with very ricketty bits of wood or string; something easily broken so that if he tripped he wouldn't injure himself. Until eventually the time came to do the thing with real vases. He would be weeks ahead, trying out his stunts, and they would be worked out almost to a metronome, rather like a dance.'

Although this pre-planning supported the fiction that Fairbanks was never doubled, stunt men, particularly on his later films, often replaced him. Dwan admitted:

We only used stunt men when there was danger – when there was a chance the man might get hurt. In one of his pictures that I wasn't on, Doug insisted on doing a stunt that I would never let him do – and he got hurt. He jumped over a balcony railing to a horse waiting below. Horses, you know, instinctively move when they feel something coming. That's what this one did, and Doug fell and was hurt. Now I'd have used a stunt man for that shot. That wasn't graceful. It was just foolish.[25]

Fairbanks wrenched his left hand, back and neck in the fall. Anita Loos also remembers an occasion when Fairbanks

turned coward in the presence of us all. It was during a scene where the hero had to deflate an automobile tyre by sticking a hat pin in it. John Emerson shot the action several times, but Doug bungled every take just at the point of sticking the pin into the tyre. Finally he broke down and confessed, 'I can't do this. I'm scared.' We all thought Doug was kidding, but he was actually afraid the tyre would blow up and blind him, so John had to make use of a stunt man.[26]

(One wonders if his fear of blindness stemmed from the accident on *Manhattan Madness*.) Acrobats obviously doubled scenes on *Robin Hood* and *The Thief of Baghdad*, notably a shot in the latter where the thief, escaping from the palace, is thrown over the wall on a springy tree. J. Theodore Reed, second-unit director on *The Mark of Zorro* (Fred Niblo, 1920) and thereafter a Fairbanks stunt designer, claimed 'Doug didn't use doubles until *The Gaucho* [F. Richard Jones, 1927] and only then because he failed to show up and Chuck Lewis substituted for him to keep from wasting time',[27] but obviously the involvement of stunt men went farther than this, and began earlier. In many cases Fairbanks hired acrobats like Richard Talmadge to execute a stunt while he watched, analysing the movements he would later perform with apparently instinctive ease on camera. It soon became simpler for the double to execute the stunt himself, and it is likely that Talmadge doubled Fairbanks in the famous *Black Pirate* 'sail' shot, among others. But on one occasion during *Robin Hood* on the enormous castle set, taller than the walls of Babylon in *Intolerance*, the old Fairbanks bravado reasserted itself. On Dwan's insistence that a double should climb the huge drawbridge chain for Robin's entry into the castle, Fairbanks grudgingly agreed. The first shot was discarded because the stunt man looked, to Fairbanks's eyes, 'ungraceful', and while a replacement was sought Fairbanks left, allegedly to try out some new routines in the gym. Shortly after, a new figure was seen climbing the chain. It was not until he reached the top that Dwan recognized Fairbanks.

5 I'm Still Alive

Through the post-war period and into the twenties, scores of stunt people drifted to California. A stunter of the time remembers them as a mixed bag.

Western doubles are products of ranches, rodeos and round-ups, good cowboys who have been bucked off many a horse before they ever saw a camera, men to whom trick horsemanship is an old story. The high divers into water, or good swimmers, usually come from circuses, water carnivals; lifeguards and such. Other boys are old circus acrobats who know how to go from heights to nets safely. Others were small-time, and a few big-time auto racers who know what to do with an automobile at high speed in case something goes wrong.[28]

Motives for making the trip varied. Cliff Lyons, who came down from South Dakota in 1922, and Yakima Canutt, famous in rodeos before signing a 1923 movie contract, were typical of the professional cowboys lured by the success of Tom Mix (for whom both eventually stunted). Buck Jones and Fred Thompson soon joined them. Many others, like Dave Sharpe, were athletes who, unable to earn money from their agility elsewhere, went into movies. Every kind of circus artist headed for Hollywood, from Aaron Bernhard, a 192-pound German who specialized in strong man roles, to Janos Prohaska, who did nothing but gorilla imitations. Joe Bonomo, the son of a Coney Island candy concessionaire and destined for the same trade, won a 1921 New York 'Modern Apollo' contest in which the prizes were $1,000 and a ten week movie contract. Al Wilson, Bob Rose and Dick Grace were typical of the fliers who often wintered in California and drifted into films during the wartime ban on civil flying, staying with the movies when its 1919 repeal led Hollywood to create its own cycle of air films whose risks and rewards were greater than those of county fairs.

The greatest lure was money. Until 1920 stunt men had been lumped with extras in Hollywood's primitive accounting system based on a daily payment with additional 'margins for skill'. An extra received a standard $5 or $7 a day, with a few dollars more for the 'dress extras' who supplied their own dinner suit or evening dress. A man with make-up skill might turn up in the bull-pen one morning with a convincing Mexican or pirate make-up and be written into an action film on the strength of it, getting a few dollars more for his enterprise. In the same way, extras would earn more by doing the occasional dangerous stunt. Working on *Intolerance*

Left *Joe Bonomo:*
The Chinatown
Mystery

in 1916, young Woody Van Dyke, employed to put beards and
sun-tan on fifteen hundred Babylonian warriors, noticed the sign
'Acrobats Wanted' in the bull-pen and spent his afternoon falling
off the walls into a net. (He later drove a chariot, and nearly
wrecked the scene when his horse ran out of control.) Gradually
expert tumblers gravitated to Hollywood and took the jobs
which amateurs like Van Dyke had risked their necks doing, but
the pay was always based on that of the other extras. They were
casual actors on a flat daily rate, with an 'adjustment' for danger,
and if injured were entitled, under California law, to the first two
weeks of incapacity at full pay, usually $10 a day, and thereafter
sixty-five per cent of full pay for a year, with the right to sue the
studio when this ran out.

For the studios this was far too expensive, and they privately
agreed to separate stunt men from the main body of extras. The
'adjustment' was replaced by a flat fee based on an agreed scale
of charges. It meant more money for the stunter – in a few years
the basic charge for any stunt rose from $10 to $25, and by the
late twenties had stabilized at $50 – but it also made him re-
sponsible for the satisfactory completion of the stunt and for his

own safety. If he died, the studio might pay a moderate sum to the next-of-kin – Dick Grace claimed his contract guaranteed $5,000 in case of death – but a stunt man was expected to allow in his fee for the possibility of medical treatment. It was also recognized that a stunt man contracted for a particular job, not for the day's work. If the director wasn't satisfied with the stunt, he had to do it over again.

The change threw stunting into the melting pot, where it has remained ever since. In this highly competitive field men scuffled for work, undercutting one another and often paring down their

Below Harvey Parry in a high dive for a John Ford film of the early twenties

safety margin to offer a more spectacular stunt. Even when Will
Hays's 'clean-up' administration of 1925 forced the studios to
found Central Casting, an industry-controlled talent agency with
which all film performers had to register (a move to prevent
vagrants and prostitutes ducking a fine by claiming to be un-
employed extras), stunt men remained independent of it. Work
went to the man with a reputation, with friends among the assistant
directors who did the hiring, or, in the last resort, to the lowest
bidder. Without collective bargaining, wages for ordinary stunt
people stayed low and risks high. Understandably, the best
learned to specialize, and although there was plenty of work for
all-rounders like Bob Rose, Harvey Parry, Paul Malvern and Ray
'Red' Thompson, able to handle horse work, falls or car stunts
equally well, they soon joined the trend. Rose exploited his background as a parachutist in wing-walking and other aerial feats,
Red Thompson his success in jumping horses into water by corner-
ing the market in this stunt. Leo Noomis and Harvey Parry became
famous for their motor-cycle and automobile work respectively,
and Joe Bonomo was also a motor-cycle specialist before diversi-
fying. The successful stunt man aimed to identify himself with one
'gag' – the terminology of the comedy days had stuck – and to
come to an assistant director's mind the moment this stunt was
contemplated. It exaggerated the isolationism that has always
afflicted the stunt field. A man whose living depended on knowing
how to dive safely into water was unwilling to tell a cowboy of his
methods for fear his own work would be taken away, and it was
not unknown for established men to let others go into a stunt
fatally ill-prepared; an injury or death could only establish the
expert more strongly.

A few stunt men, usually those with more courage and tenacity
than skill, tried to improve their position with self-publicity,
adopting picturesque nicknames and courting the fan press.
'Suicide' Buddy Mason was perhaps the best-known stunt man of
the twenties, but his actual exploits are meagre. Fred 'Speed'
Osborne, a mechanic who hoped for stardom as a stunter, earned
only a reputation for recklessness in a brief career that ended with
crippling disablement. But generally the stunt men avoided personal publicity, cultivating a laconic style that, in a field where the
average professional life was five years – after which one had
either retired or been killed – served to disguise deep personal
relationships. The amateur or newcomer was despised less for

inexperience than for his lack of allegiance in a tight-knit community. Dick Grace's description of a man who died in an unsafe plane stunt has more malice than can be explained by outraged professionalism.

The poor damned fool. He ought to have known better. There he was, all crushed to hell – his head spattered to the size of a washtub, one arm grotesquely stuck through his right side and protruding on the left, just below the heart. His legs were still entangled in the jumbled mass of wire, linen and wood. . . . His name? It doesn't matter. After all he was an amateur, and who the hell cares about one of them?[29]

In a 1927 article, Dick Hylan expressed the nervousness most outsiders felt on encountering this odd brigade. 'Some of them talked sane enough – for a time. But talk to them long enough and you find that a wheel is missing somewhere.'[30]

For a stunt man in the silent cinema, the only promotion was into acting. Few had the desire or ability to direct films, and those who did soon found places in an expanding industry. Directors who claim to have 'begun as stunt men' may have done the occasional fall when they first came to Hollywood, but examples of established stunt doubles in the twenties who went behind the camera are rare – a contrast to the present day. On the other hand, many of them traded on the popularity of 'thrill pictures' and the shortage of athletic stars to become 'actors' themselves. Most were indifferent, and faded when the action boom waned, but a few were good enough to hang on. Monte Blue earned his reputation as a stunter and, after some leading roles in the late twenties and thirties, followed by character parts as his patent-leather hair whitened in middle age, retreated into action films again before ending his career in 1963, aged seventy-six, as he had begun, in the circus, a publicity 'advance man' for the Hamid-Morton show.

One of the few actors of the twenties whose alleged Indian blood was genuine – he was half Cherokee – Blue worked as a lumberjack, railroader, seaman, forest ranger, miner, cowboy and general roustabout before joining the Ringling Circus as a member of its drill team. In 1914 he came to Hollywood hoping to put his riding ability to use in movies, but the only job he could find was labouring for Triangle's *Enoch Arden*; he dug graves for a funeral scene. For two years he was a prop man, mainly at Triangle, the huge consortium of Griffith, Sennett and Ince that dominated Hollywood until the egos of its flamboyant principals tore it apart.

Triangle's backer, Harry Aitken, spent most of his capital hiring the best talents of Broadway to make their film debuts, and found too late that few had the energy or willingness to accept the movies' exhausting methods. Humorist DeWolf Hopper, hired to play in *Don Quixote* (1916), did well enough in the dramatic scenes, which in Triangle's broad version hardly mattered, but flatly refused to joust with a windmill constructed at some expense on the Culver City lot. They had reached an impasse when Blue, who had been patiently manning the capstan that moved the blades, offered to double the star.

Blue doubled Hopper, Sir Herbert Beerbohm Tree and other Triangle stage stars for three years, also doing extra work on *Birth of a Nation* and *Intolerance* (Griffith later featured him as Danton in *Orphans of the Storm*). Since Sir Herbert, then appearing in *Macbeth*, received $100,000 for six months of very little effort, and Blue, risking his neck daily in duels and fights for the star, got only $30 a week, he took the opportunity of the company's sliding fortunes to leave as Douglas Fairbanks had done. He haunted the 'extra' bull-pens in a futile search for work, until an assistant director, looking for a suitably gaunt mob leader, chose

Left *Monte Blue as the fighting schoolmaster in* The Jucklins

Blue, who had eaten little since leaving Triangle. For the next five years Blue played thugs, bandits and wild Indians, jobs into which he threw himself and his athletic ability. Leading an Indian raid (with real Indians) on *Told in the Hills* (George Melford, 1919), he almost went too far.

I was leading the Indians in a wild charge when I met a wide ditch right in my path. There was no time to pull up the horse – I was riding him with a rope bridle and no saddle – so I just hung on to his mane and let him try the jump. He missed, throwing me about forty feet, and I got up a pretty-looking object, with blood streaming from my mouth and ears. But I didn't intend letting those Indians see me fall down on the job, so I collared the horse again, and rode him off. I was too shaken up to realize just what had happened to me, but when I went to take my shoes off after the ride, I doubled right up and couldn't straighten out again. They found when they examined me that I had broken three ribs.[31]

Later, on a mountain melodrama called *The Jucklins* (George Melford, 1920) it was his turn to save a life.

I played the part of Bill Hawes, a young fellow from Alabama who is engaged to teach school in a mountain district that is noted for the regularity and thoroughness with which the pupils thrash the teacher and drive him out of the county. Bill succeeds in knocking out the bully of the school and, in revenge, the ex-champion sets fire to the building. In order that the school house should be consumed as rapidly as possible the inside of the building was saturated with oil, and one of the property men was stationed there to fire the place on the side opposite the door and then escape through a hole in the floor, the building being on brick piles. The business was carried out as rehearsed and when I staggered from the building it was blazing away inside at a great rate. The property man followed his instructions but the oil burned so rapidly that he was overcome before he could reach the hole in the floor.[32]

Blue had to drag the man out of the burning building, then hide him behind the house before re-entering and coming out, as directed, by the front door.

Men of courage and agility like Blue were in demand, even if they had little acting ability; studios knew better than to ask for more than one Fairbanks in a decade. But when an actor appeared who was a stunt man of remarkable skill and experience, a handsome and stylish performer, and had the endorsement of Fairbanks as well, the industry snapped him up. Predictably, Richard Talmadge became one of the twenties' few successful stunt-man stars, though always barred by accidents of timing and personality from reaching the top. His career was intimately involved with that of Douglas Fairbanks Snr, his early employer and mentor. Easily Fairbanks's equal as an athlete, Talmadge might have reached the same heights, but he lacked Fairbanks's optimism, good humour and identification with American aspirations. Through a long career as stunt man, minor star, stunt coordinator and second-unit director, Talmadge acquired the image of a self-consciously remote technician, highly competent, but regarded by colleagues, even though they praise his skill and imagination,

Below *Part of the promotion for* Taking Chances

with a certain wariness. Born Sylvester Metzetti in Switzerland in 1896, he and his three brothers were trained by their father in the circus. At four, Sylvester was touring with the family troupe, a top European tumbling and aerialist act that later repeated its success in the United States. He entered the College of the City of New York, but left shortly after to return to his old business. In 1913 he did some stunts for the serial *The Million Dollar Mystery*.

I played the part of a fellow who makes a prison break and jumps off a four-storey building. The picture was made at Fort Lee, New Jersey. I had to bring my own net for the jump and also my own assistants. I got $20 for the job, and after I was done paying off my helpers I had $4 left. [33]

But he persisted. On a Californian vacation he found more prospects for stunt work in Hollywood, and moved there permanently. In the early twenties, when he became a leading man, he was to change his name to Richard Talmadge, capitalizing on the fame of the Talmadge sisters, Norma, Natalie and Constance.

His first Hollywood job, as with many new doubles, was on one of Slim Summerville's comedies. 'I had to make a seventy-two foot jump, landing in sand. It was the equivalent of six storeys. For that I got $5.' Summerville, obviously feeling guilty, approached the young Talmadge as he counted his bruises and quietly slipped him an extra $5, the 'adjustment' with which stars salved their consciences. Talmadge soon made a speciality of the high jump, which he executed from burning buildings, ships, masts and towers into cars, water or sometimes, as in a twenties serial, the hard ground.

A car in which I was jumping a ditch had turned over in mid-air and I was flung out twenty-five feet. I had to go on crutches for three weeks. Universal was making a serial and they wanted me badly for a stunt. I told them I was a cripple but they insisted I should try – they were in a spot and no one else would do. So I was hoisted up forty feet, onto a little ledge on a tower. I threw the crutches away and just stood there for a few minutes. I was so stiff I could hardly move. I was supposed to jump and land on a bunch of mattresses in a dry river bed. I jumped – but the property man had decided that I would land a few feet farther to the left and had moved the mattresses. I landed in the river bed with a terrific thud. They thought I was dead. But I got up – and walked off without crutches. The fall had straightened out my bad back. It was quite a fall! The imprint of my body was clearly visible in the river bed. [34]

By now, all four Metzettis were working in Hollywood, mainly stunting on comedies. Talmadge was on the Vitagraph set when his eldest brother, doubling Antonio Moreno, tried a difficult hand-over-hand crossing of a street and fell sixty feet to the concrete. As the doctors carried him away, Talmadge disappeared into the building, reappeared on the ledge and did the stunt. His brother was nine months in hospital and a cripple for life, but Talmadge, with brothers Otto and Vic, stayed on, Richard taking over as regular stunt man for Moreno, and for comedian Larry Semon.

Talmadge's skill attracted the attention of Douglas Fairbanks, for whom he worked on *Robin Hood* (1922), *The Black Pirate* (1926) and *The Gaucho* (1927), often doubling the star but mostly going through stunts while Fairbanks watched and memorized movements he would later make himself. Fairbanks encouraged Talmadge when he decided to launch his own series of adventure films, and publicly endorsed the first, *Taking Chances* (Grover Jones, 1922), which set the pattern for a string of others. Dick, playing himself, is an eager young man who falls for an heiress, becomes her father's secretary, and foils the Mexican bandits who try to kidnap her, demonstrating his athletic ability in the process.

Left *Richard Talmadge:* Never Too Late (1935)

ight *Richard*
almadge: Laughing
t Danger (1925)

UNITY FILM CO. LTD.
Present
Richard Talmadge *in*
"LAUGHING AT DANGER"

For *The New Reporter* (Jack Dillon, 1922) he was a newsman, for *Lucky Dick* (William K. Howard, 1923) a cowboy, but in all of them his appeal rested on stunts which, as the publicity assured audiences with fearsome insistence, he always performed himself.

Talmadge remained a minor star until sound, which ended his acting career, and then returned to stunt work, often with his brothers. They did much of the doubling on Hal Roach's late silent and early sound Laurel and Hardy comedies, which included many hazardous sequences. A mild-looking man who in middle age sported spectacles and a moustache, and spent his spare time gardening, Talmadge's apparent quiet amiability was contradicted by boundless vitality and a legendary bad temper. In 1935, Yakima Canutt worked on *The Trail of the Lonesome Pine* (Henry Hathaway), doubling Henry Fonda in a hectic fist fight with all three Metzettis. 'It was a scene where the two guys get into a fight and at the end of it the porch collapses. Dick is pretty rugged to fight with. You had to put up a pretty good sort of fight just to defend yourself from him. He wouldn't routine things out; he'd just go in there and start fighting. We were slinging them pretty tough when the director said 'Cut'. I dropped my hands and then I saw his fist just coming at my face. He'd started one and couldn't stop it. The punch put my teeth almost right through my lip. He actually cried, though of course that sort of thing can happen to anybody. His brothers were almost as energetic. When the porch collapsed in the picture, it hit one of them on the head and knocked him out. When Dick and I got through with the fight we were talking and we heard this moaning under the wreckage. What the hell's that? I thought, and we found Otto, just coming to.'

Before becoming Hollywood's car stunt specialist, Carey Loftin worked with Talmadge in the late thirties, and was forcibly impressed by his hair-trigger temper. 'We were working on an Abbott and Costello picture at Universal. I saw Dick sitting on a little flimsy box about a foot square, talking to another guy who was squatting down. So I whipped this box out and he lit on his tailbone. He's got a flash temper and he's as strong as a bull. There just happened to be a board there, about an inch square and four feet long. He picked it up and he would have cut my head off he swung it so hard, but I just got under it. I lit on my back and I started to apologize. "Dick, Dick. I'm sorry. I'm *sorry*. My God!" There was a vacant lot there and we ran all through this lot. I ran for dear life, because I know he's strong and he's got a temper. Finally when he relaxed I apologized again and he went across the street. He walked up and down for about twenty minutes, then came back over. He had tears rolling down his face. He said, "Thank God you can duck. I could have cut your head off." '

Some of Talmadge's vigour survived in Richard Grace, the self-styled 'King of Stunters'. Grace came to Hollywood, like Al Wilson, Bob Rose and Frank Clarke, as a flying barnstormer or itinerant stunt flier, but soon branched out into every aspect of stunting. Born in North Dakota in 1898, he initially studied law but turned to flying when barnstormers started appearing in his district. Enlisting in the Navy Air Corps at eighteen after lying about his age, he flew in France, and on his return started an unsuccessful barnstorming team. After its failure he came to California, worked at Fox as a property man for Slim Summerville, and took up stunt work when a nervous actor in an Al St John two-reeler balked at a jump. (He later taught St John to fly, and made him a proficient wing-walker.)

Like all top stunt men, Grace had an inquiring and technical mind. He studied the mechanics of automobile skids by racing his car on the empty streets of Los Angeles in the pouring rain, slamming on the brakes at each intersection, resentful that the car would never spin more than three and a half times. Scorning specialization, Grace sought out acrobats to learn the rudiments of tumbling, and contracted for fire gags, car crashes and every other form of stunt work. But a year of violent comedy falls taught him he could not survive another. Even at $25 a stunt, the standing rate, he seldom earned more than $50 a week, most of which went on medical expenses and the upkeep of his car. One stunt put him on the eighth floor of a building frontage stuffed with gasoline-soaked paper. The fire prevented safety men from getting near enough with a net, so Grace had to drop first to some telephone wires, and swing from them to the net. Later that day, $20 of his $25 went to the friend who had given him gas and oil on credit. Shortly after, a perfectionist director demanded four repeats of a painful jump from a speeding taxi and a car-to-car transfer, and Grace decided he had had enough. He was, at five foot eight, too tall to tumble gracefully, besides which his study convinced him that, approached with caution, the large and showy stunts were no more dangerous than those he had been doing. He decided to reserve himself for what he called 'major thrills' – jumps over fifty feet, plane-to-plane transfers, and crashes, which had fascinated him since he helped barnstormers rebuild their shattered machines. After the death of pilot Ormer Locklear in an air stunt producers were cautious, but Grace convinced one studio to commission a relatively simple crash in which a taxiing plane tips on its nose and flops over on its back. Next, doubling Tom Mix in *Eyes of the Forest* (Lambert Hillyer, 1923), he flew full-tilt into the side of a barn and walked away unharmed. Within a few months he had all the work he could use, at the high rates he demanded.

Grace became known as the man who would do anything for a price, and despite his cool calculation of the chances it is astonishing that he survived some of the stunts that built his reputation. When he wrote his autobiography in the thirties, it had the mocking title *I Am Still Alive*, the sort of gauntlet in the face of death which the most flamboyant stunters liked to think that they flung. He determined to better all the classic stunts, including Locklear's plane-to-plane transfer. Locklear had used a rope ladder; for *Wide Open* (1927) Grace agreed not only to do it as a free fall, but also while hanging head-down from the plane. He wisely hired Hollywood's best stunt fliers: Art Goebel to pilot his plane,

Frank Tomick the one below and Frank Clarke the camera plane.

We left the ground in perfect formation. When we had sufficient altitude I climbed to the end of the wing and motioned Frank Tomick to swing into position. Already I noticed that Clarke had assumed a great angle for photographing the stunt. I could see the cameraman standing up in the back cockpit, his hand on the crank, ready to start grinding the minute things began to look interesting.

At the last minute we had decided to attempt the change from the skid which was attached to the lower panel of the left wing instead of from the landing carriage. This at least would save me from the whipping of the propellor blast. As soon as the planes were in position I swung underneath the wing and locked my legs around the bamboo skid. A moment later I let my hands go and there I hung, my arms pointed earthwards, my head twisting from side to side as I watched the pilots endeavouring to bring the ships close enough for me to make the jump. But it was taking considerable time to accomplish all of these details. The muscles of my legs were beginning to feel tired. They not only had to hold the entire weight of my body, but they had to combat the force of the wind and retain their grip on the bamboo skid. . . . The nose and leading edge of Tomick's ship were almost directly below me. The time was ripe to try the leap. Unlocking my knees, I let my body slide down toward the earth. Only a few feet to go between me and the other ship, but if I miscalculated there would be two thousand more to go before I stopped.

Then, in a split second, while falling through the air, I realized that I had misjudged. It might have been because of the whipping clothes that bothered and hampered me in leaving, or it might have been that the rush of blood to my eyes had affected my judgement, but from whatever cause I realized that I would fall in front of Tomick's ship – not by mere inches but by at least a foot and a half. . . . Again there was the necessity for instantaneous decision, and my decision was not to try and divert my body from its course but to try and catch a cabane [one of the strut wires] as I passed the leading edge of the top wing of Tomick's plane. I swung my right hand backward, and made the one attempt to grasp the thin small wire. For a long second I thought I had missed. Then the two forefingers touched and slid over it – and closed. My body turned a complete somersault. Still those fingers held. With a sudden jolt my feet hit the second bay strut and I hung in front of the plane. My hand was closed on the cabane wire, my feet firmly planted on the leading edge of the lower panel.[35]

Many articles, particularly in movie magazines or *Boy's Own*-type papers, credited Grace with insane recklessness. In fact, he and his crews spent days preparing for every stunt, modifying planes, putting in safety devices and drilling the rescue teams that always stood by when he crashed. Led by an experienced pilot who could instantly diagnose the dangers, they included fire-fighters, mechanics with heavy cutting tools, a doctor and a nurse. Cautious of Hollywood's buccaneering barnstormers, Grace found and trained his own pilots, the elite 'Buzzards' whose initiation and audition consisted of following him up and for an hour imitating his hair-raising aerobatics. Cowboys used horse-breaking methods as the basis of their stunts, Grace his experience of planes; every idea had been developed in the hard school of barnstorming. He always wore street shoes or sneakers in a stunt; boots were hard to get off a broken leg or foot. Protective clothing often merely encumbered, so he relied on a leather coat and goggles, together with special belts that supported him in the cockpit no matter how the plane landed. Instruments that might cut him in a crash were removed or re-sited. Everything sharp was padded with horsehair cushions. Splinters from the propellor couldn't be avoided. He tried lining the cockpit with one-eighth inch steel plate, but slivers and stones from the propellor punched through it with ease. The problem disappeared when his growing knowledge of the physics of crashing showed that the safest crash was one in which a wing-tip went into the ground first. The energy was transferred away from the cockpit, so that the propellor when it hit would usually crumple. When Grace crashed a plane, it had been almost totally rebuilt, vital members sawn half-through, gasoline tanks drained and moved away from the cockpit, which was strongly reinforced. It was never safe, but amateur aviators faced far greater risks in their normal flying.

For ten years Grace was Hollywood's top flier, but the ambition that put him on top of this business led him into others where he was less competent. After Lindbergh's transatlantic flight in 1927, businessman John D. Dole offered prizes of $25,000 and $10,000 for the first planes to fly non-stop from California to Hawaii. Forty barnstormers entered, but Grace, thinking to steal the race's thunder, shipped a plane to Hawaii and, even though his broken neck was still in a brace after a bad crash on *Wings*, announced his intention to fly the distance in the opposite direction. The project was a disaster. Defective controls forced him to turn back almost immediately, and the plane crashed on landing; he lost most of the money he had earned in the movies. His old friend Art Goebel won the Dole Race, in which ten men died. Grace returned to

Overleaf A Dick Grace crash on The Lost Squadron

STUNT—G

California, built up his old business and did some spectacular flying in *Lilac Time* (George Fitzmaurice, 1928), *Young Eagles* (William Wellman, 1930) and the vaguely autobiographical *The Lost Squadron* (George Archainbaud, 1932) but his neck injury and increased competition forced him to retire. Incredibly for such a man, he had a distinguished combat career in the Second World War and died quietly, in bed.

Not all were so lucky. Gene Perkins, whom many consider the greatest stunt man of all time, was killed at twenty-four on Christmas Eve, 1925. 'The secret of Perkins's greatness,' *Photoplay* noted, 'lay in his amazing ability to figure out a stunt ahead of time and distance, and in the icy clear-headedness which enabled him to carry it out to the hairline the way he had planned it.' Perkins doubled many serial stars, including Ruth Roland, Helen Holmes and Eddie Polo. Clarence Brown hired him to swim the rapids immediately above the seven hundred foot Nevada Falls in Yosemite National Park, as *Photoplay* recalled.

Brown and Perkins went to the river bank and shouted at each other above the roar of the falls. 'Can you make it, Perk?' Brown asked. 'I want you to jump in here' – indicating a spot some forty feet from the edge of the falls – 'and go as near to the edge as you think safe.' 'Just a minute and I'll tell you,' said Perk. He broke the branch off a tree and threw it into the water at the spot the jump was to be made. His eyes narrowed as he watched it intently. 'Sure, I can do it,' he said. 'When I get here' – he pointed to a spot only two feet from the brink – 'throw me a rope and try not to miss me. That water looks cold.' According to Brown he did the thing with the perfection of a machine. 'When I saw him I thought he was the coolest looking person I'd ever seen. His self-control was astounding. His eyes were like ice, yet they were always smiling. I wanted him to jump out of a fourth-storey window. It was a night shot. We stalled around most of the afternoon waiting for it to get dark enough to shoot and about dusk I decided we could do it. I went looking for Perk and found him shooting craps with some of the boys. "All ready, Perk?" I said. And he looked at his watch. "Excuse me a minute while I telephone," he said. I heard him behind me talking over the phone to his wife. "I'm sorry, honey," he said, "I'm going to be little late for supper. I've got to jump out of a fourth-storey window and then I'll be right along home."'[36]

Brown warned Perkins against the stunt that killed him, a plane-to-train transfer shot at Riverside. Some suggest that the film was a William Duncan serial, but most evidence points to it being *Hogan's Alley* (Roy del Ruth, 1925) in which Monte Blue

Right *Cliff Bergere repeats the stunt on which Gene Perkins was killed*

plays a young boxer on the run from the police because an opponent has been badly injured in a fight. Perkins had asked Dick Grace
to fly the plane, but since the company wouldn't meet Grace's high
fee a friend of Perkins who had recently bought his own plane
took over. He was to bring the plane in above the train with
Perkins hanging below on a rope ladder, and put him down on the
carriage where Paul Malvern was waiting to stage a fist fight.
Crosswinds confused the flier, who showed his lack of skill by
missing the first two approaches. Perkins, hanging on the ladder,
was tired, and when the third run left him clinging by outstretched
arms to the last rung he couldn't climb back. Swinging around
again, the pilot misjudged the wind even more and Perkins was
slammed violently against the side of the train. As the plane veered
off, Perkins, exhausted and probably injured by hitting the
carriage, let go. So perfect was his coordination that he hit the
ground standing after a fifty foot fall. At almost the same moment
Malvern jumped from the moving train and ran to him. Perkins
was terribly injured. The impact had driven his leg bones through
the heels of his shoes and he had extensive internal injuries. He
died a few hours afterwards. Four days later Al Wilson and newcomer Cliff Bergere completed the stunt for which Perkins had
died; business was business.

Perkins was far from the only stunt man to suffer in this
dangerous and competitive field. Fred 'Speed' Osborne, a mechanic
who hoped for fame with his reckless stunts, accepted a 1925 job
to race a motor cycle off the cliffs of the New York Palisades and
stop his fall with a parachute. The effects man decided he would
need to pull the ripcord thirty feet *before* going over the edge for it
to open in time, but as Osborne reached that point the engine lost
power slightly and he wasted vital seconds adjusting the carbur-
ettor. When he hit the ground at the bottom of the cliff, his
parachute was only half open. Legs and pelvis smashed, Osborne
never walked properly again, but became what he should have
remained, a mechanic and one of Dick Grace's most valued
engineers.

The same year that Osborne was hurt, R. D. Jones was drowned
on Irvin Willatt's *The Ancient Highway* and Max Marx fell to his
death on *Strings of Steel*. Three men drowned in the elaborate
recreation of the Flood for *Noah's Ark* (1928), which young
producer Darryl Zanuck had promised to make 'the greatest
picture of all time'. Director Michael Curtiz, recently arrived from

Right *Three extras
drowned in this scene
from* Noah's Ark

Vienna, was vague about the operation of 'dump tanks' and failed
to graduate the load. Extras struggling in the water were inun-
dated in crushing fifteen thousand gallon sluices. Another three
men died on Clarence Brown's 1928 Klondike epic, *The Trail of '98*,
in a scene of miners shooting the rapids of a snow-swollen river.
Brown spent a year making the film under appalling conditions
in the mountains of Colorado, and though he took precautions to
protect his stunt men, accidents were inevitable. For the rapids
sequence he chose a rough stretch of the Cooper River. A cable was
strung below the location with safety ropes hanging down into
the water, and a bosun's chair was fitted to carry a safety man. The
stunt men, who included Paul Malvern, Harvey Parry, Joe
Bonomo, Gordon Carveth and Ray Thompson, all wore suits with
inflated panels, and for maximum stability Brown chose flat-
bottomed halibut dories to carry them. As is often the case with
stunt disasters, stories vary. *Photoplay* reported that the scene
had been shot when the safety man in the bosun's chair caused the
cable to break and that, in falling, he capsized the boats. Joe
Bonomo claims the boats went over during the stunt, and that
eight men died, including the safety man on the cable, but there is

little evidence to support this. Of the three who definitely drowned, one was Red Thompson; ironic, since he had survived more water gags than any of them, including jumping onto the back of a whale with a harpoon in Frank Lloyd's 1926 version of *Moby Dick, The Sea Beast*.

Sound had a drastic effect on the stunt field. Performers whose only acquaintance with the stage had been in vaudeville adapted poorly to the necessities of primitive sound recording which favoured the booming Broadway projection, and serial stars like Allene Ray and Art Acord were abruptly out of work. (Acord later killed himself.) But sound was hardly the prime cause of mass retirements among action stars that has often been suggested. Despite his Italian accent, Richard Talmadge hung on, though precariously, and Yakima Canutt, his voice reduced to a growl by an influenza bout during the First World War that affected his vocal chords, still had a productive career at Republic as actor and stunt coordinator. The real causes lie elsewhere. Stunt men who had come into the business after the First World War were now reaching their forties, and viewed the prospect of another decade of hard and punishing work without enthusiasm. Some retired, or sought new jobs. Paul Malvern, after hurting himself in an eighty-five foot fall, became a producer of B-films, one of the few stunt men to graduate in this way, and most of the barn-stormers looked for work in the booming aviation industry. Sound also materially affected the quality of Hollywood films. Action movies, though not outlawed, had been slowed down. A succession of small thrills was replaced by a coherent story in which most of the excitement was reserved for one sequence. Such sequences needed a single coordinating mind, and the second-unit director assumed the importance he was later to have in Hollywood. Rose, Canutt, Lyons, Talmadge and the other greats stayed on, to have their recognition in the forties, but many of those who built the stunt legends of the twenties had retired or died. Dick Grace's 'I'm still alive!' echoed in the empty bars and closed sets of a dead decade.

6 Yak

Yakima Canutt has changed little since he came to Los Angeles in 1923 as a twenty-seven-year-old rodeo rider anxious to 'browse around a bit' in Hollywood society, and stayed to become its most famous stunt man. His natural courtesy and pride are those of a man who has no need to inflate his exploits, which even in his wry, clipped telling have the quality of myth. He still chews tobacco, the legacy of a life spent around fire-nervous horses, and his movements, though at seventy-six a little stiff, remain naturally athletic. Canutt grins at my assumption, because of the nickname 'Yakima' given him by fellow rodeo riders during his early career, that he is part-Indian. His real name is Enos Edward Canutt, son of a German/Dutch father who was a Washington state senator. Yet there is something of the Indian in his conversation and appearance, echoed by his home, its walls lined with trophies of hunting, rodeo ring and film set (including his 1966 Oscar for a lifetime of stunt work), a lodge atmosphere contradicted by the black stub of Universal City's tower lurking behind a nearby hill. He unearths a box filled with miscellaneous awards: gold buckles as big as his hand and embossed with forgotten distinctions, bucking horses and bulls' heads in the unmistakable style of the 1910s. When I ask automatically to use one of two straight-backed chairs that stand against the wall, he is agreeable but a little hesitant. Picking one up, I find it is hand-made, pegged not nailed, its seat woven from hide strips; the chairs, he explains, were made by his grandfather last century. They are probably as old as anything that still survives from the West. And suddenly one smells the hot dust, sweat and wood smoke of a lost, legendary age.

'I started major rodeos in 1914, and went through to 1923. There was quite a crop of us travelling together, and we would have special railroad cars and cars for the horses. We'd play anywhere from three, six, eight, ten-day shows. Bronc riding and bulldogging

were my specialities, but I did some roping. I did 'all-round' work.
I held the All-Round Cowboy Championship in 1917, 1919, 1920
and 1923 – that's the World Champion All-Round – and the
bronc riding – I had that off and on from 1917 right through till I
finished. Then I had the bulldogging championship a couple of
different years. The Calgary Stampede; I won that one time, in
1919. Pendleton; I won the bronc riding there three times, and
All-Round belt four times, and the bulldogging a couple of times.
I played them all: Cheyenne, Fort Worth, through Canada,
through the East. I'd got a lot of publicity and a pretty big name,
and in the fall of 1923 I won what they called the Roosevelt
Trophy. That was put up by Cheyenne and Pendleton for the
All-Round Cowboy Championship. That was the first year it was
put up, and I won the first leg of it; you had to win three years
before it became your possession. But each year they had a small
duplicate of it. I won the first leg and they presented it in Los
Angeles at Tom Mix's corrals. I came down for the presentation.
We rode some bucking horses for the newsreel cameras, put on a
little show for them, and a producer here, an independent producer
name of Ben Wilson, saw this in the newsreels and got hold of me
and made a deal for a series of pictures.

'At the Roosevelt Trophy ceremony Mix said, "I'm going to
make a picture right away. Why don't you come out and work
with me?" I had a month or two before the shows started in the
South, so I went out and Mix told me to let my whiskers grow and
wear Levis. Well, at that time I liked to go out at night and browse
around a little bit. I didn't like a bunch of whiskers growing, so I
shaved. "Jesus, you shaved!" Mix said when I came out to the set.
"I told you to let your whiskers grow." "Sure I shaved," I said.
"Can't I be the one outlaw who shaves?" He didn't say any more,
but after we'd rehearsed for four days we began shooting and the
first day the director said, "He's too clean-shaven and well-
dressed. You should mess him up a little." Mix said, "Goddammit,
why didn't you let them grow like I told you?" I don't believe in
running around at night with whiskers, so I just left the job and
went back to the rodeo.'

Canutt's return to the rodeo was relatively brief. His films for
Wilson's company and later for Arrow established him in action
Westerns, where he worked for the next fifteen years as a peren-
nial 'heavy' but increasingly as a stunt man and stunt 'ramrod',
the term for a cowboy foreman that was applied to the boss of a

bove *Yakima
anutt quails from
ohn Wayne in
aradise* Canyon
931)

elow *Canutt takes a
orse fall in* Paradise
anyon

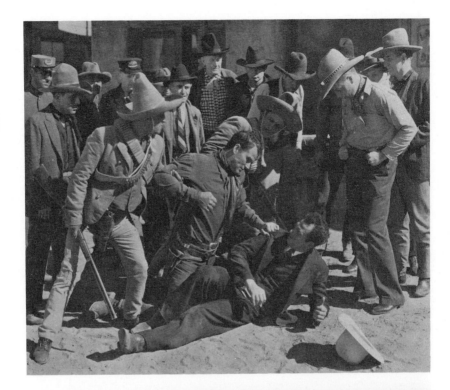

stunt team. He brought to Hollywood many techniques later
expanded and improved upon by film-makers. 'In 1925,' Cliff
Lyons said, 'there were only three basic stunts; falling off a
horse, riding a bucking bronc and getting bulldogged off a
horse.' (In rodeo bulldogging, riders compete with the clock to
catch a calf, dive onto its back, wrestle it to the ground and tie its
feet; in the movies, 'bulldogging' came to mean jumping from
horseback onto another rider, or a man on the ground.) With the
rodeo riders who took over the Hollywood stunt scene, Canutt
expanded the list of tricks, introducing a battery of horse falls
and wagon wrecks, along with the harnesses and cable rigs that
make them foolproof.

'When I first came down there weren't too many stunt men,
and they did everything the hard way; no equipment. I did all my
own stunts in my pictures, and a lot of the time stunts for someone
else. I could see the advantage of using your head a little bit and
creating equipment to do this work. Like falling off a horse, for
instance. Sometimes a man's foot would hang in the stirrup, so
he'd be dragged and hurt. Well, I had special stirrups made, open
L stirrups you couldn't hang in. In those days, you did bull-

Above *A stunter
back-somersaults out
of a Canutt L stirrup
in Blue (1968) for
which he was second
unit director*

dogging: you take a man off a horse by grabbing him, fall between
the horses, and get run over half the time. Well, I built that up to
where you jump light on the horse and go on over with the man,
and then I got to where I could make it in one jump. It became a
much more spectacular deal, and safer, because you cleared the
horses. Then wagon wrecks. They used to dig a hole to run the
wheels into or build up rocks to hit and turn the wagon over.
Half the time they'd miss, or get out of the scene before the wreck.
So I worked out equipment where you could drive the team on the
run and when they hit the spot everything would work automatic
– the team break loose, the wagon cramp and roll right on the spot.'

Canutt's technique depended on a cable of measured length
staked down at one end with the other attached under the wagon
directly beneath its front end. Another cable ran from the horses
over the wagon and was attached to the rear of the body. The
wagon tongue, which ran out between the horses and to which
they were harnessed, was cut through, then re-joined with a spring
and a pelican hook, a long hook, locked with a ring, that could be
tripped open with a cable. When the measured cable tied to the
bottom of the wagon ran out, it automatically opened the pelican

hook and released the team (whose legs were saved from damage by a sled-runner arrangement that kept the dragging harness from tangling them up); as the team ran forward, ahead of the wagon which was now on the verge of somersaulting, the cable attached to their harness pulled the wagon body up and forward, so that it crashed spectacularly, although the cable underneath ensured that it remained exactly where the director wanted it. The system has been perfected over the years; on *In Old Chicago* [Henry King, 1938] Cliff Lyons replaced Canutt's spring tongue with a small explosive charge, and the techniques of fastening cables to the wreck for various effects has become an art in itself. But it remains very much as Canutt originally planned it.

'One of the toughest things I ever had to rig was a leap off a bluff with a wagon and a team of horses with four of us on the wagon. That was on Raoul Walsh's *Dark Command* in 1940. I had to build a chute to put the team and wagon into so it'd get some momentum. It took me a week to rig this, with cables back so that automatically when the team went into the air all the harness tugs came loose. To stop the rig from landing on top of us, just before the wagon hit the water there was a cable back that stopped it.

Left *Canutt's skill laid the groundwork for such dangerous horse stunts as this jump by Steve Darrel in* Riders in the Sky (1949)

Also, I had a bunch of equipment in the wagon on a lid I'd forced down over a spring. This was tripped, and it threw this stuff into the air. The air was full of stuff, taking your eyes from this cable that stopped the wagon. We had the team out of the water, hooked up and working again in thirty minutes.'

Canutt's most controversial trick was the notorious 'Running W' system of horse falls. Like most stunt-riding techniques, it was adapted from a familiar cowboy method. To break a horse of 'running away' each time it is released, the cowboy fixes a rope to its front legs, runs it through a ring on the saddle, ties it to his own pommel and lets the horse go. Just before it reaches the end of the rope and pitches to the ground, the breaker yells 'Whoa'; after two or three falls the call will stop it instantly. For movie stunt riders, it was invaluable. 'This gag has caused more talk than any other. You hear stories about horses with their legs pulled off and all this stuff. Well, this is a lot of nonsense. It's like anything else. If you do it right, it was all right. But unfortunately, somebody will always see it done a few times, then offer to do it at half price, and if he didn't know how to do it he would go out and cripple a horse. I myself, personally, rode three hundred Running Ws and never crippled a horse.

'You have a band around the horse's belly with a ring with three compartments in it. The cable is staked down, and it runs through a hole in one of the compartments, down through a hobble ring on one of the front legs, back up through another ring, down to another hobble on the other front leg, back up, and ties in the bottom compartment of the ring. The ring looks like a W – that's where it gets the name. When the cable tightens, it pulls the horse's legs up to that ring; all the strain and pull and jerk is on the saddle – it's not on the legs. The pull just snaps them up to the ring, and as the two rings on the hobbles go on either side of the ring, it cuts the cable, but by that time he's got his feet up so far he can't get them back in time to save himself, so he turns a somersault. Then he gets up and away he goes. When I first came to Hollywood, they'd do this with a crew of men on a rope pulling at the horse's legs so he fell and floundered around. I did about two of them and I said, "Hell, there's a better way to do this than that." They were just using the old work harness cowboys used to break horses to drive, but the ring was worked from up on the side for that sort of thing and wasn't any good for picture work. So I created this ring with three compartments in it, then tested weights with a

small horse and a big horse. I found that about a $\frac{1}{32}$ inch flexible aeroplane cable would break in a fall without it being noticed, leaving the horse free so he can get up again. You need a good place to do the fall, of course; soft ground for them to fall in. And the hobbles are sheepskin-lined.

'For years I kept reading these things about tying wires on horses' legs and so on, so finally I got hold of a couple of Humane Society officers and said, "You people put these silly write-ups around. Why don't you come out and see how it's really done?" and they said, "Well, nobody will let us see them." I had a couple of days' work coming up so I said, "Bring two of your men out. I'll show you every detail of it." "Fine," they said, "but remember – if you kill a horse we'll arrest you." I said, "You're perfectly welcome." Three of them came out, in fact. I showed them how we

Left *A classic
Running W on* The
Wild Bunch *(1971).
The ring can be
clearly seen under
the horse's belly
with the cable
running away to
right, marked by
line of dust*

prepared the ground. Then I laced the horse up and explained everything to them as I laced it up. I told them that after the fall there'd be a few inches of cable and the knot attached to the ring. "Do you want to bet on that?" they said. I said, "I'll buy you all a brand new hat if it doesn't come out that way." I put them where they could watch the whole thing. Then, after the stunt, I brought the horse over to them and said, "Now check him good." They couldn't find anything wrong with any of the horses we used that day. They said, "If they were all done that way it'd be all right." But every now and then somebody will cut the price and hurt a horse.'

Although Canutt was generally well-liked, his technical skill and ability to lick even the toughest stunt urged many of his friends into a mild revenge. Joe Bonomo was particularly irritated that Canutt could do the difficult transfer from his horse to a speeding covered wagon. Most horses shied away from the flapping canvas and made a safe jump impossible. Betting Canutt $20 he could do the stunt, Bonomo quietly asked the special effects men to lash a pole onto the wagon on the side away from the camera. By grabbing this he was able to swing aboard. A puzzled Canutt, surprised at Bonomo's new expertise, paid up.

As well as coordinating stunts at Republic, Canutt doubled top stars, notably Henry Fonda. He replaced Fonda on *The Farmer Takes a Wife* (Victor Fleming, 1935) to find that growing specialization had made him an outsider in some sections of the stunt business. The scene called for a violent fist fight on the edge of a canal with stunt man Jack Stoney, doubling Charles Bickford. 'Stoney was an ex-fighter. He got sort of mad. "What the hell are they sending a cowboy out here to do a fight for? I'll teach him to stay in his own department." The assistant told me, "You'd better watch this bird. He doesn't like it because you're a cowboy doing a fight here." We started working out the routine and I said, "Well, Stoney, I've never worked with you before, so you set the pace and I'll just follow you. You want to work out a routine?" He said, "We'll ad lib it." He started hitting pretty hard, socking them in, but the harder he hit, the harder I hit, and after three or four takes we were both getting kind of sore. I laid one in that hurt him, and he threw everything he had at me. One punch hit me on the shoulder and nearly broke my arm, so I stepped back and right-crossed him, then jumped on top of him. The director said, "Cut! Jesus Christ, what's wrong with you fellows?" I said, "Don't worry, it's just a picture fight'', and when Stoney got up I said, ''You know, Stoney, that's just the way I like it; nice and easy.'' He was all right after that, and we got to be good friends.'

Most of Canutt's thirties work was in Westerns at Republic, where his technical imagination and ability to enliven stock stunts made him invaluable. 'That was why I did so well doing stunt work. I'd take a script and rewrite the action to put things in. In fact, when I was with Republic writers would come to a place where the action started, leave fifteen or twenty [shot] numbers and write beside the space ''See Yakima Canutt.'' I didn't do only horse work, but there was a lot of it. There are so many different things you can do. Bulldogging, for instance. You can jump two horses, not just one. I even did some bullfighting on one Republic film. We got two bullfighters up from Mexico, but when they checked the brands on the bulls we had they found they'd been in a few films already and got too smart. They wouldn't go into the ring with them, so I put on the costume and did the scene. I decided that as long as they didn't get a good run at me, I was safe. I had this cape, and I put the bull round the tree a couple of times, then went for the fence. I dropped the cape, and just as I got to the fence his horn hit me and boosted me over.'

His usual collaborator on the Republic serials was John Wayne who, after breaking into films in the late twenties as John Ford's property man and occasional stunter, made a minor career at Republic as a Western hero to Canutt's eternal villain. Canutt respects Wayne for his natural athleticism. 'John Wayne can do a fight better than most stunt men I know,' he says. Journalist James Bacon, reminiscing about 'Duke' Wayne, recalled visiting the Republic lot in the mid-thirties when Wayne was a regular there.

Herbert J. Yates [the head of Republic] came on the outdoor Western street. Duke took a running jump on a horse and rode like the wind, rolling under the saddle and hanging beneath the horse's belly. As the speeding horse neared Yates, Duke rolled completely off with a perfectly executed fall – just like the stunt men do. . . . He got up, dusted off his cowboy clothes and walked over to Yates. 'Let's see your Roy Rogers do *that*, Herb.'

Wayne was responsible for getting Canutt the job that was to change his career. When Ford cast *Stagecoach* in 1939 and asked Wayne to take the role of Ringo that was to make him a star, Duke suggested Canutt to ramrod the stunts. Knowing that this major film might mean a boost in status, Canutt created sequences that are Western classics.

'Well, Enos, how are you?' Ford said to me when we met. That set me back on my heels. Hardly anyone in Hollywood knew that my real name was Enos. I said to Ford, 'I see Wayne has given you the inside dope on me.' 'That's right,' said Ford. 'In fact, he said so much about you that you're going to find it hard to live up to all of it.' Ford gave me the script to read, and I found it a darned good Western. I went back to Ford and told him some ideas I had about doing the stunts. I was going to hire the stunt men and ramrod 'em through the picture. One of the things I started to discuss with Ford was a sequence in which the stagecoach came to a stream and saw the stage station burned by Indians on the other side. The script called for the coach to be lashed with logs and floated down the stream to escape the danger. 'You can forget about that,' said Ford. 'They tell me it can't be done.' 'I don't know about that, Mr Ford,' I answered. 'It seems to me you can do almost anything if you have enough time and money.' With Ford's approval I went to work on devising a way to float that stagecoach. Some fellows over at Paramount helped me devise some hollowed-out logs which could be attached to the coach, two on each side. They had to be planned just right; big enough to float

Right. Stagecoach:
*Yakima Canutt and
Chief Big Tree in
Running Ws*

Overleaf *The famous
Stagecoach stunt*

the coach, but high enough for the wheels to reach the ground. Then I devised an underwater cable which could be fastened to the front lead tongue and pulled by an offstage truck on the other side of the river. It was attached to a pelican hook which could be tripped when the coach reached the shore. I had the six horses in regular harness, but hooked together so they could be towed along if they quit swimming.[37]

Canutt tested the rig successfully on location, and the scene was shot with him driving, padded to look like Andy Devine. Impressed with the safety of the stunt, Ford reshot the scene with Devine and the other principals. They then moved to a salt lake location at Victorville for the film's high point, the coach chase as Indians pursue it across the lake. As well as a series of horse falls by Canutt and Chief Big Tree (so many of them that Canutt dispensed with sand pits and had the whole area ploughed by a local farmer) Canutt decided to repeat and expand a stunt he had developed in serials. An Indian jumps from his pony onto the lead horse of the coach team and takes the reins. The driver shoots the Indian, who drops to the tongue between the lead horses, drags a moment, then lets go, the horses and coach passing over him. But the reins are now dragging along the ground so a passenger jumps to the wagon tongue and, crawling out between the teams, mounts one of the lead horses, replaces the bit and rides it to a stop. Canutt knew that, as stunt ramrod, he must do all the work on the sequence himself, doubling both the Indian and Wayne, the passenger. The risks were obvious. He had already experienced one of the worst when, doing the stunt on an earlier film, a horse stumbled and fell. Since it was in the 'wheel team', nearest the coach, it had merely been pulled along without tripping the others, but should a lead horse fall the remaining five, as well as the coach, would pile on top of him. Once again, his technical skill came in handy. 'The first time I did the gag, the thing that had worried me more than anything was: how fast can I turn loose without rolling? I knew that to make sure the horses couldn't turn and have the coach run over me, they would have to be running fast, and the speed of a horse running fast is about thirty-eight or forty m.p.h. So I put a boom on the back of the camera truck and had them run it at different speeds so I could practise turning loose. I found I could drop off as fast as fifty miles an hour, and as long as I was relaxed from the belt down I wouldn't roll.'

Knowing that if he fell cleanly under the horses at the right speed the first part of the stunt was safe enough, he turned to the second, which required some modifications to the coach design. A special yoke was made for the wheel team, keeping the horses well apart and providing a rigid foothold for his first jump. Extra tongues were added between the other teams to give handholds, and additional harness to the outside horses to keep their heads out and the line of their gallop straight. A sudden swerve, crushing him as he did the drop, became less likely. He had made the stunt as safe as possible. It remained only to do it.

First I did the transfer, and it wasn't easy. The pinto I was riding shied away from the team, and I had a long jump to make. Next, we shot the drop. It was kind of spooky, dragging along and looking back at those horses' hooves. But they were running straight, so I let go. I kept my legs together and my arms flat against my body, and nothing hit. [Canutt admitted to me later that a hoof had cut his leg, a fact confirmed by a close look at the sequence.] As soon as the coach passed over me, I did a little roll, then fell back and laid still. That was an added touch of my own. Afterwards the cameramen weren't sure whether they had gotten the shot. 'They'd better have it,' said Ford. 'I'll *never* shoot that again.'[38]

7 The Squadron of Death

'Barnstormer'. No word evokes quite so well the uncomplicated days of personal courage and indifference to danger, the wise-cracking and cameraderie of an America where all choices were simple. The cinema, automobile and aviation industries thrived on its incautious optimism. A wartime ban on civil flying to conserve the country's feeble air strength froze the aircraft industry almost at birth, but when the law was repealed in 1919 growth resumed at a feverish rate. After investing heavily in planes and pilot-training during the war, the army, embarrassed by its accumulated resources of now unusable men and machines, dumped them on the open market, often for scrap. Curtiss JN4 'Jennies' could be bought, still crated, for $600, and pilots to fly them, mostly men in their twenties who had trained in the Army Air Corps but missed action when the war ended abruptly, were resigning in droves from an air service which the short-sighted government was cutting back to a survey and courier arm of the army. It was not until Colonel Billy Mitchell and other veterans made their stand, Mitchell enduring court martial to publicize his case, that the air force was revived, but in the intervening years most of its young pilots disappeared into other branches of government aviation, the air-mail service, into the precarious worlds of stunt flying, or movies.

Hollywood took up aviation with its usual giddy enthusiasm. By 1919, Thomas Ince was offering prizes for long-distance flights, and every star had to have his own plane or at least be photographed flying in one. Director Marshal Neilan ostentatiously made the four-hour San Francisco–Los Angeles flight for meetings, and Mary Miles Minter announced her intention to buy a plane for scouting locations. In August 1920 MGM flew a print of *Shore Acres* to Reno, Nevada, for a special screening, and nearly lost pilots, plane and film in a Sierra snowstorm. In suburban Los

Angeles, dusty cow-pastures shaded by pepper trees became airfields where the amateur pilots could overhaul their planes, clown or show off to curious visitors. Often the loungers included parachute jumpers or air-mail pilots wintering in California, and occasionally one of the fields would get a visit from a barnstormer. Making a precarious living with joyrides and stunts at county fairs, these aerial showmen led a dangerous gypsy life. With radio and navigational aids unknown, they steered by the railroads, their 'iron beam'; in bad weather they landed in a convenient field (checking wind direction from the cows, who always faced into it) and sheltered their plane behind a farmer's barn, hence their name. At the county shows they vied with each other in aerobatics, parachute jumps and simulated crashes which often ended in death when an ill-serviced aircraft crumpled in the air. And, like the cowboys of the 101 Ranch, when winter came and the shows closed, they drifted to California to work in the movies.

Newsreels were the first to see their film potential. A dull reel would often be given spice by hiring a pilot to do a dangerous stunt for the camera. When aerobatics palled, they flew under bridges or through hangars, often with wing-walkers clinging to

Above *Barnstormer Lillian Boyer in 1922*

Below *Gladys Roy in a blindfold wing wal over Los Angeles in 1924*

the upper wing, only inches from death in the propellor or from the masonry above. Gladys Ingle gave aerial archery demonstrations, standing on one wing-tip and shooting at a target set up at the other. But even these stunts soon lost their novelty, as did aviation in general. In 1920, a theatre-owner complained that the popular dodge of dropping leaflets from a plane to advertise a film had lost its appeal unless one gave it 'the jazz', usually consisting of ending the flight in a crash. Even so, Hollywood had seen what aircraft could do to speed up production and add thrills to the films themselves. Feature directors hired the best barnstorming pilots either as instructors or stunters. 'Daredevil' Al Wilson, later to figure in the tragedies of *Hell's Angels*, became Hollywood's flying teacher, instructing Cecil B. DeMille and becoming a regular pilot at the two fields which DeMille built in what is now central Los Angeles. Wilson even starred in his own films; his stunts for *The Phantom Flyer* (Bruce Mitchell, 1928) included replacing the wheel of a crippled plane while standing on the wing of another flying beneath it. Frank Clarke, also an ex-barnstormer, gained a reputation for imaginative courage when, for a film called *Stranger Than Fiction* (J. A. Barry, 1921), he agreed to fly a Jenny from the roof of a Los Angeles office building, taking the dismantled plane piece by piece to the roof and getting airborne from a hundred foot runway. He also walked wings, and earned the nickname 'Spook' by converting a Canuck (the Canadian version of the JN4) to fly apparently pilotless while he controlled it with wires from a second hidden cockpit. By the mid-twenties, the handsome and buccaneering Clarke, dashing in modified Army Air Corps gear and hairline moustache, was one of Hollywood's most respected stunt fliers, famous for his recklessness and capacity for whisky.

Wilson and Clarke were competent movie pilots and no more; Ormer Lester Locklear was a performer and, by the end of his short, violent career, a legend. With him, the mythology of movie flying began. Stunt man Cliff Bergere claims he entered the movies after admiring Locklear's full-length leather coat (he probably confused Locklear with his friend 'Skeets' Elliott, who always wore one; Locklear habitually flew in a business suit, part of the nonchalance that charmed his contemporaries). Even as an Army Air Corps instructor at Barron Field, Texas, the handsome Lt Locklear earned a reputation for reckless courage. When the radiator cap of a Jenny blew off during a training flight, he climbed onto the upper wing and stuffed a rag into the hole to stop boiling water blowing back into the cockpits, and to prove the wings of the JN4 would take the weight of extra guns he demonstrated the plane's stability by walking to the end of each wing, without a parachute. In January 1919 he made the first public transfer from one plane to another in mid-air, soon a barnstorming cliché, and in May 1919 when he was honourably discharged from the army, still only twenty-six, he formed a barnstorming team with Lt Shirley Short and his regular pilot and inseparable friend, twenty-three-year-old Arkansan Milton 'Skeets' Elliott.

Even for a celebrity like Locklear the barnstorming business offered little profit, and late in 1919 the team visited Los Angeles to pick up some money flying for films. Locklear and Elliott worked on *The Great Air Robbery* with cameraman Milton Moore

Below *Ormer Locklear*

for which Locklear changed planes at 2,500 feet and dropped to the roof of a speeding train. But the jobs petered out until, on 7 April, 1920, Locklear was summonsed by the Aero Club of Los Angeles for 'disturbing the peace in the air', the first such charge recorded. He had looped the loop, then a novelty, over a city park. Carl Laemmle's Universal promptly offered him a contract, which Locklear celebrated – earning more headlines in the process – by changing planes over the Toledo stadium at which Jack Dempsey and Jess Willard were fighting for the world title. After some successful thrill films for Universal, he was signed by William Fox to star in James P. Hogan's *The Skywayman*, with a barnstorming publicity tour of county fairs to follow. Locklear and Elliott were now Hollywood characters, intimates of Grace, Clarke and the stunt flying community. Probably with some encouragement from the couple, MGM worked up a public romance between Locklear and actress Viola Dana, who were alleged to be engaged, despite Viola's widely known romance with Buster Keaton and the less well publicized fact that Locklear had a wife and two children in Fort Worth. Flickering between elation and deep, almost suicidal gloom, taking risks that disturbed even hardened professional pilots, Locklear slid towards the inevitable disaster.

Jules Furthman's script for *The Skywayman* included almost every aerial stunt Locklear knew, as well as a number never before filmed. He had done the dangerous train-to-plane transfer, walked wings by day and, later, with the aid of searchlights, at night. Heavy lamps were still fitted to the end of each wing on the night of 2 August, 1920 when Locklear went to the DeMille field at the corner of 3rd and Fairfax to shoot the last and most dangerous sequence, in which the aerial bandit spirals to earth around a flare representing a parachuting victim. Locklear knew the stunt's dangers. Dick Grace recalls him dropping in at the bar where the pilots hung out and urging them to see the sequence; some of them, including Frank Clarke, Bob Rose and Grace himself, were disturbed by Locklear's nervous, almost hysterical manner, and went with him to the field. Before going up, mechanics heard Locklear tell Elliott, 'I have a hunch I shouldn't be flying tonight.' Elliott laughed and said, 'It's too late in life for you to be getting old maid ideas. Let's go.' At 10 p.m. they climbed to three thousand feet, glided to two thousand, then spiralled down into camera range. Fifteen minutes after take-off, Locklear dropped flares to signal he was ready and turned on the powerful wing-tip lamps; from the ground below, banks of blinding searchlights caught the plane, silver against the black sky. Frank Clarke remembers the beauty of the spiralling wings as Locklear dropped the flare and spun down around it. Nobody is clear what happened next. Two hundred feet from the ground the plane broke from its head spin, as if Locklear was making some violent correction. Clarke believed the lights blinded him, others suggest the flare threatened to ignite the wing fabric and Locklear, shying away, lost control. A third theory is that he may have mistaken lights on the top of nearby oil derricks for ground lights and, thinking himself lower than he was, pulled up sharply.

Whatever the reason, the plane went out of control and crashed on the edge of an oil-filled sump, then exploded. Protected by his leather coat, Elliott's body was only partly burned, but Locklear, in his tweed suit, was unrecognizable. They identified him formally by two things he always carried: the army identification tag around his right wrist and, in an inside pocket, a farewell letter to his mother.

Never one for sentiment, Fox rushed *The Skywayman* into release within three weeks, with Locklear described in the advertising as 'a Crusader in the conquest of the air'. Ten per cent of the film's profits went, with wide publicity, to the bereaved families. A few weeks later Ted McLaughlin, who replaced Locklear at Fox and completed *The Skywayman*, died when the ladder on which he was doing a transfer swung into the propellor; he had ignored Locklear's safety measure, a rope to the tail skid which held the ladder vertical. Shirley Short, who had been flying the plane, left to become an air-mail pilot.

But in an expanding industry there was no shortage of actors or pilots prepared to risk their lives for a foothold. Douglas Fairbanks Jnr, who had been pressed into a film career to capitalize on his father's name, appeared in *The Air Mail* (Irvin Willatt, 1925) when he was seventeen. 'I was supposed to jump off the wing of a plane with a parachute. I'd never parachuted before but they told me what to do. Count ten, pull the string, then roll over and so on. I thought it was great fun till I got up there. It was a two-seater plane, the pilot having a camera and piloting at the same time. I crawled out onto the wing and got to the end, but I was absolutely terrified. I started to cry, absolutely chickened out and crawled back, much to my shame afterwards and terrible abuse given me by everybody.' Until the mid-twenties, parachutes were far from obligatory for stunt fliers, the most common safety measure being a rope knotted to a strut and tied round the stunter's ankle. If he fell, he swung head-down until he could grab the undercarriage and climb back into shot. Even pioneer stunt parachutist Earl Burgess, who came to Hollywood in 1910 and became one of its top early stunt men, was not wearing a parachute when he went up with Walter Hawkins in February 1920 to shoot a comedy sequence for a Slim Summerville film. Dick Grace tells a blood-curdling story of an ageing and out-of-condition Burgess hanging onto a wing skid until his muscles gradually 'crystallized' and he fell, but news reports, which record only that Burgess was supposed to drop a dummy from the plane, then crawl back along the wing – a stunt the crew thought had been accomplished until they went to recover the dummy and found instead Burgess's corpse entangled in high tension wires – have a more brutal finality.

Neither death nor danger discouraged the service fliers who, drawn by the excitement lacking in the scaled-down Air Corps, flocked to Hollywood. The straightest stretch of railroad in southern California ran in front of the March Field Army Air Corps Base, and the Southern Pacific rented the track and a train to film companies for $500 a day. Bored army pilots watched in admiration as stunt fliers like Clarke and Wilson executed train-to-plane transfers and other stunts, and occasionally helped out. One of them, an instructor, was Frank Tomick, and after a few films producer Fred McConnell invited him to take up movie flying full-time. Tomick promptly resigned his commission and became a specialist camera plane pilot, a risky new sideline in the mushrooming aerial film business. Newsreels had bred a generation of cameramen who thought nothing of going up in a barnstormer's plane to shoot a bridge stunt or footage for a thrill serial. Harry Perry emerged as the dean of these uninsurables. After a few jobs as assistant cameraman, he shot *The Broken Wing* (Tom Forman, 1923), and was horrified at the primitive technique of aerial filming. Kneeling in the second cockpit of a Jenny with his back to the pilot, he was expected to operate the camera on a wooden mounting fastened to the fuselage with leather straps. Icy slipstream blew around his ears, often mixed with hot oil from the engine. Since both hands were needed to run the camera, one to crank, the other to focus and pan, he couldn't hold on, and the awkward position made a parachute impossible.

Right *Early aerial shooting techniques. A machine-gun ring mounting adapted to hold a camera for* Men With Wings *(1938)*

When he went up for the first time, Perry had no idea that cranking a camera during aerobatics was even feasible, but finding that his pilot was 'Loop' Murphy, holder of the world's record for consecutive loops – 175 – he let him experiment. Eleven loops later, Perry knew it was possible, if uncomfortable, to film under such conditions. He went on to develop a remote-control camera which could be attached to a wing or tailplane and be operated automatically by the pilot or an actor, making it unnecessary for a cameraman to go up in the plane. His electrician, Jimmy Deck, converted a sewing machine motor to drive it, and Perry a mounting by which it could be fastened to the airframe. But even this advance had its risks, as aircraft speed and manoeuvrability outstripped the cameraman's jury-rigged gear. Working on *The Flying Marine* (Albert Rogell, 1929) Ben Lyon, who had earned his flying licence while working on *Hell's Angels*, was asked to fly a new Waco monoplane to which a wing-tip camera was fitted. 'I could have killed both myself and Shirley Mason, the female lead. The novelty was that I would fly the plane myself, and a wide-angle lens would take in both the nose and tail to show that nobody else was flying it but me. The cameraman put the camera out on the wing, and we started running down the runway (which wasn't even a runway but a grass field). . . . I didn't realize that with the camera head weighing about fifty or seventy-five pounds on the extreme end of the wing, the whole plane would go over on one wheel. I had to give stick all the way over to the left to keep that wing up and get off the ground. I finally got off the ground and up to 2,500 feet and did a stall and a loop, things I never should have done with that camera on there. I looked at Shirley and said, 'Are you all right?' She said she was, but I saw her head go down in the cockpit and I knew she was being very sick, so I landed. I had to land with the stick right over and full left rudder; it could easily have ground-looped.'

Perry's skill made him indispensable when the boom in flying films climaxed with Paramount's *Wings* (1927), a First World War flying adventure directed by William A. Wellman, himself a veteran of the Lafayette Flying Corps and an accomplished pilot who liked to fly back to Beverley Hills from location and land in his friends' gardens. Screenwriter John Monk Saunders had also done some combat flying, and both wanted realism. 'He was probably the ruggedest director I've worked for,' Charles 'Buddy' Rogers said:

Dick Arlen and I had a fight scene in *Wings* so he came to me the night before and he said, 'You know, Buddy, Arlen says he can smash your face up.' I said, 'What?!' He said, 'Yes, he says he's going to beat the hell out of you.' He went to Dick and said the same thing, and he got the best fight scene out of us you've ever seen. He was that type of director. And the drunk scene when I drank champagne; he made me get drunk. He wanted the real thing.[39]

Even so, with his flying scenes Wellman was admirably cautious. Experts like Clarke and Tomick flew camera planes at generous $100-plus a day salaries, and although Tomick nearly crashed when the bombs which were dropped around him from above to simulate anti-aircraft explosions came too close and smashed his aileron controls, the film was a relatively safe one. Wellman's resourceful production manager Frank Blount avoided the cut-rate barnstorming pilots, most of them untrained in combat, and persuaded the Air Service to relinquish some of its war veterans, many of whom were friends of the director, to fly the stunt planes. Majors Frank Andrews, Hoyt Vandenberg, Bill Taylor, Earl Partridge and Hal George, all later USAF generals, were among those who agreed. The army also supplied a few of its veteran planes, though most had to be found among the barnstormers. Tomick was one of many agents sent out to persuade them to relinquish their pets. For the French Spad, needed for one of the film's most important crashes, he paid Earl Daugherty $3,500.

For the two major stunts on *Wings* – a crashing-landing by a Spad and the difficult crash of a Fokker just as it leaves the ground – Wellman hired Dick Grace. Arriving at Kelly Field in Texas where the film was shot, Grace looked over the accumulated planes with distaste. Outwardly sound, they had deteriorated in years of disuse.

The wood in the longerons of the Spads had probably wood-rotted; they would need strengthening and bolstering. The Fokkers would be no better. The steel tubing had undoubtedly corroded, for in several instances of just straight flying the fuselage had folded while in mid-air. Two hangars at Kelly Field were turned over to me, and there, day and night, the reconstruction crews worked under the command of Lieutenant Commander Harry Reynolds. Reynolds was one who could be thoroughly depended upon. With years of experience as an engineer in naval and aeronautical affairs, not even the slightest detail escaped him. The pressure system of the Spads was removed and small gravity tanks placed on the top wings instead. The linen was stripped from fuselages, and sections of wood and steel taken to laboratories for tests. In the cockpits of the French-type ships a network of tubing was constructed. New and stronger fire-walls were placed behind the motors, asbestos sheets planted between the carburettors and other fire hazards and myself. Every rib and spar was tested. A piece of control wire was attached from the landing-gear struts to the interbay braces of the baby Spads, so that when I hit, the wooden members would not come up through the bottom of the cockpit and pierce my legs.[40]

With the planes rebuilt, Grace meticulously went over his chosen Spad and Fokker and sawed through vital frame members, weakening them so that they would crumple on impact. The Spad crash was a complete success. Crawling from the inverted cockpit as smoke streamed around him from artificial explosions, Grace saw his ninety m.p.h. crash landing had put him seventeen inches from the nearest camera, whose operator had cranked on throughout the incident. Examining the plane later, he found the jagged end of a cedar airframe member jutting from the fabric only eleven inches from where his head had been. Wellman and Grace then went on to the second and more difficult job. The steel-framed

Fokker, more substantial than the Spad, needed extensive altera-
tions. Both the steel landing gear and the wing struts had to be
sawn, as did the main wing spar. Buckled into his special harness,
Grace dipped towards the ground on cue and dug his left wing-tip
into the turf. But though the wing crumpled, the half-sawn landing
gear remained intact and bounced the plane drunkenly back into
the air before it crashed heavily on its nose. All the weight was
thrown not sideways, as it would have been if the wing had
taken the shock, but down the fuselage and through the cockpit.
The straps holding Grace snapped, and his head went through the
instrument panel. When the rescue crew pulled him out he
seemed miraculously uninjured except for cuts, and was photographed smiling in front of the nosed-in wreck. Later, however,
he collapsed and it was found his neck had been broken; four
cervical vertebrae were crushed and a fifth dislocated. Doctors
told Grace he would be laid up for at least a year with his neck
in a cast, but six weeks later Wellman looked across the dance
floor in a San Antonio hotel and saw Grace, agile as ever, dancing
with a beautiful girl. He had chipped off the cast and escaped
from hospital through the window, and though the doctors
insisted that he wear a brace to support his injured neck he was
soon planning the Hawaii–California flight which was to be a
personal and financial disaster.

Grace attributed his survival to the superstitions with which
he and other stunt pilots fended off disaster. German airmen of
the First World War had used the ritual greeting 'Hals und Bein-
bruch' – 'Break your neck and legs' – and stunt men had similar
usages, based on the assumption that death would only come when
it was not expected. *Photoplay* recorded a 1930 incident during the
shooting of Wellman's *Young Eagles* that suggests such things help.
Grace, again doubling Buddy Rogers, was to spin and crash a
Jenny.

Dick stepped towards his ship. At the last moment a Paramount employee
dashed up, hand extended. 'Here's wishing you good luck, Dick,' came
the voice. It might have been a stab in the back. '————!' he said.
'That's the worst luck that can happen.' Superstition seized him. The
bravest fliers bow before it. He wanted to postpone the crash for a day,
to escape the jinx. But there were dollar signs on every passing second;
they prevailed on Dick to go. He muttered as he climbed into his ship.
He circled and dipped. Sighted the spot – in the semi-circle of cameras.
Dipped his nose. Came screaming down for the crash. . . . It was done.

Dick crawled out of the wreckage, two ribs cracked. A perfect stunt crash – perfect, but nowhere near the cameras. It was a full field distant from the spot marked X.[41]

Grace later re-did the crash, as well as another for the film and, without the benefit of good wishes, succeeded on both occasions.

None of the flying films that followed *Wings* were as professionally executed, and showed a callous disregard for safety. The most famous was *Hell's Angels* (1929), Howard Hughes's historic flying romance which set new standards both for realism in its aerial scenes and fatalities during its production. *Hell's Angels* was symbolic of a changing fashion in action films during the late twenties, the evolution of a 'blockbuster' mystique in which the pursuit of excellence gave way to a quest for sensational footage, often achieved, like the *Ben-Hur* chariot race and the deluge of *Noah's Ark*, at the expense of life. It brought the stunt man to new eminence, but also decimated the ranks of those who had survived the dangerous twenties. The risks of *Hell's Angels* were characteristic of many major action films of the period, though its producer/director was anything but ordinary. Hughes, only twenty-three in 1927 when he first conceived the film, had

Below *The converted Sikorsky 'Gotha' in* Hell's Angels

Above Some of the Hell's Angels personalities; (left to right) parachute jumper Ralph Douglas, stunt man Leo Noomis, Frank Clarke, stars James Hall and Ben Lyon, Frank Tomick and Roy Wilson

left the lucrative Hughes Tool Co., with its stranglehold on the oil-drilling equipment business, to dabble in aviation and film-making, hobbies for which the company's enormous profits gave him ample capital. His early mentor in Hollywood was veteran director Marshal 'Mickey' Neilan, an amateur pilot as well as a shrewd film-maker. Hughes financed his *Everybody's Acting* in 1926, and it was to Neilan that he suggested making a lavish air war film to outdo the popular *Wings*. Neilan wrote an outline which Hughes worked on for months, adding to it with the help of Luther Reed, a minor Paramount staffer Hughes hired to direct the film when he found he had been aviation correspondent of the *New York Herald*. For his stars Hughes chose Ben Lyon, a popular romantic lead at First National, the Swedish actress Greta Nissen, and James Hall, a refugee from the ailing Broadway stage. But the film's real stars were its aircraft, eighty-nine of which were bought and renovated in Europe and the US at a cost of $562,000. Thirty-five cameramen (twenty-six of them aerial experts) were hired, including Harry Perry, who directed the air camera team. Frank Clarke was chief pilot, with Al Wilson, Frank Tomick and other graduates of *Wings* on his staff. (Since the pilots would be shot close-up by Perry's automated cameras, most of them were given featured roles; Clarke appears as Von Bruen, Tomick as Von Richtofen, Roy – not Al – Wilson is the American 'Baldy', Clinton Herberger plays Oswald Boelcke.) Hughes's greatest disappointment was his agents' inability to find a Gotha bomber and he compromised by converting a Sikorsky S29 airliner, structurally identical with the Gotha, though he resented the subterfuge and berated his aide Noah Dietrich when he let newsmen photograph the plane. With the Sikorsky, he also got its owner/pilot, an extraordinary man who became the most flamboyant of barnstormers and a startling personality at a time when the film colony glittered with eccentrics, 'Colonel' Roscoe Turner.

Turner was the most successful and dramatic of all barnstormers to enter films. Demobilized like Locklear as an army lieutenant, he bought a decrepit plane and made a living around Columbia, South Carolina, giving exhibition flights. His career was checked in January 1922, when he was arrested by the Federal authorities. The previous September, Marine Corps gunner John L. McCoy returned to his field in Savannah, Georgia, on foot, claiming that the plane he had taken up to test had crashed in a lake. In fact, it was later discovered, he had landed on a country road and sold the plane to Turner and his partner Harry Runser. The case put only a temporary stop to Turner's plans, and by the mid-twenties he and fellow pilot Arthur Starnes had turned a borrowed $1,000 into 'Roscoe Turner's Flying Circus'. In a field of daredevils, Turner stood out less for his recklessness, which was minimal, than for his ability as an impresario. His specialities were show-stoppers like 'Falling a Mile in Flames', a dive with black smoke streaming from a movie smudge-pot, or 'the Dive of Death', a night version with flares at his wing-tips. Both combined maximum dramatic effect with minimum risk. When he heard that the first Sikorsky S29 built in the USA was for sale, he bought it and converted the plane for radio broadcasts, aerial tea-parties and charter work. The matrons and businessmen using it had little idea it would shortly figure in a grotesque death.

Turner resourcefully searched out personal publicity. Contracting with Gilmore Gasoline as a PR man, he bought a lion cub which he christened 'Gilmore' and took with him on his record-breaking inter-city flights; his arrival in a provincial hotel lobby with Gilmore on a leash guaranteed front-page publicity the next day for himself and his product. To exploit public adulation of

ight 'Colonel'
Roscoe Turner (right)
nd wife with James
Hall

Right 'Colonel' Roscoe Turner (right) and wife with James Hall

'the flying colonels' Mitchell and Rickenbacker, he acquired an honorary colonelcy as personal pilot to James 'Sunny Jim' Rolph, Governor of California, designing his own uniform, a quasi-official ensemble of blue jacket, scarlet helmet, fawn cavalry breeches, high boots and a wardrobe of wings and decorations accentuated by a large moustache waxed to two points. It was predictable that Turner would end up in Hollywood, and for five years he was the most famous of movie fliers, charter member of the Motion Picture Pilots' Association, a violent sub-group of the stunt establishment founded by a pudgy cigar-smoking pilot named Florence 'Pancho' Barnes. The MPPA made Hollywood a closed shop for fliers, and its scale of charges, ranging from $100 for a plane change through $225 for a wing fight in which one man falls off, up to $1500 for an aerial explosion and bail-out, kept its members in the necessities of life – in their case mainly whisky and big cigars.

Hell's Angels began shooting, inauspiciously, on Hallowe'en 1927, with Luther Reed replaced as director by Hughes himself. The gangling, boyish Hughes, whose poor hearing gave him an air of detachment some mistook for stupidity, was little respected by the pilots who, though happy to accept his $200 a week salaries, patronized him as 'Sonny', 'Kid', 'Skinny' or 'Punk'. Since Hughes lacked the USAF cooperation of *Wings*, Clarke had been forced to recruit freelance pilots, many of them inexperienced and reckless, among whom the veterans kept an uneasy discipline. Harry Perry remembers them as a dangerous crowd.

They would stay up most of the night and then have to roll out at daylight and fly. One day, Frank Clarke hired two fliers who were supposed to be unusually sharp and they went up to practise for the great dogfight scene. In about half an hour they were back on the ground. They said they wouldn't get mixed up with a crazy bunch of fliers like that for all the pay in the world.[42]

The first flying casualty on the film, fittingly, was Hughes himself. Ben Lyon was there. 'One day we had a scene where seven or eight Thomas-Morse Scouts were supposed to take off in formation, and each time they went down this grass runway they would all get off excepting one man. He never got his plane off the ground in time, and Howard was furious because the time was running out. "You're just trying to spread this deal out!" he said. "Get out. *I'll* get it off the ground." The Thomas-Morse has a rotary motor – the whole engine spins. Howard got it off the ground. He was up about seventy-five feet, about two thousand feet down the runway, but instead of turning against the torque of the revolving motor, he turned with it and went right into the ground. From our position, all we could see were pieces of plane going up into the air, and smoke. We got into our cars and drove like mad down there. Howard got up and staggered out, walked about fifty feet and collapsed.' Hughes was only shaken and continued directing after a week. Frank Clarke had been seen by the other spectators to be particularly solicitous of Hughes's safety; he later admitted that the prospect of his meal-ticket dying on him moved him very deeply indeed.

Other accidents quickly followed. Stunter Al Johnson was burned to death in a collision with telephone cables while ferrying a plane between two of the eight airfields Hughes had leased or built around Los Angeles as locations for the film. Two Thomas-Morses collided in the dogfight scene, but both pilots parachuted out. For a year, shooting continued in precarious safety, Hughes infuriating the cast and crew by demanding as many as 150 re-takes of a simple scene. In March 1928 Roscoe Turner flew in with the converted Sikorsky, already notorious. 'The twin-motor bomber arrived from New York piloted by one Captain Roscoe Turner,' *Photoplay* said, 'whose skill and daring were attested to by the fact that he was the only human being in the world who could or would fly it. It was that kind of aeroplane.'[43] It was promptly sent up for the scenes in which Lyon and Hall, RAF aviators piloting a captured Gotha into Germany on a sneak bombing raid, first destroy an arms dump and then fight off the attacks of Von Richtofen's Flying Circus. A set of controls had been placed well back along the fuselage so that Turner could pilot the plane without being visible to the cameras fixed on wings and nose. Hall 'flew' the plane from the normal cockpit while Lyon stood shivering in the gunner's gallery in the nose.

'The Sikorsky only did 125 or 130 m.p.h. but if you're standing in the nose of a ship exposed from the waist up, the wind hits you terribly. It would blow in your mouth and your cheeks – you couldn't talk. I tried to talk to Jimmy one time and words wouldn't come out.' Perry and Hughes planned the shots with extreme care, Perry going up often each day to check angles and light. 'I was told to go to three thousand or five thousand feet in a certain direction,' Lyon said, 'so the sun would be in a certain angle to our faces. The cameras were put on iron extension stanchions on the nose or the wing and worked by battery. We'd go to the right altitude and the right position for light and I'd signal Jimmy, "Are you ready?" He'd nod. I'd press the button and you'd see the sprockets turning. When I saw it turning Jimmy and I would enact the scene, and when we'd finished just switch it off, and then we'd turn around and come in for a run again. Then they might put the camera on the wing so they got a side angle. It would take us days maybe to get one shot.' Hughes's perfectionism led to endless re-takes in the dog-fighting; insufficient cloud in the sky or a chance flight of birds would cause him to scrap a day's shooting. There were more casualties. Clement 'Phil' Phillips, a protégé of Dick Grace – as an army cadet at Kelly Field in Texas when they were making *Wings*, Phillips had offered to clean his plane in his spare time, which Grace rewarded by giving him his first flight – made a forced landing into a ditch just after take-off when his engine failed, and although the plane was undamaged they found Phillips sitting in the cockpit with a broken neck. Al Wilson was flying a recondi-tioned Fokker over Los Angeles when its propellor came off. Indifferent to where the plane landed, Wilson bailed out and a few minutes later climbed down from a suburban housetop with nothing more serious than a slightly injured arm. The plane, miraculously, plunged into the generous grounds of writer Frank Spearman and producer Joseph Schenck. For years Schenck and his wife Norma Talmadge left the wreck where it landed in a tree; Schenck's United Artists was, after all, financing the film.

Hughes meanwhile urged Turner into stunts with the Gotha that the pilot knew would be close to suicidal. Ben Lyon: 'Hughes used to ask him at times to do things in the air with Jimmy supposedly flying and me standing in the nose, and Roscoe would say, "No, I'm sorry, Howard. I won't do that. The ship will not stand up to it."' Flying it solo he was less cautious, as Harry Perry found out.

One shot I remember very well was a dive down upon two motor-driven Mitchell cameras worth $5,000 each. Turner had made half a dozen dives but none was close enough to suit Howard. So, on a Sunday morning, Roscoe told me that he was really going to shave the cameras. He got the Gotha up in the air and started a steep dive from about two thousand feet right at the cameras. He came too low and hit both of them, knocked them to pieces, broke both his props, and ended up in a bean field a hundred yards beyond. The film was scattered all over the ground.[44]

When the plane was repaired, Hughes asked Turner to fly it in the last big scene, in which the Gotha is hit by German fighters, spins to the earth and crashes. Ben Lyon: 'He wanted Roscoe to take the ship, with Jimmy and myself in it, to seven thousand feet, with camera ships all around shooting from different angles, and pull it up into a stall, fall off into a spin, and then pull out. Turner said, "I certainly won't do it. The ship wouldn't stand up to the strain. The wings might come off."' Clarke offered Dick Grace $250 for the job. Grace, knowing the risks, told Clarke he would attempt it for only $25; if he did the stunt, Hughes would pay him $10,000; if he died, Grace's estate would pay Hughes the same sum. Meanwhile, however, Al Wilson had volunteered. 'Howard gave him $2,500 bonus to do the shot,' Lyon says. 'They waited until they had made all the shots with the bomber. Wilson went up to seven thousand feet, with four or five camera ships around photographing. They had a man in the cabin with smoke pots – a mechanic named Phil Jones – and there were strings to signal when to start the smoke. Al pulled it up into a stall, and *before* it went off into a spin a parachute opened – they cut around that in the film – and it spun down to the ground with this man in the cabin still pulling smoke, not realizing the pilot had left the ship. The motors were six or eight feet into the ground and of course the boy was killed.'

The incident created a furore among Hollywood pilots, who had always found Wilson's methods, even by their standards, reckless. Wilson claimed he heard a wing spar snap as the plane fell off into its spin, and had yanked a warning to Jones on the string before jumping himself. Frank Tomick, flying a camera plane, wrote: 'I could see the fabric on the leading edge ripping away and then an engine cowl tore loose', but most people, knowing Wilson's record, were sceptical. The Department of Commerce temporarily revoked his pilot's licence, and the Professional Pilots' Association demanded his resignation. Few pilots were prepared to fly on films that employed him, and shortly afterwards he left movies for good, to die in a 1933 air show crash.

The deaths on *Hell's Angels* poisoned Hollywood's response to it. *Photoplay* headlined its coverage 'Four Million Dollars and Four Men's Lives' (the fourth being cameraman Burton Steene, whose death from natural causes may have been due to strain of high-altitude shooting), but Hughes's decision to remake the film's non-aerial sections with sound delayed release until the chill had faded. (It also gained stardom for Jean Harlow, who replaced Greta Nissen, made obsolete by her Swedish accent.) For the première on 7 June, 1930, Hollywood Boulevard became a one-way street to smooth the flow of celebrities to the cinema, planes flew low over the crowd dropping flares and parachutes, and Roscoe Turner, with Gilmore, made a record 24 hours 20 minutes flight from New York to Los Angeles to celebrate the event. By this time, however, Turner had almost retired from movies, part of the reason being a bizarre postscript to *Hell's Angels* in which he was again involved.

During the making of the film, Hollywood flying accidents had become increasingly common. Earl Daugherty, a flamboyant pilot in the Turner mould who had been married in the air and executed the first aerial refuelling in 1921 (hopping from one plane to another with a can of gasoline) was killed in December 1929 when a wing came off over Long Beach during a film stunt. On 2 January 1930 three cabin planes hired by Fox flew out over the ocean at Redondo Beach, twenty-five miles from Los Angeles, to shoot scenes for *Such Men Are Dangerous*, based on the death of financier Oscar Loewenstein, who disappeared from his private plane in 1928. Star Warner Baxter was in one plane, with a double who would do a free-fall parachute jump for his death. In the second and third were ten members of the film's crew, including director Kenneth Hawks, brother of Howard Hawks and husband of Mary Astor. The plane with Baxter on board was flown by Roscoe Turner, one of the others by Ross Cook, the commander of Dick Grace's safety team on *Wings* and a top pilot. Later Turner said:

We left Clover Field and were to meet near Point Firmin. I had straightened out and was making a direct line for Point Firmin. The other ships were a little behind and above me. Suddenly one of my companions shouted, 'Look, they have hit each other!' I winged over and turned around to get a look at them. They were tangled together, both afire, and plunging towards the ocean. Just as they were about to hit, two or three of the men either jumped or were thrown out of the burning planes. I saw the bodies splash into the ocean a little distance away from the point where the planes hit the sea.[45]

No one survived, and the accident ended an era in flying films.

By comparison with *Wings* and *Hell's Angels*, 1931's big flying film, *The Dawn Patrol* (Howard Hawks), was a tame affair, though Elmer Dyer shot some remarkable air combat footage and special effects men nearly killed Frank Tomick when charges set along the

Left *John P. Fulton (standing) with Paul Mantz*

field to imitate bombs dropped on him by Robbie Robinson exploded prematurely and left him struggling to land a tattered wreck. Star Richard Barthelmess refused point blank to go up in a plane, so for aerial shots a Jenny was supported on cables twenty-five feet in the air and its engine run for short periods to duplicate flying. On one occasion a cable snapped and the plane sagged fifteen feet towards the ground, but this was Barthelmess's most perilous moment. Safety consciousness could have its own risks. Making Frank Capra's *Flight* in 1929, Jack Holt agreed to play some aerial scenes as a rear gunner in an exposed cockpit only on the condition that he wear a parachute. When Elmer Dyer in the camera plane moved in for his shot, Holt refused to stand up and could be seen shaking his head vehemently. It wasn't until an infuriated Capra was back on the ground that he discovered the actor, testing his parachute ring, had accidentally released it in the cockpit. Only by holding himself tightly in his seat (and lacerating his hands on the metal edge) could he save himself from being yanked out of the plane and smashed against the tail.

Producers were more than anxious to be seen protecting the lives of their fliers. Ex-army flier Charles Delaney, survivor of two hundred flying stunts, told the public:

There are fewer accidents in the air during the production of a stunt picture for the simple reason that the producers insist on the best possible flying equipment piloted by the best possible freelance aviators in the business. Even the parachutes used in the current film were scrapped immediately after they were returned to the warehouse.[46]

Some months after the Hawks fatality, director John Ford and cameraman Elmer Dyer were impressed when a pilot named Paul Mantz coolly flew through the open doors of a hangar for the film *Air Mail*, a stunt every MPPA member had refused. It was the culmination of Mantz's two-year fight to crash the exclusive Hollywood flying establishment which the MPPA had closed entirely to outsiders. His first methods had been the familiar ones of self-advertisement. In July 1930 he made an attempt on the world record for outside loops. He was congratulating himself on having broken it when another plane flew alongside with the number '35' painted on it; a second stunter had upped the record yet again. Mantz looped on and landed, dizzy and bleeding from the nose, the holder of a new record of forty-six. But studios still refused to employ any flier not a member of the MPPA for fear of

black-listing, and Mantz appealed to Pancho Barnes. 'You'll get your chance,' she said. 'There's some work around the boys won't touch.' His opportunity came on *The Galloping Ghost* (B. Reeves Eason, 1931); for the first time, the MPPA pilots didn't oppose his application, though they did demand a $100 entrance fee – all he was getting for the stunt – in advance. Puzzled at the sudden acceptance and the grinning pilots, Mantz gave Pancho Barnes his IOU and readied his old Stearman for the stunt, a simple one in which he had to fly past the camera with Bob Rose clinging to the upper wing. As a huge tree loomed before him in the narrow canyon and he banked to avoid it, he realized why the others had let him take the job; Rose's body jammed the ailerons, making the plane almost unmanoeuvrable. Seeing only one chance to complete the stunt without crashing, Mantz pushed the stick forward. The plane's wheels hit the ground, and he bounced over the tree, leaving Rose unhurt but festooned with leaves from the upper branches.

His second stunt, on *Air Mail*, had a similar secret trap; as he arrived at the location he saw what the MPPA pilots had seen, a storm rolling down the mountains that made flying almost suicidal. But knowing his plane was in better condition than those of the other fliers, Mantz took off and did the job. Among those who watched was cameraman John Fulton, head of Universal's special effects department and later a keen pilot. That evening he told his wife, 'I talked to a young flier today. I'm really impressed with him. For one thing he keeps his plane up in top shape. I'm not about to go and fly in some of these planes I've looked at. This guy only has an old Stearman, but he's very particular. I'm going to get him to do all my trick flying.' In a remarkably short time, Mantz was Hollywood's top stunt flier, with his own company, United Air Services, for which many of the top MPPA pilots worked, and a rapidly expanding reputation. His skill in personal publicity rivalled that of Roscoe Turner, who was one of his first employees; he became adviser to Amelia Earhart on her long-distance flights, installed California's first Link flight simulator on which she practised night flying, established the 'Honeymoon Express' to ferry eloping film stars to Reno for quick weddings, and was involved in all the thirties' most publicized publicity junkets. His rates made those of the MPPA seem generous; for a Mantz pilot, studios paid a basic $50 a day, with an additional $250 for every full week, on top of which Mantz

demanded an obligatory $250 weekly for himself as 'aerial director'. Special stunts, which Mantz usually performed personally, cost more.

Though most of the MPPA pilots were forced to work for Mantz as his influence increased, few hid their resentment, both of Mantz personally and his automated system of stunt flying. Frank Clarke, a rival and friend in Mantz's early days, showed particular animosity. One by one the old pilots retired. Al Wilson had already gone into show stunting, and Roscoe Turner, after making a fortune on the suicidal pylon races of the thirties, the Bendix Cup speed tests and inter-city record breaking – in 1932 he established a new trans-continental record of 10 hours 2 minutes 52 seconds – opened his own airfield and flying school in Indianapolis, where he died in 1970, a respected local businessman. Soon Mantz had tied up the Bendix Cup races as well – he won the race three times – and when he, Clarke and Howard Batt formed the Hollywood Trio to give exhibitions of close-formation flying at air shows, that field gradually became closed to the barnstormers. Mantz's arrogance was legendary; he repudiated his friendship with John Fulton when it was no longer professionally valuable to him, exploited his monopoly of the stunt business by increasing prices but passing little of his profit on to the men who worked for him. When the war came, he was an important figure in the air combat film unit that occupied the old Hal Roach studios, commissioned as 'Fort Roach' for the duration, a team in which Clarke rose to lieutenant colonel as a skilled producer of air instructional movies. Mantz's army career was shadowed by charges (brought by Clarke) that his planes had been used to transport black-market meat, and though Mantz was exonerated the mud still stuck.

When the flying boom ended, Frank Tomick had bought a gold mine at Lake Isabella on the Kern River in California and worked it in addition to his business interests. He still kept in touch with old colleagues, and one day in June 1948 was not surprised to hear a single-engined plane circling over his property. The pilot swooped low and, as Tomick watched in horror, suddenly lost control, lurched towards the ground and crashed. In the front cockpit of the plane he found the body of Frank Clarke, and in the second, slumped against the controls and jamming them, a sack of cow manure his old friend had planned to drop as a ribald practical joke. The last barnstormer had gone to an appropriately grotesque death.

8 I Don't Want to Die in Africa

For cinema thrills, the wild animal has no equal. A man armed only with whip and chair against a cage-full of lions, the latent menace of the pendant python, the onslaught of a charging rhinoceros evoke instantly our ancient fear of the beast, and predictably the cinema has exploited this, filming every permutation of man–animal conflict from circus lion-taming to the attack of giant ants. Pioneer producers, nervous about real animals, preferred fakes. In 1900, when the Australian Salvation Army produced *Soldiers of the Cross*, the first religious epic, on a Melbourne tennis court, the Coliseum's lions were played by the director's children in skins with string-operated jaws. One recalled:

My elder brother and I, dressed as a lion, approached the poor Christians kneeling in the centre of the arena, waiting to be devoured, and we clamped the jaws on one of the victims, probably one of my own sisters.[47]

Mechanical animals were common for decades. In 1907 D. W. Griffith, then a hopeful playwright pushing his script of *Tosca* at the Edison company's Bronx studio, agreed half-heartedly to act in Edwin S. Porter's *Rescued From the Eagle's Nest*, playing a woodcutter who rescues a child kidnapped by a mechanical eagle manufactured by property man Richard Murphy, who spent days adapting a taxidermist's stuffed specimen and animating its wings with black thread. Murphy later became one of the cinema's top special effects men, and the prop animal an accepted part of the movies; but by 1908, when Adam Kessel shot a wolf as the dramatic climax to *Davy Crockett in Hearts Divided*, photography had improved enough for it to be hilariously obvious that it was a pelt on a stick.

Such howlers forced film-makers to replace skins and fakes with the real thing, and only the gorilla suit persisted. These suits,

Above *Baby and mechanical eagle in* Rescued From the Eagle's Nest (1907)

Below *Members of the Australian Salvation Army, including children in lion skins, take part in* Soldiers of the Cross (1900), *the first religious epic*

Left *Joe Bonomo as Eric the gorilla with Bela Lugosi in* The Murders in the Rue Morgue (1932)

usually sewn out of monkey skin and worth more than $1,000, were always in demand, and the stockier stunt men spent their share of time sweating inside them. The best suits had extensions to the arms for a realistic ape-like effect, convincing features that used the wearer's eyes and mouth, extensive foam-rubber padding, and a fifty pound bag of sand in the crotch to lower the centre of gravity. Besides the smell and heat, they had their dangers. Playing an ape man in *The Island of Lost Souls*, Erle C. Kenton's 1933 adaptation of H. G. Wells's *The Island of Doctor Moreau*, Joe Bonomo, clowning on the boat that took the cast back from location on Catalina Island, fell overboard. The suit instantly filled with water, and it needed three men and two life preservers to keep him afloat. Gorillas became so popular in serials that Universal circulated detailed plans of how local cinema managers could manufacture their own suits for publicity stunts out of cut-up black crêpe paper, a task with all the attractions of one-handed chicken plucking.

Realistic animal stunts began in 1908 with Chicago producer William Selig, who thrived on topicality and was awake to the film value of any nationally popular event. When in the autumn of 1908

President Theodore Roosevelt announced his safari to Africa, Selig offered to train young Kermit Roosevelt in movie camerawork so that he could make a film of it for Selig release. Roosevelt had agreed but the Smithsonian Institution, which was sponsoring the trip for scientific reasons, persuaded him to take an English cameraman instead. Selig was furious when the expedition sailed in May 1909, and promptly began his own version of the Roosevelt safari. For $400 he bought an aged lion from a Milwaukee zoo, hired some black 'porters' from the Chicago work-force, put them in raffia grass skirts, and turned one end of his studio into a moderately realistic jungle, fencing off a corner for the lion. Director Otis Turner explained to the anonymous actor hired to play Roosevelt that, as he came upon the lion at the head of his safari and shot it with stage bullets, an army marksman would kill the animal. But the actor was plainly nervous – even more so when the paper wadding from his blanks stung the animal, and the marksman missed completely. As the lion stood roaring in the centre of the studio, the rifleman shot again, wounding it in the jaw. Furious, it charged. 'Roosevelt' grabbed the bars of the cage to hang precariously beyond the animal's reach, while porters erupted from the building into the long grass around a drainage canal behind the studio. It took some time to reassemble the cast, placate the lion and re-shoot the scene, after which the actor posed with his foot proudly on his quarry. When Roosevelt landed in Europe after his African trip, he was astonished to find cinemas screening what purported to be a film of his adventures.

American interest in Africa and big-game hunting gathered momentum after the Roosevelt safari, and most early studios tried animal films. Vitagraph, which had already been successful with films featuring a collie, 'Jean, the Vitagraph Dog', made the logical connection. 'If a dog picture can succeed,' producer Albert E. Smith reasoned, 'why not a lion picture, a monkey picture, a bear picture?' Selig had now bought a whole zoo, and Vitagraph countered by hiring two well-stocked travelling menageries. For their first animal film Smith used the undoubted star of both shows, a tiger, around which a one-reel comedy was built. An eccentric gentleman brings the beast back from India, to the horror of his fiancée and friends, but it lives comfortably enough in the house until the night of a party, when, with disastrous results, it mingles with the guests. Urged by its trainer, the tiger did all that was asked of it until the party scene; then, excited by the crowd, it leaped at his throat. Al Smith's brother Victor, standing by with a ·303 rifle, shot it dead, whereupon the trainer demanded damages for killing his precious animal which, he argued, was just being playful. Vitagraph sceptically paid him $500, and produced a version of *Daniel in the Lions' Den* with the zoos' accumulated stock of seven lions. When the actor playing Daniel refused to go in the cage, director Fred 'Bing' Thompson doubled him, establishing a dangerous precedent. The film was a success, and the Smiths next launched a near-epic, *Wild Animals at Large*.

The plot was simple, combining two popular Vitagraph specialities, the animal film and the train wreck; one of the studio's pioneering moves in action films had been to buy the motion picture rights to the staged train wrecks often put on at shows, and work them into story films. In *Wild Animals at Large*, a circus train comes off the track and its contents roam the countryside until captured. Ten acres of New Jersey were fenced off, and the train duly derailed, breakaway cages releasing the animals. Nobody noticed in the confusion that a leopard had leapt the fence and run into a nearby village. It bounded into a barber's shop where a man was having a shave, playfully lacerated his trousers and loped on to terrify most of the townspeople before Victor Smith and trainers recaptured it. Vitagraph paid $3,000 to the man in the barber's chair who, though hardly hurt, claimed his hair had gone white and fallen out three months later, and left animal movies to Selig, who by now had become expert. He and the other studios found that circuses were happy to sell their old and toothless lions as an alternative to destroying them. Those that proved too playful could be repelled by evil-smelling aromatics rubbed on an actor's face and hands, and, in the last resort, even the liveliest succumbed to chloroform. By the First World War, Selig's zoo, soon supplemented by 'lion farms' like Charlie Gay's in the Los Angeles satellite town of El Monte, which at one time boasted two hundred big cats, supplied Hollywood with animals for what had become a thriving sub-industry.

Animal films really took off with Tarzan. For years Edgar Rice Burroughs tried to interest the movies in his stories of the king of the jungle, but even Selig, who bought and filmed his original story *The Lad and the Lion* in 1917, would not commit himself to the big-budget production visualized by Burroughs for *Tarzan of the Apes*. Insurance salesman William Parsons at last coaxed the film rights out of Burroughs by promising to raise enough money on a free option for a truly epic film. To grease the wheels, Burroughs wrote a glowing prospectus which Parsons pressed on potential investors. In it, he promised 'not two or three lions, but a herd of twenty or thirty; the lions will be actually roped and killed by Tarzan; two or three thousand cannibals will take part in the battle; the largest and finest specimens of apes will be used.' Needless to say, Burroughs had never been to Africa, and stayed well away from that continent throughout his life.

With part of the money raised on these promises, Parsons went to the American Film Company, Thomas Ricketts's Western and adventure studio. They agreed to supply a director, camera and crew, but pointed out that Parsons's limited funds made economies unavoidable. The first casualties were the 'largest and finest apes'. Since no real gorillas could be found, skin-draped members of the New Orleans Athletic Club had to do. The twenty or thirty lions were reduced to one, a moth-eaten Selig veteran affectionately known as 'Old Charlie'. Dozens of actors auditioned as Tarzan, but professional acrobats able to swing lithely through the trees had as little talent for acting as professional actors had for athletics. Director Scott Sidney at last found a man named Winslow Wilson who had a little of both skills. He was muscular, and though most of his stage experience had been as a professional ukelele player, he knew enough acting to go through the motions. But before the film could begin, America entered the war and Wilson patriotically joined up. Very much as a last resort, the company signed a powerful, vain and not very bright actor named Elmo Lincoln.

A former deckhand, boxer and locomotive brakeman, Lincoln, whose real name was Otto Linkenhalt, had drifted into movies as an extra with D. W. Griffith. After manful service on the actor-starved *Birth of a Nation* in 1915, where he played twelve parts, from a Negro renegade to a black 'mammy', Griffith featured him in *Intolerance* as the 'Mighty Man of Valour' who hacks off heads in a battle scene. Acting as an extra on *The Last Drop of Water*, a 1911 wagon train drama for the climax of which Griffith obtained a pack of real wolves, Lincoln showed a new side to his character. The wolves, though muzzled and otherwise pacified, still had their legs, which they used to make for the hills the moment their handler opened the cage. When Griffith offered $1 for every one recaptured, Lincoln triumphantly returned with five, dragging them snapping and howling by their back legs. But despite his barrel chest and dubious prowess with animals, Lincoln made an

unconvincing Tarzan. Sidney, who did not hide his disappoint-
ment, put him in a loin cloth, covered his bald spot with a thick
wig held in place by a head-band, and ordered the bewildered
actor to shave the hair that matted his chest and legs, a practice
that continued weekly through the film. Not especially dexterous,
Lincoln fumbled the scenes requiring him to move along tree
branches or swing on vines. Finally an exasperated director found
a spot on the coast where winds had so distorted some trees that
their branches ran almost parallel to the ground and a few feet
above it. Where shots couldn't be faked in this way, wires were
strung on either side of a branch to steady him.

Covered in rope burns, cuts and bruises, and bleeding where
shaving had left large abrasions, Lincoln almost gave up when
Sidney told him his last job on the film would be to stab the lion to
death. The unit had by then formed an affection for toothless Old
Charlie, but his death at Tarzan's hands as he crashed into the hut
to menace Jane (Enid Markey) was a high point of the film, and
Lincoln reluctantly set to work.

The lion was doped and tied up. I was supposed to jump on his back and
stab him with a knife, but they gave me an old butcher's knife and the
damn thing broke when I tried to stab him.[48]

That night he honed down a bayonet and the next day messily
dispatched Charlie with it. Sidney then set up the climax. Tarzan
stands over the dead beast, one foot on its side and, with a cry,
leaps the body to embrace Jane. As the cameras rolled, Lincoln put
his weight experimentally on the lion and froze as from under his
foot came a rumbling cough. 'I set a new record for the broad
jump,' he said. Only after a cautious handler crept back did they
discover that Lincoln's weight had merely expelled the air from
Charlie's lungs in a posthumous growl. With the film finished – it
was released in 1918 and became one of the first six features to
gross more than $1 million – Lincoln, who by then had expanded
to fill the role of Tarzan, went on a publicity tour, announcing
that he would wrestle a live lion on stage before each performance.
The body of Old Charlie displayed in the foyer of the Broadway
theatre where the film was premièred hinted at high drama, and
when the curtain rose on Lincoln romping with a lion cub audiences were generally not amused.

In all his films, Lincoln religiously avoided risks. After *Tarzan*

Right. Tarzan of the Apes (1918): Enid Markey, Elmo Lincoln and 'Old Charlie'

of the Apes he starred in some minor imitations that played on his strength and endurance. While making *Elmo the Fearless* (J. P. McGowan, 1920) he noticed a young acrobat hired to play a heavy and throw some falls. Monty Montague had been a circus tumbler since he was seven, but left at twenty-one to join the army. Wounded in the Philippines, he was invalided out after six years' service and briefly returned to the circus before trying Hollywood. Impressed by his agility, Lincoln put him on as his regular double. He stunted for him on *Elmo the Fearless*, was given two parts in his next serial, *The Flaming Disk* (Robert F. Hill, 1921) and went on, when he was not replacing Lincoln, to become a serviceable action double in Westerns. His wife Scotty also doubled actress Louise Lorraine, Lincoln's regular leading lady who, though only seventeen when she began her film career, was an accomplished stunter, accepting a double only when she broke two ribs on a Tarzan serial. Later, deciding to concentrate on Westerns, Montague handed the job of doubling Lincoln to gymnast Frank Merrill, who graduated to the lead in 1928 when Joe Bonomo, who began in *Tarzan the Mighty*, broke his leg while swinging from a vine. Merrill held the role for a few films before retiring into business and local politics;

he later became Parks Commissioner of Los Angeles.

By 1921 Lincoln, though as inept as ever, was an action star with a series of films to his credit. In the same year he played Tarzan in a serial, *The Adventures of Tarzan* (Robert F. Hill), a production fraught with problems. Shooting the last episode, Lincoln picked up Louise Lorraine, only to drop her with a howl of pain as a pin in her hurriedly altered costume pricked his finger. The crew laughed and Lincoln, offended, returned to his dressing tent. Hill, not to be blackmailed, called cameraman Jerry Ash and, in Monty Montague's hearing, outlined a fictitious new ending for the film which he proposed to shoot without Lincoln; a witch doctor curses Tarzan, who then walks into the river and emerges as a nine-year-old boy. Hill and Ash saw Montague slip away, and shortly afterwards Lincoln returned, contrite. Unfortunately the 'new' ending got to Universal's boss Carl Laemmle, who liked it so much that Hill spent days persuading him it couldn't be used.

In the same year, husky, handsome Hawaiian actor Kamuela C. Searle was cast in the name role of *The Son of Tarzan* (Henry Sevier, Arthur J. Flaven) with P. Dempsey Tabler, a sub-Lincoln strong man, as his father. The final shot called for Searle, being burned at the stake, to be rescued by an elephant, which uproots both stake and victim and carries them into the forest. The shot proved impossible, with either stake or actor falling to the ground as soon as the elephant grasped them. Searle, exhausted, was finally lashed to the stake and the whole thing tied to the elephant's trunk and head, necessitating more agonizing re-takes. After these scenes, Searle was too weak to stand and had to lean against a tree while Sevier got the final close-ups. He died three years later, allegedly of cancer aggravated by First World War injuries but actually, many on the film believe, as a result of these stunts.

No ambitious producer could now think of a major film without animals. Cecil B. deMille, whose fascination with Biblical subjects demanded a constant supply – 'Bring my zebras!' an imperious Mary Magdalen orders in his 1927 *King of Kings* and a moment later her chariot with a matched pair is at the door – wrote a Babylonian flashback into his 1919 version of Barrie's *The Admirable Crichton, Male and Female* (he thought people would mistake 'admirable' for 'admiral' and assume it was a naval picture) to show Gloria Swanson going to her death in a pit of wild beasts, a delightful sequence but remote from Barrie's social satire. Thomas

Meighan, who also played the butler.Crichton, was to enter from the hunt with a dead leopard around his neck, and Miss Swanson to expire with a lion resting its paw on her neck. The plan had been to use a stuffed leopard, but hearing that Selig intended to shoot a leopard that had turned on its trainer, DeMille decided to have it brought to the studio, killed just prior to the scene and draped over Meighan's back. One look at the handsome animal softened his heart, and with Meighan's nervous agreement he used chloroform instead. After a few re-takes, the leopard began to growl restlessly, and Meighan finished the scene with the animal stirring angrily around his ears. In the same film Miss Swanson, draped in lamé and plumes, lay resignedly under a lion, its purr shaking her like an electric motor.

DeMille demanded complete confidence from his players, and imagined all shared his immunity to injury. He called in Joe Bonomo for a dangerous stunt on *The Sign of the Cross* (1932) where a Christian slave is thrown into a pit of alligators. 'Just remember this was your decision, Joe,' DeMille said, 'and if any alligator gets you the studio won't be responsible.' The script had originally called for a pit of crocodiles, but Bonomo changed this.

The reasons for my choosing alligators was that a 'gator is built all along one vertebrae from the tip of his nose to the end of his tail. Though the tail is flexible, the forward end is fairly rigid. He lacks the double hinged jaw the crocodile possesses. Only his lower jaw moves and that hinges down. If you can catch this lower jaw when it is open, you can hold it open, unless he twists away. Of course, there is always the danger of being knocked senseless, perhaps having your head smashed by his powerful thrashing tail, but I'd have to risk that. . . . As I walked toward them I wondered how many legs I'd have left to walk back on, if any. I had taken one precaution. Just out of camera range I had stationed five men with long poles with big cloth wads on the ends of them. They had instructions to watch the other five 'gators and shove the wads into their mouths if they started to mix in. Meanwhile the make-up man sprayed both me and the 'gators with oil, to make everything glisten ominously, not realizing an oily alligator would be twice as hard to wrestle with and pin down.

But it was too late now – the cameras were set. We waited until my particular alligator was a little apart from the rest, then two husky Roman soldiers threw me in beside him. As I hit the mud I grabbed him by the front leg, the one away from the side where the cameras were going to shoot the death scene. We wrestled for a moment, and he opened his big lower jaw. I grabbed it with my left hand, held it open and half put my head in his mouth, but from the side away from the cameras. From the camera side it looked as though my head was in his mouth. Then I slammed it shut and held it shut. Had my head actually been in that mouth, I would have been decapitated. I quickly pulled him down on top of me, kicking my legs violently just once, then stiffened them out suddenly . . . slowly relaxed and fell 'lifeless'. Actually the death scene was so realistic that for a moment DeMille thought the world had seen the last of Joe Bonomo. He was torn between delight over having captured a sensational scene, what he should wire my family and what he would tell the papers.[49]

As a reward, Joe received a half-dollar gold piece from DeMille, one of a whole issue he bought up and handed out for decades as his 'Congressional Medal of Honour' for heroic service on his films.

Some companies, like Pathé Lehrman's Sunshine Comedies, built their fortune entirely on animal films. When Lehrman left the business to join Fox, the Sunshine holdings, including his star lion 'Old Friday', went to the E and R Jungle Studios, which accumulated a large collection of animals for rental and use in its own films. Stunts became progressively more dangerous. A reporter described Billy Campbell and cameraman Lee Garmes making a 1920 animal film at E and R.

Little Albert Austin, a two-and-a-half year old that beats anything for nerve I've ever seen, gets lost in a zoo. He wanders around having hair's breadth escapes from the animals until he finally gets caught on the sloping roof of a woodshed. He slips down to the edge of the roof and gets caught on a nail, and a lion comes along and tries to get him. There is a wall behind the lion with a hole in one of the planks. Snookie, the monk, who has been right on the job and saved the kid about a dozen times already, comes along at this point, pulls the lion's tail through the hole, ties the knot in it and saves the kid.[50]

In the same report, Campbell is understandably wary of the dangers of using prop guns with animals as Selig rashly did in the Roosevelt film. 'A gun, even though full of blanks, in the hands of an excited property man is more dangerous than the lion.'

Training had improved so much that not only action stars and stunt men became involved with animals. Comedienne Marian Nixon, who had no circus background, regarded working with wild animals as part of the job. 'I did a circus picture called *Spangles* (Frank O'Connor, 1926) at Universal in which I did stunts with an elephant. The elephant's name was Jewel. You'd just say "Docko, Jewel" and she'd put her head down. You'd put your hands up over her eyes – there are two little sort of bumps over the eyes – and you'd hang on and say "Docko, Jewel" again and put your foot up in back of you and she'd lift you onto her head.' Near-disasters like those on the DeMille films and the serious wounding of serial star Marie Walcamp on *The Lion's Claws* (Jacques Jaccard, Harry Harvey, 1918) when a lioness lacerated her hands and face – she retired in 1920, permanently scarred – merely added spice to the use of animals in films, and serials in particular stepped up the supply. Understandably, it was to serial directors that studios turned in the twenties for animal films with the authentic spark of danger.

The years following his Grace Cunard serials had been eventful for Woody Van Dyke. Noted for his forceful working methods and ability to deliver a serial on time, he had become a trouble-shooter, accepting bonuses from studios in return for guaranteeing prompt delivery. For *Daredevil Jack*, with boxer Jack Dempsey, who had been signed for only twelve weeks, he received an extra $500 for every episode shot and delivered in under a week, a bonus he rarely missed. Later, he moved on to directing trick rider and ex-Tom Mix stunt man Buck Jones, then became the regular director of Tim McCoy, a Cavalry colonel and Indian expert who exploited his true frontier background as Mix had a false one. With all of these people Van Dyke established his usual contradictory relationship, the sting of sadistic and brutal working methods drawn by a breezy informality, and claims that he forced the pace only for the good of the film. On the McCoy feature *War Paint* (1927) Van Dyke saved on dummies in a massacre scene by having extras lie on the ground among them as the Indians rode through giving the *coup de grâce* with their tomahawks. Prop man Harry Albiez, Van Dyke's regular effects man and assistant, patiently explained to the Indians that they were to chop only the dummies, but not all got it right and there were some broken heads. Bob Rose, who stunted on this and other Van Dyke films, threw Running Ws in threes, at an alleged $150 each, and otherwise knocked himself about for the man who, a few years before, had scalded him in a Cunard serial and subjected him to other indignities. The final disaster came when McCoy, racing from a band of Indians, was shot in the back of the neck by an ebullient extra. The blank charge peppered his neck and shoulder with black powder grains which took hours to remove. As McCoy was jounced back to the unit's headquarters in the prop car, Woody sat by, laughing uproariously at the actor's discomfort and mocking his groans.

Van Dyke's biographer noted the incident and explained, without conviction: 'This, Colonel McCoy soon discovered, was Van Dyke's way of covering up his real sentimentality with this outward appearance of utter brutality.'[51] Van Dyke again moved on, this time to Universal, where he caused havoc on the set of *The Chicago Fire* by calling the police to deal with a riot on the set. Some say Van Dyke provoked a revolt among extras and stunt men with his demands for ever more violent takes in a bar-room brawl, others that he deliberately put in a false riot call to set off a confrontation between angry stunt men and the cops. In any event, he soon left Universal too, and went to MGM, where he was to remain until his death in 1942.

The source of Van Dyke's popularity at MGM was his work on *White Shadows in the South Seas* in 1927. Documentarist Robert Flaherty used the commercial success of *Grass* and *Chang*, actuality films shot on location by adventurers Merian Cooper and Ernest Schoedsack, and his own *Nanook of the North* to extract finance from MGM for a film on Polynesia. Van Dyke was sent as 'associate'

Left *Woody Van Dyke and skulls of dikdik antelopes shot on his* Trader Horn *safari*

or 'assistant' director – opinions vary – to shoot second-unit material of Raquel Torres and ex-stunt star Monte Blue as a framing story for Flaherty's ethnographic footage. From the start, the project was unstable, each director resenting the other. As Flaherty fell farther behind schedule, Van Dyke gained influence, and got permission to shoot a contrived love story with the principals which eventually took up most of the film. Just as it was completed, Warner Brothers made the pioneering break with sound, and MGM added synchronized music and effects to make *White Shadows in the South Seas* its first sound film. Overnight, Woody Van Dyke became a talkie expert, and MGM's most valued director.

His alleged grasp of sound shooting made Van Dyke the only logical choice to direct *Trader Horn*, the African melodrama MGM were determined to shoot on location. The cast, like that of *White Shadows*, was divided between young hopefuls and Van Dyke's acquaintances from the action days, with Western star Harry Carey in the title role. Duncan Renaldo had the romantic lead opposite a nineteen-year-old unknown, Constance Woodruff, who called herself Edwina Booth. She couldn't act, but Van Dyke, first hearing of her when, as an extra, she refused to pose for a still shot unless paid a day's wages, recognized the spirit his jungle goddess would need. A talent quest was faked by the publicity department and Miss Booth 'chosen' from among a number of candidates. Irving Thalberg wanted Wallace Beery for the grizzled Horn, but Beery, with some idea of how rough a trip it would be, refused. His second choice was Harry Carey, who survived a year's grinding sub-zero location work in Colorado on Clarence Brown's *The Trail of '98* (1928) only to return and find his personal fortune lost through bad investments. Knowing this, Thalberg offered him $600 a week, a quarter of his usual salary. Carey reluctantly agreed, on condition that a part be made for his wife, Olive Fuller Golden. (Mrs Carey had her revenge. When extensive re-takes were necessary after the film, she charged MGM a top star's salary for what was merely a supporting role.) The thirty-one person *Trader Horn* crew left for Africa on the *Ile de France* in March 1929, with a nine-ton generator and enormous quantities of sound equipment and film stock. At Mombasa they picked up some additional help, including 'white hunter' W. V. D. Dickinson, a doctor of suspect credentials, and 180 bearers led by a trapper named Waller. Trekking into the interior, Van Dyke made a base ninety miles west of

Farajo, near the northern border of the Belgian Congo, and set out to photograph everything in sight.

Shooting was dangerous. A rhinoceros charged the camera car and came close to overturning it. One of the crew fell out of a tree and was concussed. Others caught malaria and various other tropical diseases, which the doctor treated universally with whisky. Van Dyke solaced himself with the gin he had imported in liberal quantities along with the film equipment, and enlivened the trip with practical jokes, for which he had become famous. On *Daredevil Jack*, Dempsey had woken from a between-takes snooze to find himself roped to his chair while Van Dyke and his minions danced around beating him with rolled-up newspapers, and *White Shadows in the South Seas* had been spiced up by such gags as putting land crabs into the beds of cast and crew. Van Dyke exploited to the full Africa's potential for practical joking, placing a prop rubber crocodile on a path much used by crewmen suffering from one of the many intestinal complaints common to the area, dragging a rope across sleeping members of the cast in imitation of a snake, and feeding some of his gin to a baboon. Edwina Booth, terrified one night to see her shoe moving, apparently of its own accord, across the floor, found a toad inside. Her skimpy clothing for the jungle goddess role exposed her constantly to insect bites and sunburn, from which she suffered agonies, and she later won a substantial settlement from MGM for damage to her health, though the story that she subsequently died from a lingering ailment contracted on the trip is apparently apocryphal.

The script caused more problems than the location. Written in Hollywood from a fanciful quasi-autobiography, it bore little relationship to African life. Van Dyke's biography has fevered descriptions of how the crew solved this problem.

An important scene . . . was the one that called for Harry Carey and Renchero, his gun-boy, to leap across a croc-infested stream while escaping from 'cannibals'. There were plenty of crocodiles there all right but no living being, not even Tarzan, could leap across the Victoria Nile. Van had a quick consultation with his engineers and an artificial stream bed was made close to the river bank. An island was built in the middle of the moat and then an inlet out into the river so that it would fill up with water.

To attract the crocodiles, Dickinson suggested throwing some hippopotamus carcases into the water for bait, and after a few days the stream was filled.

The minute they got into the artificial bed far enough, the gang quickly placed barriers across the inlet, cutting them off from the river. . . . [But] the crew didn't know the wallop a crocodile packs in its tail and crocodiles eighteen feet long are not alligators.

The crocodiles broke out, and the angry Van Dyke, who had wasted ten days on the project, ordered a larger and stronger stockade built. The rotting carcases were dumped inside, and by nightfall the stream was thrashing with two hundred reptiles.

To keep them from getting out of the pen, a twenty-four hour watch was posted. The crews changed shifts every four hours. In addition to clubs and heavy calibre guns they prepared torches with which to drive the beasts back if they should rush the gate. These torches consisted of burlap bags soaked in oil and wound around the ends of long bamboo poles. The idea was to ignite the burlap and ram the flaming bags down the crocs' throats if they charged. The first rush came at two a.m. It reminded Van Dyke of the stories he had read as a kid about knights of old running their lances down dragons' throats. The crocs snatched the torches off the ends of the poles and chewed them up like nice juicy steaks, coming back for more. The gang managed to hold the fort and drove them back with yells, clubs, bamboo poles and a few heavy shells. The next day was cloudy and they couldn't photograph so had to keep the crocs penned up for another night. This night was the worst of all. By this time the beasts were vicious, and charged several times. The gates held, but Van had to kill three of them. The following day the battle went on. The tail of one croc blasted through the fence and caught Harry Carey on the leg, laying him up for a week. Another croc dislodged some sandbags which served as a dam at the lower end of the moat. Duncan Renaldo crawled inside to attempt repairs while diminutive Harry Albiez held one of the beasts at bay. Albiez was on one end of a large pole while the other end was stuffed down the croc's throat. The croc was shaking Harry like a Mixmaster with Harry yodelling to Renaldo to hurry up. Renaldo got out all right but Harry wouldn't drop the pole. Van Dyke yelled 'Let go, you fool!' but Albiez wouldn't let go. 'This is a prop and has to be used in the picture. Damned if I'll find another one.' It cost Van Dyke four shells to save the pole as well as his property man before the croc shook him to death.[52]

Photoplay gave the returning unit a hero's welcome.

The longest, hardest, cruelest location trip in the history of motion pictures is over [for] Harry Carey, Duncan Renaldo, and Edwina Booth. . . . Following on the next boat was director W. S. Van Dyke. With him were many metal cans containing the perishable fruit of nine months of hunger, fever, danger and backbreaking toil.[53]

MGM's editors were less elated when, viewing Van Dyke's 200,000 feet of film, they found most of it useless except as back projection. Long shots of animals, however authentic, bored audiences who had been accustomed in the serials to vivid close-ups and savage action. Van Dyke, who had brought back his leading native bearers as technical advisers, used them to cook up some more exciting scenes on the Culver City backlot, but the increasingly active Society for the Prevention of Cruelty to Animals, as well as a shortage of trained beasts, made this difficult. Knowing that Mexico as well as being free of interfering regulations also had a thriving animal-training industry based partly on their use in pornographic films, Van Dyke moved the whole unit to Tacate in Mexico, built an artificial jungle and recreated in close-up the bloody scenes he had missed in Africa. Lions unwilling to fight for meat were starved until they would, after which one of them was set on some live zebras. Among the records of film production casualties is a note that one Donald Gooch received worker's compensation for a shoulder wrenched when a haltered zebra

Left. Trader Horn: *a starving lion kills a zebra during the additional shooting in Mexico*

broke away from him at Tacate, a hint of the brutality of this location shooting.

Trader Horn was a hit, but as most of the film had been shot in Hollywood or Mexico with Van Dyke's African material as background, no other studio bothered to waste money on overseas shooting. Animal-trainer Frank Buck, hoping to film his book *Bring 'Em Back Alive* about his adventures capturing animals for the world's zoos, found no studio willing to put up the money. Finally the Van Beuren Corporation, a minor RKO subsidiary, agreed to sponsor short films on the subject. Buck spent the same nine months' period in Malaya, Sumatra, India and Ceylon as Van Dyke had in Africa, but shot only half the amount of film, concentrating on close-ups and unconventional scenes, including a battle between a tiger and a python. A delighted RKO cut the film into a feature, and *Bring 'Em Back Alive* (Clyde E. Elliott, 1932) grossed $2 million. Studios that had turned down Buck's proposition searched the circuses for comparable animal experts, and Universal's Carl Laemmle, who approached Buck after the success of *Bring 'Em Back Alive* only to be told that his own story editor had been one of the first people to reject the idea, chose diminutive but dynamic Clyde Beatty, then Ringling's top lion-tamer. His first film, *The Big Cage* (Kurt Neumann, 1933) recreated some incidents from his eventful career, including the occasion when a lion named Nero dragged him around the cage by one leg and hospitalized him for sixteen weeks. Nothing if not audacious, Beatty hired forty-three of Ringling's animals, including Nero, for $3,000 a week, packed them into two extra-long baggage cars, and shipped them to Hollywood.

The 5ft. 5 in. Beatty had grown up in the circus. At fifteen, determined to be an acrobat, he ran away from his parents' Ohio farm and joined a travelling show. This lasted only until he broke his ankle in a fall, and the manager offered him the choice between dismissal and a job as the animal-trainer's assistant. At nineteen, he was urged into a cage with five polar bears and, surviving, found he had become an expert. Four years later his boss had a nervous breakdown and Clyde replaced him. Beatty's arrival with his entourage of half-tame beasts, a contrast to the complacent contents of the Selig Zoo, galvanized Universal. Only one stage was large enough to hold them, the vast studio on which Lon Chaney had made *The Hunchback of Notre Dame*. Tom Mix and Slim Summerville, who appreciated a good stunt, as well as Pat O'Brien,

Ralph Bellamy, Lew Ayers and other Universal players were constantly on Beatty's set, and Laemmle finally barred visitors except between eleven a.m. and one p.m. Beatty and Laemmle got on well.

Mr Laemmle was a kindly little man with a big heart. Deeply interested in my approaching battle with Nero and other exciting scenes, he demanded that no shooting be done until he was personally present. When we at last got ready to begin shooting the first day, director Neumann called for him. Quite a while later he arrived. Stepping briskly over to me with real sincerity and earnestness shining from his eyes, he said, 'Now, Clyde, I don't want you to take any unnecessary chances. We'll get enough thrills as it is. I'm going to sit right here and see that you don't.' Then he sat gingerly down on a special chair and, with his small hands gripping the arms, began keeping his determined vigil over me. Around him on all sides were cameras focused from many angles. I was in the arena with the cats; everybody else was outside. As the cameras ground away, I brought the animals out and pedestalled them. Mr Laemmle sat there tense, staring at me. Suddenly, a lion broke the calm by leaping at a tiger. Firing my gun, I leaped in to separate them. The lion roared, shot a paw at me, and I ducked and advanced on him. There was a panicky yell from the sidelines. Throwing his hands wildly above his head, Mr Laemmle had jumped from his special chair, shrieked his alarm and dashed off the set as fast as his legs would carry him.[54]

Not only Beatty took risks. The crew too worked close to these wild cats, a fact on which the unit's practical jokers traded.

Andy Devine and Vincent Barnett were comedy cage boys, and in one scene wore tiger skins. They discovered that George Robinson, the head cameraman, was quaking with fear inside the four foot by four foot cage on wheels he was using inside the arena. The big camera poked its lens out through a specially cut hole, and in this way the action could be filmed without any arena bars showing. It was, however, an obstacle for me; besides, it was unpleasant for George. One afternoon a lion named Tuffy took a swing at the camera lens, upset the camera, tried to reach through the hole to seize George and his assistant, and finally knocked the cage over. Both were safe enough, but they went sprawling. When the afternoon was over, George was justifiably upset when the time came for him to leave his own cage. Poking his head out nervously, he said. 'Have you got all the animals out, Clyde?' 'Sure, they're all out and in their own cages.' George came hesitantly from his cage – and at that moment two ferocious-looking tigers rushed at him from around the corner of his shelter. He and his assistant almost upset the cage getting back into it. When George discovered the two tigers were Andy Devine and Vincent Barnett clad in tiger skins with a dummy tiger head apiece, he went after the pranksters with his fists.[55]

Beatty became a Universal regular, his wife Harriet often doubling his leading ladies, but as the jungle film fashion declined in the less-affluent Hollywood of the late thirties he retired to his own Florida animal show. Jungle films contracted to the level of Tarzan romances. Johnny Weissmuller wrestled drugged lions or, more often, dummies, with *Trader Horn* footage, progressively more faded, on the back projection screen. It wasn't until 1951 that a Tarzan unit actually took a star to Africa, and for most producers even Florida locations were a luxury. Good animal action scenes were like gold. Devotees claim to have seen the same crocodile battle in five different Tarzan adventures, but duplication was cheaper and safer than going to Africa.

In the efforts to save stars the rigours of African locations, studios often blundered deeper into confusion. Twentieth Century Fox intended its 1939 *Stanley and Livingstone* (Henry King) to star Tyrone Power, and the second unit sent to Africa under Otto

Brower contained a double well-coached in Power's ungainly walk. Brower returned with miles of scenic material to find Darryl Zanuck had borrowed Spencer Tracy for the role, making many hazardous sequences useless. When risks were taken on jungle films, it was seldom by the stars. Animal-handler Bert Nelson was almost killed by one of his own lionesses when she failed to recognize him in Johnny Weissmuller loin cloth and wig; Paul Stader, an ex-lifeguard who broke into stunting with a high dive for Jon Hall on *The Hurricane* in 1937, doubled Weissmuller in the 1948 *Tarzan and the Huntress* and was tossed 150 feet into a tree when a vine on which he was swinging broke. Also in 1948, Mexican diver Angel Garcia, standing in for the star in a dive from the cliffs of Acapulco on *Tarzan and the Mermaids* (Robert Florey), struck a rock and was killed.

Predictably, a producer at last decided to try a stunt man in the role. Jock Mahoney had tested for Tarzan when Weissmuller abandoned the part, losing to handsome but unathletic Lex Barker. Ten years later he was luckier, and got the lead in *Tarzan Goes to India* (John Guillermin, 1962). The 6ft. 4 in. 220 pound Mahoney was one of Hollywood's most audacious and ambitious post-war stunt men. Born Jacques O'Mahoney in 1919, he was a college sports champion and a Marine before turning to horse-breeding for the movies. When this failed he took on stunt work, first in Westerns, where he doubled Charles Starrett and Gene Autry, but establishing his reputation with a dangerous leap down a flight of stairs in the duel scene at the end of *The Adventures of Don Juan* (Vincent Sherman, 1948). He also doubled Gregory Peck and John Wayne in later films, and had a career in TV Westerns as well as in the part of Tarzan.

Serious location films in Africa didn't revive until the fifties, when a slump in studio film-making sent units once again on long journeys for their material. One of the first to make the trip was another MGM team shooting a 1950 remake of *King Solomon's Mines*. Deborah Kerr and Stewart Granger starred; the directors were Englishman Compton 'Bob' Bennett and Andrew Marton, who remembers the occasion without affection. 'Bob Bennett was the original director, but I replaced him when he became ill. We split the credit. Out of forty-six American technicians we were down to eleven, yet we still had to run two units.' Richard Rosson directed the animal stampede, one of the film's action highlights. 'He had terrific trouble with it. He spotted the herds by plane but

Below. King Solomon's Mines: *Deborah Kerr and Stewart Granger momentarily impede the rhino on his walk into Africa*

by the time he came down they had gone. At about the fourth or fifth try he did it, and then we had to put Granger and the girl into it, which we did on the backlot at the studio. We had a few animals and we turned them around in a kind of cyclorama because we didn't have enough footage of the herd. We built a barricade on the set and the animals had to jump over it. Granger almost lost an eye when he fired his gun to turn them away. His old 1880 rifle misfired; you could see the flame hit him in the eye. He was almost blinded.' Some scenes in this film are classics of animal photography, including an encounter with a rhinoceros. It stares crossly at the party for a moment, then turns away, to the protests of Miss Kerr. But Granger is adamant. 'He wasn't going to harm us. Must you have another trophy?' Marton says: 'Bennett built a large enclosure out in the wilderness, and they actually turned a wild rhino loose on Deborah Kerr and Stewart Granger. They had eleven white hunters on high positions aiming in such a way that they could not hit each other or the actors. If the rhino had charged them, Granger would have fired, and the hunters also. They turned him loose, with two cameras going. The rhino came up, looked at the actors, and very quietly went off screen, kept

walking right to the fence and disappeared into Africa.'

A trip to Africa soon became obligatory for all studios. To enliven John Ford's *Mogambo*, a 1953 remake of Victor Fleming's 1932 jungle drama *Red Dust*, Richard Rossen was again sent to Africa to shoot some gorilla-hunting in the jungle. When he became ill with the tropical disease from which he later died, Yakima Canutt replaced him, returning with a memorable sequence, shot in gorilla country but against a canvas backdrop and with the help of an electric cattle fence. But the ultimate African picture was delayed until 1966, when actor/director Cornel Wilde made *The Naked*

Prey, in which a lone hunter, played by Wilde, eludes his native captors and flees across Africa with them in pursuit. Naked and unprotected, he faces heat, hunger and predators, but learns to survive.

Wilde planned the whole film while suffering from an infection contracted on his research trip that necessitated a catheter inserted into his bladder, and experienced after-effects of the illness right through the pre-production period. To convince a studio doctor that he was fit to begin, he had to feign 'flu to explain a high temperature. His English crew suffered as much as the director/ star. Three caught the parasitic disease bilharzia, six succumbed to heat exhaustion, and others were badly stung by 'killer bees'. But Wilde remembers the production almost with nostalgia. 'I got used to the running and really enjoyed it. I ran eight or ten miles a day and lost a lot of weight, which was right for the film. We got up to 115 degrees, but fortunately most of the locations were dry. Humid heat in the hundred-degree area is just terrible. The heat didn't bother me but it bothered a lot of my unit. We worked like hell – I knew that in forty days the monsoon would begin – and some of them wanted to quit. My English assistant director said, "I don't want to die in Africa". I said "Neither do I, and I don't think we will, but this is the way we're going to work all through the picture. It isn't going to get any easier." He stayed, but he bitched and cursed through the whole film and so did a lot of the others.'

To heat, disease and exhaustion were added the problems of working with wild and untrained animals. One scene called for the man to stumble into a pit of spiders. 'There *was* a place where giant spiders had been breeding but three years of drought had eliminated them, and I was stuck. I thought "What else?" and snakes came up as a good possibility. We found a place where there were a lot of snakes and we had an extra man from the zoo as well as our own snake man to look them over. They said there was one poisonous variety, a bird snake, grey and white and very, very fast, but though they're very poisonous the fangs are in the back and the snake has to chew up on whatever he's grabbed before he can get them into play. That takes maybe six or eight seconds. I thought: well, there are very few places he could grab me where I can't reach and even then somebody will pull him off. They counted about sixty snakes around when the scene started. I could hear the slithering and hissing. My eyes were almost closed and I couldn't see a lot of what was happening, but I heard a gasp from the crew. They told me afterwards that one of the snakes had struck at me. I never saw rushes but weeks later we saw the film and the snake actually struck, but stopped about an inch away from my leg.

'Five or six of us got tick bite fever. A lousy experience. It used to be fatal before antibiotics and it still makes you pretty sick. A day later I had to do a scene in a mountain pool where I'm under water, presumably dead, and a little girl pulls me out. That was a cold, *cold* pool. I was still weak from the fever and got the shakes so badly that we couldn't shoot until I got numb enough to lie still under the water. Then there were the thorns, some of them four or five inches long. Every day I'd be cut or scratched and people were always stepping on them. They go right through the sole of a shoe.' For the last scenes Wilde and a small crew went to Bechuanaland for some shots of a swamp and all contracted a stomach infection from brackish water. But the film was shot and Wilde thankfully returned to England. As a precaution all the crew went through the London Hospital for Tropical Diseases. Most were suffering from some after-effects of their ordeal or a lingering infection. Wilde, however, had only one symptom: his knee joints were inflamed from too much running.

Left *Steward Rafill wrestles a leopard in* Tarzan and the Valley of Gold. *(From the grip Rafill has on the animal's ear it is probably more attacked than attacker)*

9 Magicians

The words 'special effects', like 'additional dialogue' or 'from an idea', cover some of the cinema's greatest mysteries. At one end of the scale, a special effects man can be someone who supervises the back projection, or juggles some miniatures; at the other, he can script, design, photograph, produce and direct sequences vital to a film's success. But the distinction is always blurred. Pearl White's 'Pitch' Revada, technically a property man, supervised and acted as safety man on her stunts, as well as playing minor roles. Fred Gabourie was more than a mere technician, but worked closely with Buster Keaton on important sequences. Until German cinematographers like Rittau and Schuftan gave a lazy industry the crutch of camera trickery, these men were vital to a film's success, and even today the special effects technician, part inventor, part artist, part engineer, is one of the cinema's key people, playing a role that is seldom appreciated.

The development of techniques for the simple fall show in microcosm the inter-reliance of special effects and stunting. Silent comedians used acrobatic ability to protect them, but as jumps got higher a shock-absorber became essential. The carpet held by Pearl White's unit to catch Eddie Kelly and the nets rigged by Richard Talmadge for his falls gave way to kapok pads, auto tyres, excelsior and other crushable combinations. Later, cardboard boxes became standard; three dozen of them, specially folded or trimmed of their corners to expel air on impact, covered with mattresses and roped down under tarpaulins or nets, made an effective but bulky cushion. For falls in confined spaces, some men used flexible wooden slats laid across sawhorses with mattresses on top and underneath; compact but risky. Today, the most common device is the air pad, a rubberized canvas mattress developed by sixties stunt men from those used by pole vaulters. Easily folded, it can be carried to a job on a pick-up, inflated

quickly with compressed air and adjusted to any fall. There has
been the same development in the use of the pads with which stunt
men protect hips, elbows and knees, the special harnesses for
'drags' – being pulled, often by arm or leg, behind a horse – and
other apparently simple techniques. In the stunt business, everything can be improved; a life may depend on it.

Sennett's Keystone lot was a laboratory of effects technique,
its property men adapting most of vaudeville's ideas for use in
the cinema as Keaton was to do. The first bricks thrown by comics
were made of felt and, when their lightness impaired accuracy, of

Below *A Spanish
stunt man falls into
cardboard boxes in*
King of Kings (1961

sand-filled cloth. Walls that cars or comedians crashed through were built of balsa wood which, with the dried stems of the yucca plant, went to make 'breakaway' furniture. Balsa chairs or tables held together with glue or toothpicks, bottles and lamps baked from bread dough, props cast in paraffin wax, resin, sugar or from plaster of paris weakened with sand or sawdust could all safely be broken over a comedian's head, though constant blows from break- aways led, twenties stunt man Buddy Mason claimed, to a state of punch-drunkenness known as 'Yucca Nutty'. When comics complained that sand from breakaway pots got in their eyes, they switched to stearic acid, an extract of vegetable and animal fats, reasonably transparent but inclined to distort if left for too long. The first breakaway windows were made from sugar boiled into a murky candy. Stunt men showing off to journalists by somer- saulting through a window and calmly munching a scrap of 'glass' may not have known the additives prop men put in the mixture to clear it; cream of tartar was only the most prosaic of them.

With the advent of arc lights after the First World War, sugar props, which melted, gave way to resin. Today, plastics like polyurethane and styrofoam are the basic materials of all break-

aways, from disintegrating violins to artificial boulders. They are even used for movie snow, replacing the salt, alum and bleached cornflakes of earlier years. But risks remain even in such simple stunts. Christopher Lee and Robert Beatty nearly choked to death when the snow machine on a Douglas Fairbanks Jnr TV show went wild and filled the studio. Dry ice used to duplicate fog can also smother a man if the carbon dioxide is not dispersed, though the most grotesque dry ice accident occurred on Frank Capra's 1931 *Dirigible*. For realistic breath effects in an Arctic scene (shot in tropical studio conditions) Capra made metal cages to fit in the mouth of each actor, and filled them with scraps of dry ice. Unable to speak his lines, Hobart Bosworth threw away the cage and put the dry ice directly in his mouth. A moment later he was in agony as the cold froze his cheek. Portions of tongue, jaw and teeth had to be removed.

The error was one no good effects man would have committed. They were proud of anticipating every contingency. In one famous incident, a director needed to repair the bedraggled ear of a donkey, and was delighted when the prop man produced a realistic copy that could be glued to its head. 'Well, I read the script,' he

Left A well-prepared fall for Texas (1941) *with roof slide and sand pit*

explained to a puzzled director, 'and it mentioned making a silk purse out of a sow's ear. I've got the silk purse too.'

Hollywood in the thirties was in its golden age. Many basic techniques were still forming, and for the ambitious effects man technical imagination and a stunt man's willingness to take risks meant more than a BSc. Some came close to the mad scientists whose exploits they often had to duplicate on screen. From his Santa Monica garage, Ken Strickfaden created unique electrical effects. His 'High Amperage Pyrogeyser', 'Lightning Screen' and 'Dyna-scope' flared and crackled in most of the thirties' great horror films. For *The Mask of Fu Manchu* (Charles Brabin, 1932) MGM wanted fiendish Fu to test 'scientifically' the sword of Genghis Khan plundered from a hidden tomb. Strickfaden designed a rig that would allow Boris Karloff to play lightning from his long-nailed fingers over the blade's surface, a stunt the cautious actor refused to perform. Strickfaden confidently put on Karloff's costume, including long copper fingernails designed to slip over those of the actor, grounded himself with a wire from one leg and placed his hand in the electrical field. Sparks flared satisfyingly, but when he moved his ungrounded leg near a metal floor conduit, Strickfaden went cart-wheeling in a crackling short circuit. 'They said I spun around in the air,' he says nonchalantly. 'All I know is that I had a sore back for a long time.' On a Superman serial of the forties, Kirk Allyn, playing the Man of Steel, had a similar un-pleasant moment when rescuing Lois Lane from an electrical trap in which the villains had imprisoned her. Lightning flared from two terminals as he moved purposefully towards her, but he was horrified when the sparks wavered and then homed on the metal buckle of his belt. For a moment he stood, the nervous point of an electrical triangle, before backing hastily away.

Some of Strickfaden's flamboyance crept into the career of John P. Fulton, perhaps Hollywood's greatest special effects technician. A tall and athletic Nebraskan, Fulton came to Hollywood in 1914 with his father, a theatrical scene painter who established himself in the movies creating backdrops; among his biggest jobs were the scenic backgrounds for *Gone With the Wind*. John broke into films as an assistant cameraman, but after training with Frank Williams, pioneer process photographer and inventor of the travelling matte technique, he freelanced in process work and joined Universal as head of its trick department. Fulton was to win three Academy Awards and create the complex trick work for *The Invisible*

Man (James Whale, 1933) and the parting of the Red Sea for Cecil B. DeMille's 1956 *The Ten Commandments*. He lived for his work, relishing every detail, even the most hazardous. A keen flier – his instructor was Paul Mantz – he supervised his own aerial shooting, usually from the cockpit, and handled animals with total lack of fear. Seeking 'killer ants' for *The Naked Jungle* (Byron Haskin, 1954) in which Charlton Heston's surly Amazonian planter fights off an army of them, Fulton took his team, including assistants Paul Lerpae and Charlie Baker, into the mountains after a particularly large but non-biting variety of wood ant, hundreds of which they unearthed from rotted logs and transported triumphantly back to the studio. Bathed in syrup, Heston spent uncomfortable days with these crawling all over him, but in his zeal Fulton forgot their mobility until roars of discomfort from the next stage, where Bob Hope was shooting a costume comedy, showed they had strayed. As head of special photographic effects for Universal and later Paramount, Fulton had time to experiment. On *Elephant Walk* (William Dieterle, 1954) he brought in thirteen circus elephants (which were quartered in the drained studio tank), supplementing them with automated elephant heads for close work to mollify the nervous Elizabeth Taylor. Highly ambitious, Fulton was poised to begin a new career as director when he was taken ill in Spain while planning second-unit shooting for *The Battle of Britain*. He died in 1966.

The technicians who built the elaborate studios of Sennett and Hal Roach were anonymous, but many special effects ideas began there. Both had water pipes in floors and walls to deliver squirts on cue. Roach went one better and installed ceiling 'dump tanks' that instantly flooded a scene. Such tanks have been the basis of some striking sequences. Duplicating the crash of an airliner into the sea for *Foreign Correspondent* in 1940, a grim scene in which pilots and crew seem to drown horribly in a sinking cabin, Alfred Hitchcock, a natural inventor who delights in tinkering up complex stunts for his films, exploited tank facilities.

I had Paul Mantz go up over the Pacific and do some nose dives with the camera stuck out in front of the plane and pull out of the dive at the last minute, so that the plane was practically touching the water. He did two or three of those. Then we brought those films back. When you looked at them on the screen you felt you were diving towards the water, and at the last minute you came out of the dive. Now I built the cockpit in the studio with the glass front and the two men in it, and on a screen, back-projected, I had the dive towards the ocean. How did the water come in and envelop the people? I had the screen made of rice paper, without any seams, twelve feet wide and eight feet high, and behind the screen two dump tanks with 2,700 gallons of water in each, and a chute pointing at the screen. So, at the crucial moment, when I felt we were just about to touch the water, I pressed a button and let the whole of that 5,400 gallons go. It tore through the screen in such a volume that you never saw the screen go, and the whole cockpit was filled with water. All in the one shot.

To achieve that shot of the people apparently drowning in the cabin we had a tank, and lowered the set with the people in it into the tank, so you got the effect of the water coming in. We had the ceiling made of paper so their heads went through the paper; we cut just before the paper ceiling broke. Herbert Marshall presented a special problem because he had only one leg. So we built a chest-high tub for him, photographed him in the water, and just skimmed over the top of that tub.[56]

Hitchcock, like most Hollywood directors, also used the 'studio tank', a concrete pond employed for everything from miniature sea battles to beach parties. The complexity of these tanks – MGM's

Left. In Which We
Serve: *Noel Coward
and crew before a
take . . . and after*

could create, among other effects, fifteen foot waves – made them dangerous to the uninitiated. Three extras drowned in one on Warner Brothers' 1929 *Noah's Ark*. On Hitchcock's *Lifeboat* (1944) Tallulah Bankhead was at the centre of a multiple water dump in which 100,000 gallons of water sluiced down on the boat. Cast and crew gave her a round of applause. On Curtis Bernhardt's *A Stolen Life* (1946) Bette Davis was dragged under by wires in a yacht sinking scene and nearly drowned in seventeen feet of water, but more often the tank is less dangerous than merely unpleasant. Over a long period of shooting, the water, generally warmed for the actors' comfort, becomes stagnant. Shooting *In Which We Serve* (Noel Coward, David Lean, 1942) the cast, including Coward as the captain, spent days bobbing in life-preservers, daubed with oil and soot, after having survived the sinking of their ship. Richard Attenborough remembers that the sawdust around the tank was mouldy, the water foul with debris, oil and scum. As the cast gingerly immersed themselves on the last day, Coward poised himself on the edge, made a perfect dive and, rising covered with grease, called encouragingly, 'There's dysentery on every ripple.'

One of the best 'tank stories' surrounds Poppaea's milk bath

for *The Sign of the Cross* (1932); this scene which took Cecil B. De-Mille a week to film, has Claudette Colbert as the dissolute empress luxuriating in a marble bath of milk at which kittens lap and into which her handmaidens pour scented oils. The bath was first filled with four hundred gallons of real milk to precisely the level of Miss Colbert's nipples. To duplicate globs of cream floating on top, lard was used, since real cream would have melted under the lights, but as shooting continued the melting grease and rapidly souring milk made the scene a noisome one for the star. 'Excuse me,' she is reported to have said, 'but my bath is turning to cheese.' When the scene was finished and Miss Colbert had escaped to a real bath, De Mille left the milk, by now coagulated and glazed with melted fat, to be drained the next morning. A publicity man, showing visitors over the set, mistook the surface for a marble floor and, stepping experimentally onto it, disappeared from sight.

DeMille also had early experience of yet another complex special effect, the gunshot. His brother William, shooting *Rose of the Rancho* on location in 1914, wrote:

I can't begin to tell you all the exciting things we have been doing. You'll see when you see the picture. I was one of the sharpshooters today, shooting with powerful rifles to break down doors, smashing the top of a stone wall, breaking water jugs, etc. It was very exciting Friday. If I shot badly, I would be apt to kill someone, but the effect will be fine for the picture . . .[57]

For years a rifleman, often as unskilled as DeMille, was a standard member of any Western film unit, though nervous actors soon persuaded directors to use slingshots firing marbles (or pieces of chalk for richochets) and to suggest a shot by whisking off their hat with a black thread. But as late as the mid-thirties, stunt driver Carey Loftin found the shot gun still had its place. 'I've blown tyres, on purpose and accidental, and I've never lost a car yet that way, even on films where I drove alongside the camera car and the guy blew it with a shotgun and double O buckshot. But that was in the old days. After that, we did them with a charge bouncing around on the inside of the tyre, with some wires to fire it, but that didn't always work. When you pressed the switch, the thing mightn't even be making contact. The best is what they call a "shaped charge"; it looks like putty and you put it on a heavy backing. Whatever hole it makes on one side of the tyre it makes one exactly the same shape on the other. It's instant blowout.'

Right *A squib at the moment of explosion:* Lawman (1971). *Special effects by Leon Ortega*

Bullet 'hits' on the human body also went through a similar refinement. At the climax of *Hell's Angels* in 1928, Ben Lyon had to be shot in the back by his brother James Hall. The 'bullet' was an ink-soaked plug of sponge rubber fired from a starting pistol, and while it made a realistic mark, even two heavy sweaters and towels wrapped around his body didn't save Lyon from bruises. Thirties technology transformed this with the invention of two small but vital devices. One was a gelatin capsule solid enough to be shot from a compressed air rifle but so soft it exploded on impact, spattering its target with realistic blood. (For a starred windscreen or window, clear gel, aluminium dust and a disc of black cloth give a startlingly accurate effect.) The other was the 'squib', a tiny plaque of explosive, sometimes no larger than a coin, that could be detonated electrically. Squibs taped to a metal plate and sewn into a solid leather jerkin allowed effects men to duplicate the impact of a real bullet, even to the ripped and charred clothing, without hurting or even distracting the stunt man. For greater realism, rubber sacs of 'blood' taped over the squib made the wound spurt sickeningly. (The sacs were usually condoms, yet another use found by film-makers for this indispensable device. British composer Tristram Cary recently achieved new effects for the score of Richard Williams's animated feature *I Vor Pittfalks* by scratching a condom stretched across a microphone, and director Jack Arnold, unable to find means in his 1957 *The Incredible Shrinking Man* to show how simple drops of water would appear to his micro-miniaturized hero, filled condoms with water, dropped them to a concrete floor and back-projected the enlarged image, with remarkable veracity.) Movie gunshot technology still relies on the squib and gelatin capsule and, except for refinements like the use of sound switches to explode a squib at the mere bang of a gun, little has changed since the forties.

A violent new cinema has kept the effects men – 190 in Holly-wood in 1972, and a handful in Britain and Europe – more than busy, with scenes that go far beyond simple mayhem. For *Bonnie and Clyde* (1967), a sequence where the bandit lovers die in a machine-gun ambush involved hundreds of squibs, and half a day's preparation for each take. Since director Arthur Penn demanded absolute realism, with bullets punching through the car body into Faye Dunaway, the realistic jerk of impact and the correct welling of blood, effects man Danny Lee spent hours drilling holes in the car, taping in squibs which were then painted over, and fixing corresponding charges to the actress's body so that, as he touched his battery to a pinboard linking the charges, they exploded in proper sequence. Four cameras covered the scene, shooting at speeds ranging from twenty-four to the extreme slow motion of 168 frames a second. Penn later intercut their footage to create a bloody ballet, disguising the complex mechanics behind the sequence. Sam Peckinpah, whose *The Wild Bunch* (1970) with its gouts of blood from shot-gun wounds and spouting slit throat encouraged Hollywood to pull out all the special effects stops, demanded new horrors from British effects technicians Cliff and John Richardson for *Straw Dogs* (1971). They obliged with a con-vincing severed foot – a boot filled with beefsteak and liberally baptized with a brand of stage blood known as 'Kensington Gore' – and equally realistic shot-gun impacts in which wires yanked the victim backwards, an idea first used on George Stevens's *Shane* in 1953 where Jack Palance guns down Elisha Cook Jnr (Hollywood effects boss Roland Chiniqui developed a spring-operated harness for the same job.) Although they occasionally mix powdered rub-ber with stage blood to duplicate exploding flesh, occidental effects men have not yet been asked to imitate the Hong Kong studios of

Run Run Shaw which order blood by the barrel and pig intestines by the bucket for the most realistic disembowelments ever filmed. British expert Les Bowie did, however, explode a life-size dummy filled with offal for a sequence of a soldier stepping onto a mine, creating a grotesque and almost hilarious effect soon, no doubt, to become commonplace.

The gunshot and its cousin the knife or spear 'hit', generally achieved by shooting hollow arrows or spears along a piano wire anchored to the stunt man's body, or by free-shooting into slabs of pine or end-grain balsa under his clothing, are the effects man's

bread and butter, simple to arrange and relatively free of risk, but in battles, 'fire gags', car crashes and explosions, the unpredictable makes room for danger and death. To prepare for this responsibility, the modern Hollywood special effects man goes through an elaborate apprenticeship. After two years as a prop maker, he must spend at least fifteen hundred hours working at conventional effects jobs; making rain, snow or fog, handling gear for fully-trained technicians. In America, trainees must also pass a state-approved explosives course and an eighty-page examination to win their Class Three Powderman's Licence. Since explosives handlers are automatic security risks, the candidate is also investigated for unsafe political connections by the FBI. Even then, he will be only the most junior of effects men, barred for some years from major projects and the $16,000 plus salary he can draw in an industry that has an inordinate respect for technical skill.

An effects man needs every hour of his experience when he takes over the engineering of a complex battle sequence. Screen warfare has improved since D. W. Griffith, shooting *The Birth of a Nation* in 1914, demanded that the man tossing prop bombs into the fight aim lower, and cameraman Billy Bitzer saw a smoking incendiary

Below *A perfect 'pot' explosion:* Seven Guns for the MacGregors

whizz between his legs. By the twenties, the powderman who set and detonated charges for a battle scene was a key figure. Harry Redmond, who managed the battles for Raoul Walsh's *What Price Glory?* in 1926, exploded six thousand separate charges on that film without a single stunt man hurt, and although not all were as expert – on an anonymous war film of the early thirties an inept technician wired nine tons of powder to an area 880 feet square; it rained rocks for a full minute afterwards – his systems are still standard today. Conical metal 'mortars' or 'pots' are placed in the ground where explosions are needed, then filled with a measured charge of black powder or 'flash' powder, topped with Fuller's Earth, 'Bentonite', peat moss or other soft debris to create a realistic cloud. Wires connect the pots to a central 'war board' with pins or switches corresponding to each mortar or group of mortars, and at the director's order the effects man touches his battery to the pin, exploding the charge, which is funnelled upwards by the pot so as not to injure anyone. It doesn't always work properly. On *Porkchop Hill* (Lewis Milestone, 1959) stunt man Hal Needham played an American soldier advancing up a hill under cover of 'friendly' artillery. Lines of charges had been set to explode in front of the advance. 'But the effects man hooked his wires up backwards. We were supposed to go all the way across a line of pots and have them explode behind us, but just as I got two or three feet away from the one in front of me, it exploded. I had a helmet on but it burned all my hair, my eyelashes and eyebrows as well as my face. It knocked me down and all the dirt and peat moss in my eyes made me think I was blind.'

The Devil's Brigade (Andrew V. McLaglen, 1968), on which Needham ramrodded the stunts, was better managed. 'We had an effects man on that who I'd trust with my life – Logan Frazee. If he says "Hal, here's what's going to happen", you can depend that that's what *will* happen. On *The Devil's Brigade* we had ten guys out on the point of a mountain when an artillery barrage was supposed to start. We had log bunkers and Logan was blowing fifteen foot logs a hundred feet in the air. I had men in the middle of all this, but he'd given me the safe spots and I told the guys to go straight to them. We never hurt anybody. On *The Bridge at Remagen* [John Guillermin, 1968], myself, Gary McClarty and another guy had a big bridge shot. A section of the bridge was rigged so it would fall away from us and dump us all in the river twenty-five feet below. We had a series of explosions on the

bridge and two and a half kilos of TNT in the water. The director wanted a big geyser of water coming up as we went down, but we were only in the air about a second and a half at that height and if you're in the water when that thing goes off, you're in a lot of trouble. I told Logan, "You've *got* to hit that right." He said, "Don't worry." And if you look at the film, when we're just six feet off the bridge the water is boiling up, and as we fall we meet the water half way. That's how accurate and precise he is.'

Water's incompressibility is not the only complication to shooting explosions at sea. Directing *The Caine Mutiny* in 1954, Edward Dmytryk almost abandoned a simulated assault and landing sequence because of sea sickness. 'It was a big operation, with explosions going off all over,' he says. 'The effects men had the charges on inflatable rubber tyres from children's tricycles or

Above *Hal Needham's bridge fall on* The Bridge at Remagen. *Special effects by Logan Frazee* go-karts; something like that. We sat there at the edge of the surf all day while they set up the charges, blew them and set them up again. We were all right on the camera boat, but landing craft aren't made for that kind of work. They've got no stability and they roll horribly in the swell. We had seasoned navy men coming on board and they were *green*.' Similar problems were resolved more tragically in February 1935, when a second unit started shooting material for Frank Lloyd's *Mutiny on the Bounty* near Catalina Island and in the straits of Santa Barbara. Actors doubling Bligh and his castaways were in a long boat, the cameras and lights bolted to a flat-bottomed barge. When a sudden squall swept down on the unit, the long boat was able to escape, but the top-heavy barge capsized, taking a camera operator and all the equipment with it. The remaining long boat footage was shot in the studio, where effects men manned the rockers so energetically that all the actors got sea sick. The waters off Catalina have been the scene of some classic Hollywood disasters, some tragic, some hilarious. For *Captain Blood* (David Smith, 1924) Vitagraph bought two old square riggers for $5,000 each with the idea of shooting a full sea battle culminating in the explosion of one boat. An inexperienced prop man, told to distribute two hundred pounds of dynamite through the hull, fell for the explosives' salesman's persuasive line that, if a spoonful was good, the whole bottle was better, and packed in five thousand pounds. When it blew, the ship was reduced to matchsticks. All the camera got was a blur.

Fire gags are among the most dangerous of stunts, and in the early days absurd risks were taken. Making *The Fire King* in Hackensack, New Jersey, in 1914, director Walter King put actors Charles Davenport and Arthur Robinson into a prop house which was then set alight. Davenport, playing the villain who is supposed to have ignited the house, fights with Robinson and is knocked unconscious while Robinson drops through a trapdoor into the space under the house and appears triumphantly before the camera. The only safety device was an asbestos bag Robinson pulled over Davenport's head before he escaped. This should have protected him long enough for the shot to end, but when Robinson found his escape barred through the cellar, both men were scorched and Robinson badly burned before the director could get them out.

In the mid-twenties, Dick Grace, doubling an un-named female star, had a ballet dress he wore soaked in gasoline and set alight.

'In a moment I was a flaming human torch,' he wrote emotionally:

It was too much; to feel those flames searing the flesh of my back, neck, arms and face pierced my self-control. With the agonized scream of a person burning to death I cleared the balcony in a bound, then down to the main floor. 'Help, I'm burning!' Everyone seemed paralysed into inaction. Then everything began to fog before my eyes. I still had the presence of mind, however, to keep my arms locked above my head, thus preventing my face from burning seriously. I kept running, and so for the most part the flames and fumes swept behind me, although they reached ten feet higher than my head.[58]

A moment later an assistant director threw Grace down and smothered the fire in an overcoat. All the skin from the upper part of his body was gone, but the doctor's prompt action in dousing the burns with gasoline, an agonizing but effective therapy, let Grace recover in a few months.

Most stunt men are sceptical about this legend. Are we to assume Grace agreed to be set afire without protective clothing of any kind, and that nobody was standing by to douse the flames when the shot was over? Such carelessness clashes with Grace's usual caution, and it seems safest to take the story with a large grain of salt. But undoubtedly Grace did do some hazardous fire gags, seldom with more protection than a double layer of clothing and heavy leather gloves. So confident was director George Hill of his skill that when he heard Little Venice was in flames, he called up Grace immediately and had him running in and out of the blazing buildings to store up some cheap thrills for later films.

Modern technology has made the fire gag safer, but any stunt man will ask an automatic $500 just to put on the special asbestos suit, face mask and miniature breathing equipment needed to keep him alive when doused with alcohol or gasoline and set on fire. Adjustments – for running, fighting or falling into water while in flames – can push the price up to $1,000 a stunt. The so-called 'bail-out bottle' designed for high-altitude parachutists holds only three minutes of air, but no man could survive this period of continuous heat. The record is fifteen seconds by stunt man Jack Wilson on *Tobruk* (Arthur Hiller, 1966). Wilson uses a double layer of asbestos under his padded jump suit, with long underwear under the lot, and an asbestos mask and gloves capable of with-standing the two thousand degree temperature of napalm. For greater effect, he also smears his suit with rubber cement to give

Right *Denver
Mattson and Donna
Garrett in the near-
fatal fire gag on
Flare-Up*

Right *Denver Mattson and Donna Garrett in the near-fatal fire gag on Flare-Up*

greasy black smoke. Accidents are common, often for the least
likely reasons. Wilson's safety man burned his hands badly just
by touching the suit minutes after a take, and he has seen camera
gear soften and distort from coming too close. Shooting a fire sequence in *Flare-Up* (James Nielson, 1969) Denver Mattson,
doubling actor Luke Askew who has been set on fire by Raquel
Welch (replaced in the fire shot by Donna Garrett), got second-
degree burns on his hands through wearing leather gloves instead
of wool. Inside the non-porous gauntlets his sweat vapourized
into scalding super-heated steam. Others have been hurt by flame-
throwers, failing to realize that gases make a vital vapour barrier
between the suit and the flames. Effects men always incorporate
alcohol into their gasoline/benzine mixtures to provide this essential shield, but the blast of a flame-thrower used too close can strip
it away and fatally heat up the interior of a suit.

On Franklin Schaffner's *The War Lord* (1965) Hal Needham was
one of nine invading soldiers doused with burning oil by castle
defenders. It was not a pleasant experience. 'Time is important.
They have to put you in the suit, seal you up, put the stuff on you,
set you afire and get the shot all in three minutes. You can't have

claustrophobia, because when they put you in that suit it really can work on your mind. I checked my air supply, and found they'd cut it in half. Everybody else had 2,500 pounds and I had only 1,200. I could have said, "I don't have enough air, so forget it" but that would be throwing away $750, so I decided to go with what I'd got.

'The gag was for us to attack the door over the drawbridge, then be doused in oil, set afire and fall into the moat. It was a pretty wild scene, shot at night. I got in there and, to save my air, I decided to breathe the air that was inside my suit and face mask. So I was breathing my own carbon dioxide. It does funny things to your mind. I damn near panicked. My eye-piece fogged up so I couldn't see where I was. I took my sword and felt about for the wall, and then for the edge of the bridge. I started to think: when

Left and right *Joe Canutt in fire suit surviving the bridge blaze in* The War Lord

the fire starts I have to fall into the water. It's night, and the suit isn't waterproof, so if I get water up my nose I can't spit out the mouthpiece because there's not enough room in the suit. I could drown. All that was going through my mind as they poured this mixture of alcohol and benzine and gasoline down on us, and the guy dropped the torch. He was in a window eighteen feet above us but the flame burned the hair off his arm. We just exploded! It was a hell of a fire, but I didn't really know I was in trouble until I pulled my faceplate tight to get a look at what was happening and I saw an effects man with a five gallon bucket spreading more of this stuff around. I got out of that one, but it was hairy — real hairy.'

10 Nightmares

It is the essence of fantasy films' attraction that in them one sees the unseeable, and until animation and process photography minimized their contribution, horror directors relied on effects engineers and stunt men.

Like the comedy, it borrowed optical tricks from vaudeville; Georges Méliès, earliest master of screen fantasy, had been a stage conjuror, and his pioneer films of the 1890s exploited and expanded some popular illusions. But he tired of these simple effects and in 1897 built a new studio with trapdoors, concealed panels, sliding doors, as well as capstans, winches and pulleys to animate his complicated creations. A huge torso and movable arms in *The Conquest of the Pole* needed twelve operators. Over the next two decades mechanical monsters became common, used nowhere more effectively than in Fritz Lang's *Siegfried* (1922). Lang's vision of the Nibelungen legend demanded a larger than life recreation, forests gloomier than the real thing (he had them built from plaster), a hero of impossible courage, and for his battle with the dragon Fafnir, and subsequent blood bath which makes him invulnerable, a dragon of convincing size and ferocity. Refusing model work, he called in expert engineer Erich Kettelhut who built a Fafnir twenty metres long that needed a ten man crew, five pushing it along a trench hiding the wheeled structure on which it was built, the rest operating eyes, mouth, tongue and craning neck. Lang added sacs of 'blood' in the chest to create a striking sequence.

Few later film monsters were built in such detail. The most famous, King Kong, supposedly fifty feet tall, did not exist except as a number of separate limbs and features, ranging from a 'life size' articulated arm and a bust with automatic rolling eyes, to models, some only inches tall. Willis O'Brien, the animation expert responsible for the success of *The Lost World* in 1925, with its convincing dinosaur battles, created the impression of an enormous beast battling with the creatures isolated with it on a

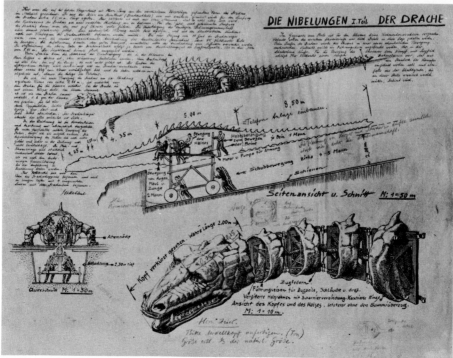

remote East Indies island, kidnapping Fay Wray and conducting with her an absurd but somehow never risible love affair. He returns with his captors, first to amuse, then to ravage New York, dying at last in a hail of bullets on top of the Empire State Building. Bruce Cabot, second lead and, with Fay Wray, the romantic interest, recalled *King Kong* (1933), his first film, with little warmth. The tough New Mexico oil-field worker met David O. Selznick at a party, and was cast in the film mainly, Cabot believes, for his obvious sexual charm. It was not until he began to work under the direction of Merian C. Cooper and Ernest B. Schoedsack, explorer/ adventurers whose reputation had been made with the documentaries *Grass* and *Chang*, that Cabot realized how dangerous his job was to be. 'I managed to get pretty skinned up and I stayed like that most of the time. Jumping out of windows into nets and so on.'[59] The stunt men on the film, including Gil Perkins, were amazed at his energy, and pointed out that, on a salary of $150 a week, he was paid less than they were. How did he know that, after the film was done, Joel McCrea wouldn't be called in to do the close-ups and Cabot's name removed altogether? Cabot promptly walked out, and was lured back by Cooper, only to find

Right *One componen of King Kong . . . anc* (below) *the film itself*

his salary cut as a punishment to $100 a week. Delayed by model and effects shooting, *King Kong* took two years to complete, Cabot taking on other roles in the interval and building a formidable reputation as a leading man.

Not all horror films demanded the degree of physical danger faced by Cabot, but in discomfort they had no equal. The complex make-up needed for even the simplest taxes the constitution of any man, and only a few unique actors, whose mentality verges on the masochistic, have endured the ultimate agonies of this field. Lon Chaney was their dean and martyr. *Photoplay*'s Ruth Waterbury, sent to do a personality piece in 1928 while he was working on *London After Midnight* (Tod Browning), found his devotion almost unhealthy. 'In his visible suffering Lon was plainly an artist in the exquisite travail of creation,' she wrote uneasily. 'To endure pain for his work brought him a strange joy.'[60] Chaney built his fame with characters so complex that they obscured the man behind them. Brought up by deaf-mute parents and by nature solitary and secretive, Chaney welcomed the anonymity that MGM made his trademark. When sound came, he was doubtful about acting in a talkie:

When you hear a person talk you begin to know him better. My whole career has been devoted to keeping people from knowing me. It has taken me years to build up a sort of mystery surrounding myself, which is my stock in trade. And I wouldn't sacrifice it by talking.[61]

(He was also concerned that mouth pads, an important part of his make-up, would muffle his voice.) Chaney starred in one sound film, a 1930 remake by Jack Conway of his 1925 classic *The Unholy Three* (Tod Browning), but he had his way in the end; of the five voices he used in his multiple role, a ventriloquist, his dummy, an old woman, a parrot and a girl, none was his own. Shortly after, in August 1930, he died of throat cancer, almost, one feels, a grotesque revenge for compromising his principles.

Although Chaney had always loved the stage he did not begin as an actor. Born in 1883 (on April Fool's Day), he left school at nine to look after a bed-ridden mother. He became a property boy and scene-painter, then a vaudeville song-and-dance man. In 1912 he went to Hollywood, and for eight years acted in Westerns and melodramas, until Universal refused to raise his salary and he joined Adolph Zukor's Paramount-Artcraft. The new studio gave him a testing first role, that of a cripple, 'The Frog', in George

Right *Lon Chaney making-up for* The Octave of Claudius (1922)

Loane Tucker's *The Miracle Man* (1919). One of the gang that exploits a sincere faith healer, 'The Frog' is reformed through love and cured of his afflictions. Chaney said later:

Tucker didn't really want me for the role of the cripple. He wanted a professional contortionist, but the contortionists he had already tried out in the part couldn't act it. . . . At home that night I unconsciously did a trick I've done since childhood. I crossed my legs, then double crossed them, wrapping my left foot round my right ankle. I caught sight of myself in the mirror and jumped up to try walking that way. I found I could do it with a little practice.[62]

He faced a double problem, since his character, though only partially paralysed, had to appear in the opening scenes as a beggar trading on public sympathy by pretending to be more crippled than he was, with limbs locked into total paralysis, eyes rolled to show the whites – the inner skin of an egg was pressed to the eyeball – and tongue protruding. Later, he reverts to partial disablement, and at the climax drags himself to the feet of the healer and painfully unfolds himself, kissing the hand of the man who has cured him. This scene, in which he wrenches every joint

out of a lifetime's statis with a horrific jerk, then falteringly lurches upright, is a classic, and Chaney called the twelve weeks of discomfort he spent making the film 'a wonderful experience'.

Paramount, oddly, didn't capitalize on Chaney's obvious flair for this work, and he made some straight dramas before appearing in *The Penalty* (Wallace Worsley, 1920) as the legless criminal 'Blizzard'. Maimed as a child, Blizzard becomes boss of San Francisco's Barbary Coast brothels, then sets out to revenge himself on the world which he feels has cheated him, but which he will now force to yield, as a title puts it, 'the pleasures of a Nero, the power of a Caesar'. He plans first to kill the doctor who amputated his legs, but instead he is captured, and doctors remove a blood clot from his brain, another result of the early injury, to make him a new, honest man. For *The Penalty*, Chaney's legs were strapped up and the knees covered in leather 'boots' that imitate stumps with surprising fidelity. He quickly became expert on crutches, and is convincing as a lifelong cripple, even though his legs were agonizingly deprived of circulation during the long hours of shooting. To make movements harder, his two canes were heavily weighted with lead. After *The Penalty*, he made an odd shift in emphasis, concentrating on Asian characters. Two years later, after the triumph of *The Hunchback of Notre Dame*, he was to write: 'Now I am through with cripple roles. . . . I prefer Orientals. Portraying the Oriental is to my mind an infinite art.'[63] Although Asian make-up is a cliché today, it was a difficult effect to achieve with the twenties' relatively primitive cosmetics (shortly to be revolutionized by Max Factor). Even in the seventies, Christopher Lee said his Asian eye make-up for the Fu Manchu films caused more discomfort than any other, and there are unpleasant stories about less successful attempts. Akim Tamiroff played a Chinese general for *The General Died at Dawn* (1936). Lewis Milestone said:

I at first instructed the make-up man to superimpose a Chinese-shaped eyelid on him, using the liquid rubber employed by dentists. They tortured the poor guy and blistered his eyelids, all to no avail. He still looked like Tamiroff. Finally I suggested they bring in a real Chinese, make a facsimile or cast of his eyelid and then apply it to Tamiroff, using the same principle as key cutters. They tried it and of course it worked.[64]

The eye make-up for Chaney's oriental roles, combined with the egg skin of *The Miracle Man* and the putty that covered his eye in *The Hunchback of Notre Dame*, later impaired his sight, forcing him to wear glasses.

In 1923, by then a major star with a string of classic roles behind him, Chaney was lured back to Universal for two films. *The Shock* (Lambert Hillyer) again cast him as a crippled San Francisco gangster, but the second was the now-famous *The Hunchback of Notre Dame*, directed by Wallace Worsley and produced by young Irving Thalberg. In the intervening years, Chaney had retreated from Hollywood society. Time between films was spent fishing, and he refused interviews unless related directly to a new role. More at ease with studio technicians than with other actors, Chaney even affected their casual clothing, and would proudly produce evidence that he still belonged to the same property men's and scene-painters' unions he had joined while still a young stagehand. Wearing the cloth cap of the technicians, or occasionally a Marine's felt hat (his favourite starring role, one of the few without special make-up, was as a sergeant in George Hill's 1927 *Tell It To the Marines*), he approached his job with a technician's casual contempt. Film shot on the *Hunchback* set shows him joking with the crew, testing a cornice by swinging from it, gibbering like an ape – curious glimpses of a man for whom work and life were inseparable. Universal advertised that Chaney did all his stunts on the towering Notre Dame set, making him un-insurable, but in fact Joe Bonomo was called in for a hazardous 150 foot rope slide with which Quasimodo descends from the cathedral. When Bonomo protested that the soft leather gloves provided were too light for the job, another man offered to do the stunt. He was carried off the set an hour later with badly burned hands and thighs, as well as a broken leg. Bonomo found heavy working gloves, lined them inside with metal foil and had strips of the same material sewn into his trousers before doing the slide without injury.

Chaney's make-up for Quasimodo is one of his masterpieces. Each day he spent four and a half hours in, as usual, complete privacy, climbing into his elaborate costume. The forty-pound rubber hump was attached to a heavy harness, itself weighing thirty pounds. Footballer's shoulder pads held it in place, and were in turn buckled to the breastplate and leg pads, holding him in a permanent stoop that reduced his five feet nine to four feet. Over these he wore a flesh-coloured rubber suit covered in clumps of animal hair. His face was distorted by mortician's wax inside his mouth, which a metal clip held permanently open, showing uneven capped teeth. A wig and medieval clothing completed the costume. The effect was horrifying, yet oddly lyrical. Charles Laughton, who played the role in 1939 with only a two pound papier-mâché hump and mask, praised his performance as that of 'a great dancer'.

Chaney was one of the stars Thalberg persuaded Louis B. Mayer to sign on when he joined him in 1924, and starred in the first film made by the amalgamated Metro, Goldwyn and Mayer companies, *He Who Gets Slapped* (Victor Sjöstrom, 1924). Backed by MGM's technical expertise, he created some memorable characters. In *The Phantom of the Opera* (Rupert Julian, 1925), false teeth and wires forced into his nose and eye sockets created the agonizingly spectacular effect of a face from which most of the flesh had been seared, and in *London After Midnight*, where he played a capering top-hatted villain, wires stretched over his eyelids, again with great discomfort, made him seem pop-eyed and insane. Even though, towards the end of his career, cosmetic technology had improved sufficiently for most make-up men to duplicate his effects, he remained a legend, and to the public a kind of wizard. 'Don't!' people would jokingly warn others about to crush a spider. 'It might be Lon Chaney.' When he died, MGM lowered its flag at the hour of his funeral and a Marine blew 'Taps', but the solitary Chaney, who had lived only for his work, left an oddly insubstantial image.

The Chaney tradition flourished at his old studio, Universal, whose structure and orientation favoured the form. MGM, looking to the American middle class, recruited new artists and directors mainly from Scandinavia, and Paramount from the talented Viennese Jews of the Weimar cinema, but Universal's diminutive 'Uncle' Carl Laemmle, whose affection for his birthplace, the tiny town of Laupheim, led him to support it all his life (a fact recognized by grateful citizens when they named a street after him) shared the German love of low-life and grotesquerie, and hired film-makers of this persuasion. He offered a home to Paul Leni, director of relentless tragedies like *Hintertreppe*, to Brecht's star Peter Lorre, and Fritz Lang's *Metropolis* cameraman Karl Freund. After a slump in 1929, when Carl Laemmle Jnr, by producing ambitious but uncommercial works like Lewis Milestone's *All Quiet On the Western Front*, nearly ruined the company, his father pulled it back to popularity with a series of Germanic horror films that remain classics today. It is ironic that the best of them were made not by a Berliner but by James Whale, a young British director whose cordial contempt for the material shows in their mocking black humour; and that they should star another Englishman, a calm, cricket-playing character actor named Henry Pratt, already in his forties when he found fame as Boris Karloff, the star of *Frankenstein*.

Much of the credit for the success of Whale's *Frankenstein* (1931), *The Old Dark House* (1932), *The Invisible Man* (1933) and *The Bride of Frankenstein* (1935) belongs to Universal's make-up man Jack Pierce, who created the familiar Frankenstein monster mask and heavy gait. Scholarly and meticulous, Pierce conceived his designs for Frankenstein's monster, the Mummy and the Wolf Man after careful study of the original stories, then of anatomy, in *Frankenstein*'s case including that of hanged corpses. Karloff patiently endured his ingenuity, despite grave physical discomfort. The *Frankenstein* costume weighed sixty-seven pounds, including weighted and built-up boots weighing twenty-one pounds each. Three and a half hours each day were needed to apply the elaborate mask, which included layers of greasepaint on the eyelids, pads of

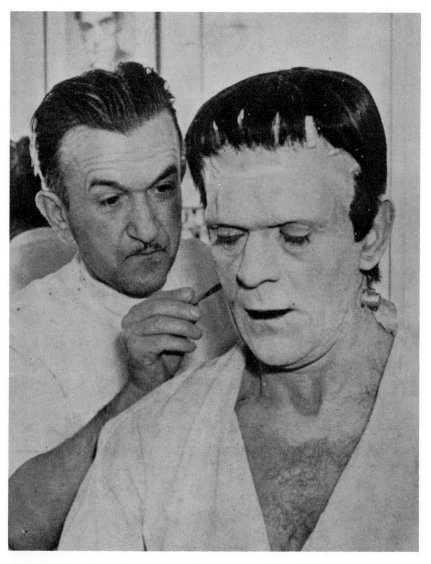

Left *Jack Pierce touches up Boris Karloff's make-up for* Frankenstein

cotton wool covered in artificial skin to change the shape of the face, and plugs glued to the side of his neck. With elevated boots increasing his height to seven feet, Karloff was prone to over-balance, and on *The Bride of Frankenstein* he wrenched his hip, spending most of the film in bandages. (During the film he lost thirty pounds.) Removing the make-up was more painful than its application. Only acetone would melt the rubber solution that held it in place, and since this dried his skin, a full oil massage had to follow each session. In later films, collodion, which contracts to pucker the skin into realistic scars, and the use of fish skin,

below Pierce surveys the result of a three-hour make-up job on Vicki Lane for Jungle Captive

layers of which were glued on with spirit gum to create realistic shrivelling, further irritated Karloff's face, leading to painful attacks of dermatitis.

The dangers and discomforts of actors who have played in versions of the classic *The Mummy* over the years show in microcosm the horror film's risks. Stories of Egyptian mummies coming to life had a vogue after the discovery of Tutankhamen's tomb, and in 1932 Karl Freund directed Karloff as Imhotep, the Egyptian priest whose sin of stealing the secret of eternal life to restore his beloved princess to life is punished by his own treatment with the spell, followed by burial, alive and immortal. Revived in the twentieth century by incautious archaeologists, Imhotep spreads ruin through Cairo in his search for the modern incarnation of his dead love until Isis strikes him down. Freund's film was one of Universal's best, and had countless sequels, none of them with the ingenuity in make-up which Jack Pierce brought to the original. Karloff's face, arms and hands, the only parts of his body not enclosed in constricting bandages, were covered in a flaking ash, eerily like the skin of a desiccated corpse, an effect Pierce achieved by applying a paste to the normal make-up base and baking it dry

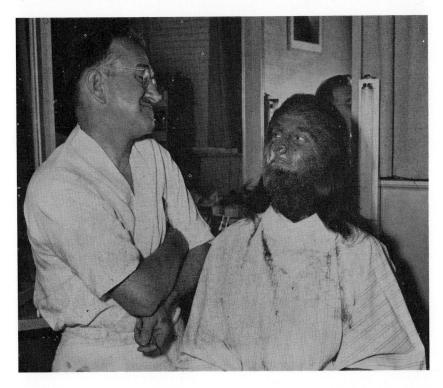

with heat lamps. Karloff was literally cooked into his costume each day.

The tradition of discomfort remained with this role. Christopher Lee, who starred in a 1959 British remake, recalls it with horror. 'I was supposed to come crashing through a door. It was a prop door of light wood but part of the trick in that sort of thing is to make sure the door isn't locked, so that it bursts open just after your blow begins to splinter it. On this occasion the door had been locked. I nearly knocked myself out going through it, and dislocated my shoulder.' Lee also attributes a cumulative back

Below. The Mummy
*Christopher Lee
emerges from a studi
swamp*

injury to the role. 'Going through these swamps holding those girls out in front of me – the strain on one's arms and back is tremendous. And with all the wires and tubes and jets and pipes in the studio tank crashing into your shins, I was torn to bits, bleeding all over the place. That doesn't sound like anything particularly unpleasant but it was. And going under water to "appear" out of the swamp – I don't like that sort of thing.'

Like the discomforts of the studio tank, claustrophobia was a familiar risk for stunters appearing in versions of *The Mummy* and other fantasy films. Doubling Claude Rains in *The Invisible Man*, one stunt man found John Fulton's special effects shooting grimly uncomfortable. Audiences were delighted when the actor un-wound his bandaged face to reveal – nothing. Updating an old vaudeville illusion, Fulton had encased the man in a helmet and suit of non-reflective black, over which the bandages were wrapped. As they unwound against a dark blackcloth the suit blended in to create invisibility. Fulton said:

The most difficult part was directing the actor. In some shots he had to work blind behind the wrappings, with air supplied by concealed tube as in a diving suit. Inside his helmet and bandages, it was sometimes impossible for him to receive instructions. When I used a large mega-phone and shouted he could just hear a faint murmur. Once, when the air supply failed, he fainted in the middle of a scene.[65]

A minor discomfort compared with that of an anonymous stunt man of the thirties doubling on a sequel to *The Mummy*, a job he called

the toughest I ever went through mentally. The gag was about some scientists or explorers in Egypt who had discovered a hidden tomb underground. There was a row of mummy coffins standing upright against the wall, each containing a mummy. One of these was supposed to have eternal life, and was intended to move out of his coffin when the explorers inspected it, and so scare them out of the tomb. I was that mummy. I was stripped and very carefully wrapped from head to foot with linen bandages until I must have looked like a soldier's putteed leg. Then they placed me in the upright coffin with the door open. My arms were wrapped flat against me under the bandages, so that I was practic-ally in a strait-jacket. I could not move, all I could do was stand.

The director looked me over and decided that my bandages were too new and clean; they did not look tattered and discoloured enough to be a few thousand years old. He decided to age me up and untidy my wrappings, so a studio painter fooled around with an air brush, spraying me with paint, while someone else tattered the bandages. Then they shoved me back in my coffin and waited for the paint to dry. Meanwhile I was dying for a cigarette, a drink of water, and wanted to go to the lavatory. I was sweating from the heat, and so far not one shot had been taken. The feeling of being tied up began to make me feel nervous.

Finally lunchtime came, and I expected a rest for an hour from the bandages, but they went to lunch and left me still tied up, because if they unwrapped me for lunch they would have to go through the whole thing over again to re-wrap me. So they left the prop man with me, and he cut a small slit in the cloth over my mouth and gave me a couple of drags of a butt and a drink of milk through a straw. That did not ease the situation.

They came back from lunch and picked up where they had left off. One of the actors did not remember his lines, and they shot re-take after re-take. By four that afternoon I was a raving maniac. Something went wrong with me. I don't remember what, because I went out entirely. The next thing I knew I was lying on the floor with the prop man and his helper wildly tearing and cutting off the remaining bandages. I was dripping wet from repeated dousings of cold water. Then the reaction set in. I shook and halloaed and cried tears until no more could come. Then I turned icy cold and they got scared, and ran for the doctor. By the time they found him I was regaining my self-control, and he told them I was lucky; a few minutes more and I would probably have been permanently deranged. I went home and shook for two days before the effects wore off. Ever since that time I cannot bear being tied up or confined in too small a space. You could not pay me enough money to lock me in a clothes closet for five minutes.[66]

11 Breezy

'He was a crazy, drunk Irish-American, happy-go-lucky, who had the uneducated man's flair for doing the right thing at the right time. He didn't know that a Roman wouldn't do this, and he didn't care. A *horse* would do it; that was all he was interested in.' Andrew Marton's memory of the second unit director B. Reeves Eason, a man who enjoyed the big triumphs, made the big mistakes and created some enduring and bloody legends is typical. Compatriots speak of 'Breezy' Eason with affection, respect, often with awe, but stunt men remember him as a ruthless technician with little respect for human or animal life. Yakima Canutt worked on many of his pictures. 'A lot of the time I used to line up the action, figure out new gags for him. Working with him really gave me quite a knowledge of directing. He was a real nice guy; loved to joke, loved to kid. We were always ribbing one another; some of the ribs were really rugged. He was a hell of an outdoors man. Go on a hunting trip with him, and if he got on a deer track he'd follow it until dark, lay down and go to sleep, get up and go on the next morning.' About his professional methods, Canutt is charitable. 'In his heart he didn't aim to be brutal, but he'd have things happen that could have been worked out a little more from the safety standpoint, but which he didn't understand all the details of. He got terrific stuff, but he also got a lot of horses and a lot of men hurt.'

Journalist Ezra Goodman interviewed Eason in 1947 and gave a convincing thumbnail sketch.

I sought out Eason on his little ranch in North Hollywood, with its smokehouse and all kinds of animals. . . . He was a sturdy, reddish-haired man in his late fifties, with a weather-beaten face and a habit of lighting matches by striking them on his teeth. He was a typical old-time Hollywood type, a bit of a roustabout and rather inarticulate. . . . Born in Fryors Point, Mississippi, in 1891, Eason broke into show business as part of a vaudeville song and dance act. But he was also a sure shot with a gun and an expert horseman, and in 1913 he joined Thomas Ricketts's American Film Company as a sort of jack of all trades. He was writer, actor, stunt man, property man and custodian of the kitchen rolled into one.[67]

Below *B. Reeves Eason*

Eason's instinctive insight into the mechanics of action, particularly when it involved horses, made him a natural Western director. He was soon being sent out with a group of cowboys to shoot chases and other lively material to be inserted into serials

later, work that made him friendly with such new stars as Art Acord and Reginald 'Snowy' Baker. An Australian, and typical of the foot-loose young men who drifted to Hollywood in the twenties, Baker, who had won most of his country's sporting and athletic prizes, including the Olympic middle and heavyweight boxing titles on the same night, made some energetic films in Australia for visiting Americans Wilfred Lucas and Bess Meredyth, and was advised by Lucas, an ex-Sennett writer and director, to try Hollywood. A stiff acting style soon made him redundant as a leading man, but Baker found his niche instructing other stars. He taught Rudolph Valentino riding tricks and spent three weeks as the house guest of Doug Fairbanks explaining the use of the bull-whip for *Don Q, Son of Zorro* (Donald Crisp, 1925), after which he retired comfortably to run the Riviera Polo Club in Santa Monica and become Hollywood's top polo teacher, a crony of the Up-lifters' Club and other movie cliques.

Eason's Westerns earned him a reputation for lively action work. In 1924 Thomas Ince sent Breezy and his brother John to Canada to film a buffalo stampede for an unfinished project, *The Vanishing Frontier*, and though the film was never made, his pounding herd appeared as stock footage for more than twenty years. This led logically to an invitation from MGM in 1925 to shoot the chariot race for its ambitious production of *Ben-Hur*. Already as much a white elephant for MGM as *Cleopatra* was to be for Twentieth Century Fox in the sixties, *Ben-Hur* changed directors and locations at a dizzying rate until Fred Niblo set it back on the rails. Eason, skilled with horse stunts and known for the ability to finish jobs on time and under budget, was an ideal choice for the race. His ruthless methods brought magnificent material, but only at the cost of injured stunt men and dead horses. Estimates of the number of animals killed on the sequence range as high as 150; rather than treat a maimed horse, it was shot.

Scores of Hollywood celebrities mingled with four thousand extras, who made the long trolley trip for $3.50 each, plus lunch, to watch the final day of shooting on the huge Circus Maximus set, re-built at Culver City in imitation of that torn down in Rome. Of the twelve four-horse chariots, ten were driven by stunt men; stars Ramon Navarro and Francis X. Bushman handled their own. Eason's encouragement of side bets and the promise of $150, $100 and $50 for the first three drivers over the line made extra direc-tion superfluous. The notoriously ill-paid stunt men, who included Cliff Lyons, outdid each other to win the race, which forty-two cameramen captured in thousands of fragments later woven into one of the most remarkable sequences of the silent cinema. Its most memorable incident was, however, shot almost by accident. E. Burton Steene, a serial and newsreel cameraman who was to work on *Wings* and *Hell's Angels*, had been placed well back with an Akeley camera and telephoto lens, a favourite newsreel combination, since the Akeley had a flywheel that steadied the cumbersome long lens. After an exciting straight-away run, nearer cameramen turned off to save film. Only Steene, still operating to catch the turn, saw a wheel on the chariot driven by cowboy Mickey Millerick work off the axle and send his vehicle swerving into the one next to it. Two others piled into the careering wreck, going down in a tangle of jagged wooden frames and rearing horses. Miraculously none of the four drivers was hurt, but five horses had to be destroyed. Steene's shot, intercut by Eason with the other material, was a pivot of the sequence.

Ben-Hur established Eason's reputation, but since such epics were rare he stayed a director of Westerns, teaming up with ex-101 Ranch star Hoot Gibson, a fellow tearaway who liked to relax by

Below *Mickey Millerick before the big accident on* Ben-Hur (1924)

ight *Some of the
ad horses from the
rst* Ben-Hur *were
sed for posed
ublicity shots*

Right *Some of the
dead horses from the
first* Ben-Hur *were
used for posed
publicity shots*

giving trick riding exhibitions at rodeos, on some dangerous films.
It was five years before a film of *Ben-Hur*'s scope came along, but
Eason was well satisfied when Wesley Ruggles asked him to
direct the Cherokee Strip land rush for *Cimarron* (1930). The rush,
which opens the film and dwarfs the story that follows it, is a
sustained explosion of action, with land-hungry settlers on horses,
wagons, even penny-farthing bicycles and foot setting out to stake
their claims in newly-released territory. It used eleven hundred
horses and four hundred wagons, all of them supplied by a horse-
handler named 'Fat' Jones. 'Fat', who at 250 pounds lived up to his
nickname, began as a stunt man with Pathé in 1912. Later he bought
his own stable, renting horses to the studios and doubling actors
like Fatty Arbuckle. When *Cimarron* was announced, Jones
decided to bid on the contract to supply horses and gear. He won,
but the project came close to putting him out of the business he had
just entered. When wagons of the kind Ruggles and Eason demanded could not be found in California, Jones and his wranglers
had to dig them out of junk yards and expensively restore them.
Horse-breaking and harnessing were also, Jones learned, even
more costly when done with large groups of animals, and by the

time the land rush unit moved to Delano, on the edge of the desert, to start shooting, he was almost broke. He had just calculated for the hundredth time that, even with the wagon and horse rentals, he would be bankrupt before the film was finished when, to his delight and Eason's despair, it began raining. It poured for a week, on each day of which Jones drew a fifty per cent stand-by fee for all his equipment and men. When the sun came out he was solvent again, and went on to found Hollywood's most famous movie stable.

Cimarron was a relatively safe film, though stunts like a river-bed horse fall by the girl doubling Estelle Taylor (probably Audrey Scott) show Eason demanding a great deal from his stunt people. In the same year, Eason directed the Red Grange serial *The Galloping Ghost*, on which Paul Mantz, doing his first film

Above. Cimarron
(1930): *the land rush*

flying, nearly crashed in a stunt Eason must have known to be fatally dangerous. Among other performers who experienced Eason's incautious technique was animal-handler Clyde Beatty, who rated *Darkest Africa* (1936) the most dangerous film of a risky career.

Breezy, whose thirst for realism exceeded that of all the other directors I had met, was extremely fond of the idea of me wrestling a tiger with my bare hands down in a pit. . . . My protestations to Breezy that I was not experienced in tiger-wrestling were brushed grandly aside. He assured me it could be very simply done. There was a Hollywood animal, Bobby the Wrestling Tiger, who would wrestle me and not hurt me a bit, he said.

Beatty found that Bobby belonged to Louis Roth, his first instructor in animal work who had retired to run a movie animal farm. He went to Goebel's Lion Farm in Ventura, looked Bobby over, and was reassured when Roth's son put on a safe but convincing wrestling act for him. Even though one of Bobby's brothers had once turned on Beatty and tried to kill him, he hired the tiger for Eason's film.

The day came. The cannibals hurled me into the pit. Remembering that this was supposed to be a wrestling match, I was planning to limit myself to a few toe-holds and half-nelsons. But as I got to my feet it became clear that Bobby had not bothered to learn wrestling rules. He charged at me with his eyes narrowed and blazing, jaws wide open. When he got close, he reared and clubbed at me with his enormous claws. Clearly the jungle atmosphere and the fact that he didn't know me had combined to drive Bobby temporarily berserk. Presently he was right on top of me, paws on my shoulders and his full five hundred pounds pushing as though he planned to splinter me. . . . With the full force of my right fist, I belted him squarely on the chin, at the same time letting out a murderous yell which distracted him a little. Dazed slightly by my blow, he plunged backwards momentarily, then recovered and came back at me, roaring with rage. I had only made him angrier. . . . As he slammed his paws down on my shoulders again I managed to let go another right-hand punch. In my terror I began shouting like a crazy man. The cage attendants suddenly seemed to discover that after all I wasn't kidding, and rattled the door. Bobby by now was hugging me with his paws and I shot punches weakly at his stomach with my free left hand, my right hand being pinioned to my side by his paws. Old wounds on that side began to burn, a recently healed cut in my right hand was reopened and blood oozed tricklingly out. My legs ached and I felt sick. Still the attendants rattled the door, and finally the noise caught

Bobby's attention. He pricked up his ears, sprang toward the door and bolted out. This old device often works on animals; they associate the rattle of the door with food. . . . I leaned against the cage, panting, perspiring and marvelling at how close I had been to death. Breezy Eason leaned down from the top of the pit where he and the cameraman were perched in safety. 'Boy, that was swell!' said Breezy excitedly. 'Get your breath, Clyde, and we'll do a re-take . . .'[68]

In the early thirties, impoverished Warner Brothers, who gained a temporary advantage over larger studios by backing the chancy sound cinema concept, exploited its lead with adventure films of the kind on which larger companies like Fox and MGM had built their reputation. No idea or actor was so exalted that Warner Brothers could not create their own cheaper version. Young Irish actor Errol Flynn was groomed as their answer to Clark Gable, and studio boss Hal Wallis cast him in costume pictures designed to achieve on a B-film budget all the grandeur of a major work. Eason, with his skill, authority and economical if ruthless methods, was a godsend to the studio, and became its resident master of spectacle. His assistants included ex-editors Stuart Heisler and Don Siegel, who later became expert action directors in the clipped Eason style. Siegel recalls Eason slumped in his chair on location,

Below Errol Flynn *leads his riders into the Turkish camp in* The Charge of the Light Brigade

cigar clamped between his teeth as he broke down the action into jobs for his assistants and stunt ramrods. 'Breezy would give you the set-up by pointing his cigar in the direction he wanted you to shoot, and muttering around the cigar butt. I learned to stand behind him and see from the angle of the cigar what he had in mind.'

It was to Eason that Warners handed the action shooting for *The Charge of the Light Brigade* (1936), its answer to Paramount's highly successful *Lives of a Bengal Lancer* (John Cromwell, 1935). The director was Michael Curtiz, hardest-driving of Warners' staffers, who combined ruthless professionalism with a paradoxically flowing and observant style. Although he left much of the action to Eason, there is no reason to believe that Curtiz, infamous for his harsh treatment of actors, was unaware of Eason's methods or inclined to criticize them. By wrenching history, the writers began their story in India, getting through a massacre and some desert chases before moving to the Crimea, where Errol Flynn leads his avenging regiment down 'the valley of death' mainly to wipe out the oriental potentate who killed their women and children in India years before. Eason recruited two hundred riders for the India sequences and the charge, and chose from these an elite of thirty-eight stunt horsemen for the major falls and leaps which, intercut with scenes of Flynn leading the attack, made up the charge.

No part of California looked much like India or the Black Sea riviera, so Eason compromised with Sonora in the north of the state, a windy plain below the snow-topped Sierras. But the area was rocky, and his cowboys nervous and angry at having to work without safeguards like sand pits. A man died when, doubling Flynn, he leaped from a high rock onto a rider; the horse shied at the man's shadow and he landed heavily, breaking his neck. Seeing the young and inexperienced Flynn as the cause of their plight, some stunt men set out to reduce him to size. As the assembled riders waited in costume for a take to begin, one leaned forward and waggled the rubber point of his spear under the tail of Flynn's horse, sending it wild. Flynn picked himself up from the dust, singled out the man responsible, and with skills learned on the Australian waterfront during his days as a coasting skipper, beat him unconscious. Thereafter he was treated with more respect, and came to share the stunters' anger at Eason's reckless methods.

A six-hundred-foot trench was driven along one edge of the valley to carry a camera tracking with the riders in low shot, and others cut at right angles across the line of the charge for 'gun pits' and camera emplacements. Since most of the sequence was shot from low angles, countless holes had to be blasted in the flinty rock, and even sand could not soften the jagged edges left by dynamite. Horrific weeks went by, with horses killed and men injured daily, as Eason accumulated the miles of film needed for the 295 fragments of the charge sequence. Eventually a party from the Glendale Society for the Prevention of Cruelty to Animals visited Sonora. When they filed charges against Warner Brothers, a shocked public heard for the first time what a badly planned 'Running W' would do. According to a news report,

an SPCA witness stated that the pits were from eight to ten feet deep, but errors in the measurement of the wire caused one animal to dangle helplessly over the edge, its back broken. It was destroyed by employees of the film company. Two other horses had to be killed. According to the same witness, a special pit was prepared to receive the bodies of injured animals.

Three crew members, including assistant director J. J. Sullivan, were given minuscule fines, the equivalent of £3, but the case dramatized the brutality often inflicted on movie horses. Encouraged, the SPCA ferretted out other examples. For a scene in Cecil B. DeMille's *Northwest Mounted Police* in 1939 where a Gatling gun is heaved over a cliff into the river, DeMille's second unit director Arthur Rosson set the gun on a rail and had two stunt riders throw Running Ws on the cliff edge. The stunt men, allegedly well numbed with whisky, were merely bruised; the horses were less lucky. The same year, Twentieth Century Fox, shooting *Jesse James* (Henry King) at the Lake of the Ozarks in Missouri, hired Cliff Lyons for $2,350, a record fee, to jump two horses seventy-five feet into the lake. Since the horses shied in terror from the drop, chutes were built and the animals and rider pushed off. Lyons survived, but both horses were killed. 'What a stink there was over *that*!' he later commented.

The *Jesse James* incident focused growing public indignation at the mistreatment of movie animals. Since 1925, the Association of Motion Picture Producers, Will Hays's self-policing guild, had paid lip service to the principles of humane treatment, but in fact brutality was common. The studios' own humane officers were usually stooges, and though provision existed to call in the SPCA to supervise animal stunts (at a token $10 a day) this seldom happened. The proliferation of animal safety organizations also hampered concerted action. As well as local, regional, state and national branches of the SPCA, various local and national Humane Associations were also involved. Laws on cruelty to animals were not uniform, but the fact that Missouri had strong legislation allowed the Missouri Humane Association to bring prosecutions against Twentieth Century Fox, a campaign taken up by, among others, Mel Morse, then a minor officer of the Californian SPCA, with a special interest in the problem. When the society refused him paid leave to attend the 1939 American Humane Association convention in Albany, NY, he borrowed on his car to make the trip, and was active in putting the case for a national policy on animal safety in movies, which he later implemented as executive director of the AHA. A new agreement was negotiated between the Motion Picture Producers Association and the AHA in December 1940, specifically outlawing the Running W and the pit fall, and pledging the MPPA to have officers of the association, at studio expense, on the set of any film in which animals appeared. Humane officers, usually AHA men working in their spare time or on holiday, became fixtures of Western movie sets, often feared or resented by stunt men who found themselves robbed of techniques that had taken years to perfect.

Meanwhile, Eason moved on. In 1938, Warners again gave him a major action film, *The Adventures of Robin Hood*, for which he was asked to create an elaborate jousting sequence (never filmed, perhaps because of SPCA agitation) and some Errol Flynn swashbuckling in Sherwood Forest. William Keighley, an inoffensive Warners contract director, began the film, but after a few weeks Hal Wallis, displeased with the material, called in Michael Curtiz for his advice. After they had watched the rushes in silence, Wallis asked the director for his reaction. 'Ziz Keighley,' Curtiz said succinctly in his heavy Hungarian accent, 'he hass no balls.' Wallis, who agreed, put Curtiz in charge, with the by-now predictable carnage. One man broke a leg in a twenty-five foot jump from a tree, another his foot in a thirty foot wall fall. A third man injured his back when the horse from which he had fallen stepped on him. Dissatisfied with conventional special effects arrows, Eason called in expert archer Howard Hill to free-shoot arrows into the stunt men, but even at a bonus of $25 an arrow and the protection of jackets padded with end-on balsa blocks, the stunters were less than enthusiastic. Not surprisingly, Warners' stunt bill on *The Adventures of Robin Hood* exceeded $50,000.

Now Hollywood's top second-unit director, Eason was in demand by all studios. When Yakima Canutt had spent most of the night trying, without success, to convince the second-unit man on the Atlanta burning scenes of *Gone With the Wind* that a team of horses, even with Canutt doubling Clark Gable at the reins, would not gallop through a raging fire, he took the opportunity of the visit by an irate David Selznick to the set to suggest privately that his old friend be called in. The director was sacked and Eason subsequently handled this and other spectacular scenes in the film, with Canutt as stunt man and actor; he played the renegade who tries to rape Scarlett on the road. Between directing B-features and serials, Eason managed what is generally agreed to be the best marathon fist fight ever done in any version of *The Spoilers* (Frank Lloyd, 1942) as well as a remarkable train wreck for the same film, repeated in 1947 for King Vidor's *Duel in the Sun*. He also did the First World War battles for *Sergeant York* (Howard Hawks, 1941) and was often called in to 'doctor' flagging melodramas. The otherwise turgid *Salome, Where She Danced* (Charles Lamont, 1945) ends in a hair-raising but quite irrelevant Eason coach chase along the rocky California coast, with stunt men clinging for dear life to a series of wildly rocking and eventually gleefully destroyed vehicles.

But even while Eason was kept busy, the emphasis in action film had shifted as studios, embarrassed if not actively influenced by the Humane Society campaign – the laws on animal safety remained as lax as ever – found how easily lavish action sequences could be assembled in the form of montages. Simulated natural disasters like the earthquake which James Basevi, A. Arnold Gillespie and the MGM special effects staff created for *San Francisco* (W. S. Van Dyke, 1936) or Basevi's tropical cyclone for John Ford's *The Hurricane* in 1937 were achieved without risk through editing and miniatures combined with judiciously shot action footage. Slavko Vorkapich, Stuart Heisler, James Basevi, John P. Fulton and Don Siegel, originally editors or cameramen, took over from the old school of second-unit men, though occasionally realism showed it had a place. On *San Francisco*, Gillespie, who had used hydraulic rams to cave in buildings without risk, and back projection to show Clark Gable staggering through the ravaged city, set up a shot in which he is apparently buried by a collapsing wall. Cardboard bricks and Fuller's Earth made a convincing effect but when preview audiences saw Gable emerge unshaken from under tons of rubble, they laughed uproariously. Basevi re-shot it to show Gable only partially buried.

Movie horse work also changed radically, as trainers like George Dolan found replacements for the outlawed Running W and pit fall. Satisfied to see the AHA code observed, humane officers seldom realized that the new methods caused more pain to the horse than the traditional techniques of Canutt and Lyons (which in fact are still widely used). Hal Needham, horse-trainer as well as stunt man, deplores the new systems he is often forced to use. 'Training a horse to fall on cue is, I think, the most difficult horse stunt there is, because it's so much against his nature. To train a "falling horse" I have to work with him for at least a year, and it isn't until you've used him three or four years that he gets really good. First you tie his leg up with a rope on a pulley, pull his head around very easy and get him to lie down. That way you assure him he isn't going to get hurt. You do this over and over and over. Then you do it at a walk; pull his leg with a rope, pull his head around, lay him down. Finally you get to the point where he knows that when you pull his head around you want him to fall. Then you try it out. Sometimes you get lucky and you've got him trained. Other times you wind up thirty feet out in front of the others and they're standing there looking at you.

'When you train a "falling horse" you really hurt him in the mouth. I have to put more pressure on his mouth than he gets when he hits the ground. The only reason he falls is that he knows I'm going to hurt him in the mouth if he doesn't. But people who don't know horses don't see that on the screen. They can't know how much abuse that horse has gone through. Running Ws can be bad; you can kill a horse with a wire if you try to do it too spectacularly, but the fact that with a Running W you know the exact spot where he'll fall lets you put down eight inches of sand in that place. You can also hurt a horse by putting the wire straight out behind him, because he'll turn end over end when he goes down, but if you put it out at a forty-five degree angle he'll turn sideways and go down safely. An animal will take care of himself if you leave him alone. Don't mess with his head, don't try to save him when he hits the end of the cable but let him save himself, and put some sand down for him to land in. I hate anything that's a farce, and that's just what we've got today. The American Humane Association is a pain in the ass.'

For all their distrust of the new methods, stunt men learned and often improved on them, though the true situation in the seventies is a synthesis of both schools. The compromise reflects the change in the stunt field during the early fifties. The first wave of top stunt men – Canutt, Lyons, Talmadge – who entered movies in the twenties had turned from active work to ramrodding and second-unit direction, often with groups of stunt men in which their own family featured. But the transition had its problems. Men within the studios who had risen from assistant positions to second-unit director status and settled themselves comfortably at that level resented and opposed the ambitious 'cowboys' who hustled for their jobs. Without the advent of Cinemascope in 1953 they might have blocked them indefinitely, but the first wide-screen features dramatized that subtle editing and elaborate montages would not satisfy an audience hungry for real spectacle. After a period of uneasy entente, the stunt men came into their own, working in collaboration with studio professionals who learned from them some new and dangerous techniques, while the stunters in turn gained from them a much-needed professionalism and detach-ment.

One director to experience at first hand the frictions of the new situation was Andrew 'Bundy' Marton. A cultured and witty Hungarian, editor on three of Lubitsch's late silents, including his lost epic *The Patriot* (1928), he became a feature director and MGM's resident second-unit expert in the forties, directing such classics as the small boat fleet's departure for Dunkirk in *Mrs Miniver*, and action sequences in *Dragon Seed*, *The Valley of Decision* and *King Solomon's Mines*. After Cinemascope, studio directors often passed to him the action they felt incapable of handling, and a Marton spectacular became one form of commer-cial insurance as it had in the case of Breezy Eason. 'In my next picture,' a comedy producer quipped, 'the only action's when the star chases his secretary around the desk. But I'm playing safe and getting Bundy Marton to do the chase.' He made a substantial contribution to *The Red Badge of Courage*, *55 Days at Peking*, *The Longest Day* and many other films, after which he went on to produce and direct TV series like *Sea Hunt*, *Man and the Challenge*, *Daktari* and *Cowboy in Africa*. But in 1958 he was briefly free-lancing, having left MGM the previous year after a dispute. His old friend producer Sam Zimbalist called him back. '''What's the assignment?'' I asked. ''It's just about the biggest assignment you can get. I want you to do the chariot race for *Ben-Hur*.'''

The second *Ben-Hur*, no less than Niblo's effort thirty years before, had elements of confusion and high drama. Anxious to beat the front-running Twentieth Century Fox, which since its pioneering break with Cinemascope dominated the epic field, MGM had William Wyler remake their silent hit, with Charlton Heston as the hero and Stephen Boyd as his antagonist Mesalla. The film was to be shot mainly in Rome at Dino de Laurentiis's Cinecitta, now offering lucrative tax advantages to a Hollywood establishment plagued with restrictive union rules and high costs. While Wyler got on with the main sequences, Zimbalist hired Yakima Canutt to manage the all-important race. Grizzled but still ramrod-straight, Canutt, then in his sixties and retired from active stunting since breaks in both legs made jumps painful and difficult, had become a major stunt coordinator heading a team that included his sons Tap and Joe, both stunt men of great ability. Canutt was bitter, and remains so, that Zimbalist called in Marton to oversee the race and act as official second-unit director, but an uneasy peace was established as the crew left for Italy.

The first problem Marton encountered was that of horses. 'Yakima found out, to our horror, that we couldn't have made the picture in America. There are not enough horses there. Quarter horses, which we use in Westerns, were no good for the work we were going to do. There were not enough in England or Spain either. The only place where we found an abundance of good horses was in Yugoslavia.' Canutt bought seventy horses in Yugoslavia and another eight in Sicily, passing them to top trainer Glenn Randall for final preparation. By tradition, Ben-Hur drives a team of four matched white horses and Mesalla matched blacks, for which Canutt used trained Lippizaner show horses. Both teams had to have two sets of understudies, while each of the seven remaining chariots – this race had only nine vehicles as opposed to Eason's twelve – needed its team, with back-ups. 'These were horses that had stood sleepily in the snow and the rain,' Marton recalled, 'but as we fed and trained them, their ears perked up and their coats changed. Our main trouble with the star teams, which we found out early, was that the blacks were faster than the whites. You couldn't rewrite the story with Mesalla winning the race, so we had to put lead weights on the chariot or a sort of sand plough behind it; anything to slow them down.' The chariots were also rebuilt and lowered to be more manouvreable, a fact which was to have near-fatal implications later.

Since the huge circus set hadn't yet been finished, Marton and Canutt began planning the race, marking out behind the set a course equal to that they would have to run inside. William Wyler's script would have puzzled anybody unused to action shooting. 'It went on and on until you turned the page and there were three words on that page: "The Chariot Race". We turn the page again, and Mesalla is messed up and dying. The race itself, our script, was thirty-eight pages long, which covered twelve minutes of screen time. It was laid out like the master score of a conductor. Every move was in there. The trouble was that anything in the race, even the most important thing, had to happen in twenty-three seconds, because we found it took that long to cover one long stretch. At the end we built up such a speed that the camera car couldn't make the turn; the chariots, but not the car. When I went into the cutting room later, there were four walls lined with film rolls, all identical in size.'

Delays in finishing the set further slowed up production. 'We

Left *Andrew Marton (next to camera) and Yakima Canutt (on tailboard) direct the second* Ben-Hur *chariot race*

found ourselves shooting in July and August, the hottest months in Italy. So, to protect the horses, we had only four runs a day, two in the morning and two in the afternoon. We could often do only one take, because the horses would end up spitting blood. But even then the race was shot in only twelve shooting days, with another ten days afterwards for reactions of the crowd and so on. I had Heston for only three days on the race, Stephen Boyd for five, and the two together for one.' When shooting began on the circus set, there were further mishaps. The surface was too soft and bogged down the chariot wheels. It had to be stripped back so that they raced on the abrasive foundation of crushed lava. Two chariots crashed into the wooden barricade from behind which Marton was shooting and, though nobody was hurt, irreplaceable cameras were damaged. On another occasion, Marton and Canutt were racing ahead of the teams in the camera car when the engine faltered and died. Luckily, the drivers swerved in time. While Marton organized the race, Canutt re-trained Heston and Boyd in handling a four-horse team; they had been coached for months, but Boyd in particular suffered badly from blistered hands and abrasions on his wrists when the reins were wrapped around them. The international stunt team, which included Joe Canutt, Mickey Gilbert and Basque stunter Joe Yrigoyen, was meanwhile busy in the sequence's two major stunts. In the first Ben-Hur, blocked by two crashed chariots and forced to the wall by Mesalla, sends his team leaping over the wreck. In the second, Mesalla's fatal fall, the villain is thrown out, dragged along the ground by the reins, then crushed and flayed under another wrecked chariot.

Canutt's technical flair was indispensable. As well as engineering these two stunts, he worked out some dangerous close-ups, including one of a bladed hub mincing the side of a chariot, for which he rode on the joined vehicles, yanking them together with a rope. For the pile-ups, he fitted some chariots with hydraulic brakes and releases that let the stunt men turn their teams loose, then cramp and crash the vehicles on cue. Adapting the cable and pelican hook quick-release of the Republic days, he fitted spring-operated chariot tongues with squibs that separated them without the risk of sticking. 'To drag Boyd, I had a chariot upside down and under it an armour thing that a man could get right into and clamp on. . . . The chariot was on top of the man in the armour, and we had a runner out of frame that kept the chariot in place so it couldn't turn over. When I'd got that all fixed, we did the wreck with a dummy, rigged so that the lines tied to its hands would drag it into a position where the chariot, when it turned over, would end up right on top of it. It looked very natural. Then we did the drag with Joe Yrigoyen, and got some nice big close shots. I got ready to do this thing with the chariot dragging on him, and Steve Boyd said, "Why don't I do that? It looks safe." I said, "Steve, it *is* safe, but believe me you can get a hell of a lot of sand kicked back in your face from horses running. It can get pretty rugged." "Hell, I can take it," he said. We dragged him the full length of the arena and got some pretty good close shots of him, but when we stopped and got him out he couldn't see a thing until we washed the sand out of his eyes.'

In contrast to the success of this stunt, the second major crash almost ended in disaster. 'We were all set up,' Marton says. 'The horses were trained to do this jump, which of course was not over a real chariot wreck but over a ramp, with a wreck on the camera side. Joe Canutt was driving, and we had four cameras on him; incredible since there were no more Panavision cameras in Europe, and only five in the world.' Canutt prepared the chariot for the stunt. 'I fixed handholds on the back-rail of the chariot for Joe and one in front, and explained to him very carefully to be sure to get hold of that back hold or it might flip him over onto the team.' Canutt and Marton watched the run begin. Marton said, '"Right. Action!" The cameras are running and Joe takes off. And Yakima and I both screamed in complete unison, "You're coming too fast!", but of course he couldn't hear. He did come too fast. He hit the thing, the chariot went up in the air, threw him in the air, and he fell out of the chariot. The chariots were four inches above the ground, and the underside was studded with nuts and bolts sticking out. Anybody caught under there would have the meat pulled off his skeleton. Suddenly Joe was heading for this. But he had the magnificent presence of mind to get hold of the hitch rail that attached the chariot to the team, so he was between the horses' hoofs and the nuts and bolts. His legs were under the chariot but only to the knee, which he could manage. Finally he crawled back up over the front of the chariot with only his chin bleeding.

'I said, "Go and have yourself fixed up before anything." People didn't know we had a first-aid station next to the chariot course just for such occasions. Yakima and I discussed the scene, and I said, "It is either the most magnificent shot ever, or it's a total failure." As we were talking, suddenly three thousand extras see

Right. Ben-Hur. Joe Yrigoyen, doubling Stephen Boyd, tips hi, chariot . . . and is dragged behind it.

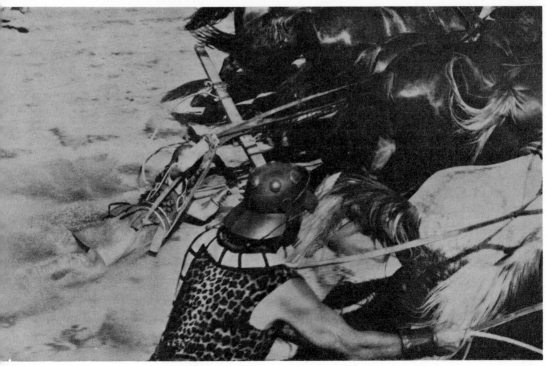

Above *Joe Canutt's almost fatal jump on Ben-Hur*

something behind our backs and break out in incredible jubilation and applause. I turn round and there is Joe Canutt coming back, still in his Roman outfit, with four stitches in the cut on his chin. We didn't shoot anything more with him that day. I told him to take the day off. That night, in the bar in his hotel, with no warning at all, Joe just keeled over. It was a delayed reaction.

'I needed time to digest the problem. How could we pick up the action after this with Heston? When we showed the rushes to Sam Zimbalist he said, "It's great, but we can't use it." "What are you saying?" I said. "Well, he fell out of the chariot," Zimbalist said. "He's out of the race." "Sam," I said. "This race isn't fought by the rules of the Marquis of Queensberry. They've got knives, cutting hubs; they *hit* each other." "How would you do it then?" he asked. "Simple. You just mount a camera on a running chariot, shooting ahead, and suddenly you see a hand coming over, and then Heston's face, bruised and bleeding. He jumps in and wins the race." And that is just what we did.'

In the aftermath of *Ben-Hur*, there were inevitable comparisons with the 1924 version and accusations of death and injury during the production. Marton, tired of the charges, shocked a press conference by telling them that twenty men had died during the race and a hundred horses. 'That's what you want to hear, isn't it?' he asked angrily, and though most reporters recognized the reproach, his comment fed rumours of hushed-up accidents. As action films go, *Ben-Hur* was relatively humane. Running Ws were used, and the AHA forced MGM to delete three seconds from a shot of horses collapsing in a crash. AHA executive director Mel L. Morse agrees, 'I have no assurance that any [horses] were actually killed', but adds, 'There certainly was a violation of the Motion Picture Production Code in that wire cables were placed on the animals. I have listened to the stunt men for a period of years telling me that they can do a Running W on a horse and not injure it. If you have ever had the opportunity to see a Running W, you have seen an animal shaken (that is of course if the neck isn't broken). The animal will stand trembling for hours afterwards and is usually not fit for anything else after it has been so used. The Motion Picture Production Code wasn't set up just to keep animals from being killed. It was to keep them from being abused.' This argument is unanswerable. But as long as we, the audience, demand our share of thrills, the stunt men will continue to use these techniques. Blaming them is irrelevant; they are only doing a job. The final moral responsibility is ours.

12 Swash

Costume films never recovered from the death of Douglas Fairbanks, and though they survived the thirties, the emphasis was more on romance, *couture* and barbed repartee than action. Errol Flynn's dashing adventures for Warner Brothers under Breezy Eason and Michael Curtiz helped preserve the form, and despite wartime restrictions on manpower and material that reduced costume filming to a flicker, swordplay and historical romance lived on, to revive in the late forties when audiences, tired of wartime austerity, turned gratefully to the past. Sinbad, Robin Hood, Zorro, the Count of Monte Cristo, Aladdin, Ali Baba and the Three Musketeers, after countless 'returns', were reincarnated in an army of sons and daughters. Richer than ever from the profits of a world hungry for entertainment, Hollywood lavished its best technicians on costume romps that the elder Fairbanks would have enjoyed. His own vehicles were, after all, the first to be remade.

Behind the scenes, special effects and stunt men worked and often suffered to create the illusion of historical style. Swashbucklers demanded much from their stars and crews, and a degree of skill and determination unknown even in the Western. Swordplay in particular is a complex skill, complicated still further by the need to broaden and simplify it for the screen. The fencing of Fairbanks Senior, the first star to employ it regularly in his films, was athletic horseplay, not swordsmanship, with the rapier used more often as a whip, goad or even toothpick than a legitimate weapon. Given a dagger, Fairbanks was apt to slide down a sail with it, or to throw a somersault before burying it in an enemy's chest. But for a film like *The Mark of Zorro* (1920) he needed an expert. Henry Uyttenhove had been Belgian fencing champion before becoming coach at the Los Angeles Athletic Club, and Fairbanks, after the usual fanfare of publicity which ominously announced the mild Uyttenhove (anglicized to 'Uttenhover') as 'the victor in several mortal affrays', put him in charge of swordplay for the film. A few years later, Doug met another Belgian, Fred Cavens, then technical adviser on Mary Pickford's *Dorothy Vernon of Haddon Hall* (Marshal Neilan, 1924) and invited him to become his permanent fencing coach. Cavens managed the duels and doubled for one or another of the principals of *Don Q, Son of Zorro* (1925), *The Black Pirate* (1926) and *The Iron Mask* (1929), becoming a regular member of Doug's *équipe*. He also planned John Barrymore's duel with Montagu Love on *Don Juan* (Alan Crosland, 1926) and those for Errol Flynn and Basil Rathbone on the 1935 *Captain Blood* (Michael Curtiz). (It's sometimes claimed that Cavens also doubled Flynn in the film instead of his regular stunt man Don Turner, but except perhaps in a few acrobatic moments the star seems to do his own work.)

By the time Warner Brothers remade *Don Juan* in 1948 as *The Adventures of Don Juan* (Vincent Sherman) with Errol Flynn, much had changed. Screen fencing had become commonplace and highly expert. Ralph Faulkner, a 1928 and 1932 Olympic champion who trained under Cavens, then branched out on his own, Joseph Vince, Cavens's son Albert and Gene Heremans, Uyttenhove's successor at the Los Angeles Athletic Club, were all active as duel-arrangers and doubles. The fights on *The Adventures of Don Juan*, again by Fred Cavens, were more spirited than those of the 1926 version, where Crosland covered up the principals' limited skill by shooting much of the duel subjectively, the star advancing on the camera and fencing with an unseen adversary. A big problem of the remake was to find a stunt man willing to duplicate Don Juan's leap onto his enemy as they battle down a wide flight of marble steps. Although Barrymore is credited with doing the jump himself, Crosland's quick switch to long shot suggests a stunt man, but on the remake neither Flynn nor his regular doubles would try it. The almost unknown Jock Mahoney took the job, and made his reputation.

The swing to costume films alarmed many stunt men who, despite their acrobatic ability, knew nothing of fencing, and less of the complicated pantomime of stage swordplay. Predictably, the first to learn were the natural acrobats. Dave Sharpe added it to his long list of stunt skills, as did Saul Gorss, an ex-University of Nevada football champion who even at forty was adaptable enough to master stage fencing. Both worked on George Sidney's 1948 *The Three Musketeers*, with Gene Kelly as a feather-brained

D'Artagnan, Gorss rating a featured role as Jussac, Captain of the Guard, and a share of Gene Heremans's liveliest routines. Except for dancers like Kelly, actors cut a sad figure in fencing scenes, and men like Cavens adopted a second-unit director's superiority to leading men, even though natural fencers like Basil Rathbone and Douglas Fairbanks Jnr were as able as any instructor to sustain a long film duel. As in most other branches of the action film, good photography soon made fencing doubles too obvious, and the search was on for actors with enough dramatic and acrobatic ability to do their own swordplay. When a studio found one, it hated to let him go, as Cornel Wilde discovered.

'I never wanted to do swashbucklers and I had constant suspensions from the studios because of that. I got into it because I fenced in high school and college. I won the 1934 inter-collegiate competition in sabre. I was on the foils championship team and the 1936 Olympic training squad in sabre. But I didn't have any money so I had to drop out. I got into stage acting, and eventually played Tybalt with Laurence Olivier and Vivien Leigh in the 1940 *Romeo and Juliet* on Broadway, and staged all the duelling scenes. Olivier had fenced very little, and he didn't have much time to take

Left *John Barrymore and Basil Rathbone:* Romeo and Juliet (1936)

lessons. He forgot the routine all the time. He'd get in such a frenzy in a scene – we were fencing with sword and dagger – that I had more scars at the end of that run than I ever got in movies. If we'd been having a *real* duel, I'd have known how to take care of myself, but here, where we had a routine, I'd expect, say, a jab on the right and the jab would come in on the left. When you're expecting anything, you're on the lookout for everything, but when you know it's supposed to come at one point, that's where you're going.'

On the strength of his showing in *Romeo and Juliet*, Warner Brothers signed Wilde up, but since they had no immediate project for him, cast him in small supporting roles, then loaned him to Columbia for Charles Vidor's 1944 biography of Chopin, *A Song To Remember*. To everybody's surprise, the film was a hit. Wilde received an Oscar nomination and hoped for meatier roles, but he was rudely disappointed. Columbia, now aware of his athleticism and effectiveness in costume parts, put him in an Eastern romp, *A Thousand and One Nights* (Alfred E. Green, 1945).

'I didn't mind too much because it was a sort of spoof. There was a good deal of swordplay in it, and I had a finger almost cut off in a scimitar fight when the prop man gave my opponent the wrong sword. In rehearsals we used dull ones with edges that had been ground down. There was a special stunt in which my opponent hurls a wooden stool at me and I catch it on the point of my sword, and then he cuts at me and I parry with the stool and he cuts the stool in half. It was a balsa wood stool but it was a very effective thing on screen. In rehearsal we had used dull swords but the prop man was saving money, or so it appears, and didn't have enough swords prepared. The only sword available for my opponent was the sharpened one used to cut the stool, and that was really sharp. So we rehearsed. I jump onto the table and my opponent comes at me. I parry and leap off the table over him, and he cuts at me as I go over. As I did the jump I felt a blow on my left hand, and when I landed I looked down. For a moment I saw the bone of my finger and then a stream of blood. They sent me quickly to the studio doctor. He sewed it up and put some tape on it. We got back to the studio where they put some camera tape on it, and make-up over that, and I went back to work.'

Columbia showed no inclination to lose its new costume star, and cast him in *The Bandit of Sherwood Forest* (George Sherman, Henry Levin, 1946) for which Ralph Faulkner planned the fencing

Left *Cornel Wilde in the scimitar duel from* A Thousand and One Nights

and doubled villain Henry Daniell. A series of swashbuckling costume romances followed, most of which Wilde despised. But few stars had his skill, or could so confidently be relied on to organize a duel scene. 'Although I never wanted to make a career of them, I loved riding and fencing. It was very easy for me. My fellow actors had to learn not only the routine but most of the time had to learn to fence first. It would take a few months before they could even do the movements; the *en garde*, the lunge, the various parries. And then they had to learn the routine. I didn't start months ahead; I started days before. I'd write down the movements of the routine, whether to parry in *sixte* or *carte*, and just follow it the way I follow dialogue. I never hurt anybody, but I frequently got hurt because my opponents had no control. If they forgot their lines the sword went in the wrong place. I was in hospital for ten days on *At Sword's Point* [Lewis Allen, 1951] with a cut on the eyeball. Maureen O'Hara, who was playing the daughter of one of the Musketeers, forgot the routine. It was no fault of hers; she hadn't fenced before. In *Forever Amber* [1947] Glen Langan and I had a duel in a park. The park had been built on a sound stage, and they put down this artificial grass, and as they wanted a nice foggy effect, sprayed "Nujol" all over the area. That looks like fog under the lights, but it settles on the grass after a while and becomes oil. We were slipping and sliding on the grass they'd put down on the floor. Every time we'd lunge or retreat we'd skid; it was very dangerous and stupid. Otto Preminger was directing, and he put more and more of this crud on because during the course of each shot it would settle and disappear. Glen had never fenced before and as Preminger had been riding him through the film he was very nervous. He forgot the routine, made some wrong move, and his sword went right through my hair. I was wearing a "fall" of false hair at the back; his sword went through my own hair and knocked that off. I'm glad it wasn't a couple of inches lower.'

Wilde soon developed a healthy respect for the risks of the costume picture, and an understanding of its implicit rules. 'When I first came here and did fencing I didn't want a double. None of the doubles fenced nearly as well as I did, and they had all learned "picture fencing". I felt very superior about that. It was wrong, because the movements were all broad and obvious, but I realized very quickly that the attitude was wrong. The way I did it, the audience wouldn't see what was happening. When two good fencers get together in competition the fencers will understand what's happening but people who don't understand fencing will miss fifty or seventy-five per cent of the action. Blade work is too fast, and I learned after the first picture to slow it down a bit. The audience had to see what was happening for it to be exciting. I soon saw that a double could add quite a bit to a sword fight if he was expert in "picture fencing", but none of the available film fencers were my build. Cavens, father and son, doubled a lot of stars, but neither resembled me at all. Cavens *père* was roly-poly and the son was much too small to double me. But there was a fellow named Gene Cetrulo I had fenced with in competition who came out to Hollywood and became a fencing double. He was very good, so he did the long shots on a couple of pictures. Later on, I had a couple of doubles for long shots, though I did the close-ups and the fancy footwork. Footwork in fencing is hard to learn, and it takes years to really get good at it. There just aren't any stunt men fencers in Hollywood who can do it.'

Douglas Fairbanks Jnr also suffered some re-education when he moved from light comedy to costume roles in the late thirties. Many professional fencers have criticized Fairbanks's swordsmanship but, though he was too tall to have the stylish 'line' favoured by stage fencers (and which Basil Rathbone cultivated by wearing special stiff boots in his screen duels), agility and careful planning compensated. 'Fencing as a sport, regardless of what kind of foils you use, is quite different from theatrical fencing, because it's relatively dull and you have to combine a lot of types of fencing from sabre to épeé and other things to make it look spectacular enough. I'd have different coaches for the various swords. Fred Cavens was particularly good with the sabre. He had lots of imagination for laying a thing out, which he did with the star and the director. The normal thing was to take a fight director on a few weeks before the film, and work out with him an hour or two every day. Get into condition for it first, and having got into condition start working out the routine. When you had got the basic routine, you'd work with the set director, the art director and the cameraman until you'd worked that out. Then, little by little, you'd bring in other people, and decide how much would be done from one angle and how much from another. I'd insist that the other man have a double for my own safety as well as his. It could be very dangerous to have playing opposite you somebody who didn't know what he was doing. At one time I very nearly plucked a fellow's eye out; he was blinded for a year by a mistake. The sword was blunted at the end but nevertheless sharp enough to open his eye up.'

The meticulously-designed fight, planned by Ralph Faulkner, for John Cromwell's 1937 *The Prisoner of Zenda*, in which Ronald Colman and Fairbanks fenced to the death, so impressed producer David O. Selznick that he had the castle set built around Faulkner's routine; Fairbanks, Cromwell, cinematographer James Wong Howe and Faulkner, who also had the small role of Fairbanks's henchman Bersonin, spent weeks planning this classic battle through the darkened castle with its winding stone stairs and narrow windows, which was then shot in a continuous take, intercut later with close-ups. It held the record for continuous screen fencing until 1942, when Fairbanks broke it again on *The Corsican Brothers* (Gregory Ratoff) with a three and a half minute duel against Akim Tamiroff. Fairbanks had influenza and a temperature of 102, but although Tamiroff was doubled by Fred Cavens the star, perhaps because he was also the producer, dosed himself with aspirin and fought on.

Fairbanks took more risks than most action stars. 'In the early days, I was precluded from doing any stunts, except perhaps in a fight scene which was close enough to be very carefully rehearsed. I remember as a young man in three films where I was supposed to win, there was a slip of the punch and I got knocked out. Once when I was a teenage boy, Noah Beery knocked me out, and then in the first self-produced film I ever made, *The Amateur Gentleman* [Thornton Freeland, 1936] I had a bare-knuckle fight with a big heavyweight. It was supposed to be a fairly effective fight and it was; we rehearsed it carefully and neither one of us really wanted to hurt the other, though we expected to take some blows. But when the time came there was a slip-up and I got one right on the jaw and went straight down to the ground. We kept it in the picture, but of course I get up later and win.' To minimize risks and make his stunt work more convincing, Fairbanks trained with ballet masters, planning routines almost as dances. 'Then I'd try to forget it, and do it naturally, but a certain element of the grace would remain. That way they looked as easy as possible.' For the action films which he also produced, Fairbanks took onto his crew the stunt man Dave Sharpe, who had a substantial effect on their success.

Born in St Louis in 1911, David Hardin Sharpe was an expert tumbler at the age of seven, and became US champion in the sport in 1925 and 1926. He went into movies, first as a child actor on Fairbanks Snr's *The Thief of Baghdad* and other films, then as a regular double with Hal Roach in 1929. Despite his height – he's only five foot five – Sharpe became one of Hollywood's most agile stunt men, and later an occasional star of Westerns. In a respectful tribute, film historian William K. Everson remarked:

Sharpe is an all-round stunt man, but he has a speciality; the acrobatic – leaps, falls from horses, high dives, unrestrained fisticuffs. In *The Perils*

Left *Dave Sharpe
(left) doubles Clayton
Moore in* The Perils
of Nyoka

of Nyoka, one of the most frenzied serials ever made, Sharpe doubled for literally everyone in the cast, the heroine included. He has doubled and stunted for Tony Curtis in *Forbidden* and *The Black Shield of Falworth* [as well as *The Great Race* and many other Curtis films] and for Alan Ladd in *Desert Legion*, for Glenn Ford in *Man From the Alamo*, and for many others. He was the stock double in Guy Madison's Wild Bill Hickock Westerns, in which he was often photographed almost close-up. His appearance in a bit part in any Universal picture was usually a tip-off lively footage was on the way. No sooner did he make his entrance in *Little Egypt* as a French sailor than all hell broke loose in a waterfront dive.[69]

Off the set, the quiet, courteous Sharpe is miles removed from the traditional image of the tough stunter, and he has the respect and admiration of the whole industry. To Hal Needham, one of today's top stunt people, 'Dave Sharpe was the best all-round stunt man in the era just before this, because he had something I try to model myself after and I think most of the new guys do too. Dave could do *anything*. He was never a great horseman, but he could do horse work along with the best of them because he had agility. When they did *The Three Musketeers* [1948] Dave doubled one of the musketeers and he did things a cowboy couldn't do; a jump from a balcony to a horse, for instance. He could work ten or twelve storeys up in the air; height didn't bother him. He was an athlete and tumbler, so he had the terrific timing and coordination you don't find in cowboys. One day we were standing over at Universal and I said, "Davey, somebody told me that you used to be able to do a standing back [somersault] on the concrete. Is that true?" He said, "Hal, don't you believe that." We talked for a few minutes and he said, "I'll see you, Hal", and he just did a standing back and walked away. At *sixty*!' Douglas Fairbanks Junior freely acknowledges Sharpe's importance to films like *Sinbad the Sailor* (Richard Wallace, 1946), Max Ophuls's *The Exile* (1947) and *The Corsican Brothers*. 'His sense of timing and training were excellent, and his imagination was awfully good. He was the ideal man to help me design fights and action, and the things that could be done on the set; various ways to make hard things look easy or easy things look hard. I would start working with him a couple of months before a film and we would outline certain things to do. I remember a thing in *The Exile* where I had to chin myself on a bar and swing myself over and swing down again. Because the camera was moving all the time and people were coming it had to be done with split-second timing. It took weeks and weeks to work out just exactly right.'

It is often only from another action star that one gets a fair assessment of the stunt man's importance to film-making, or the ability of actors who, since screen trickery makes all stars heroes on film, genuinely take the risks they appear to. English actor Christopher Lee, before his rise to fame in Hammer's stylish horror films and other dramatic roles, was a journeyman performer in costume films, and gained a large respect for the swashbuckling trade. 'It's tremendously hard work. I don't just mean mentally; the physical toll it takes, not only on your nervous system but your actual body, can be tremendous. The things I found myself doing you would normally only expect an Olympic weight-lifter to do. Somehow you get this fantastic spark that ignites the adrenalin and when the director says "Action" you step forward and throw somebody forty feet over a house.' A natural sportsman, Lee fenced, threw the javelin, ran and played most sports as a boy, experience that helped when, after a spell in the army as a Special Operations officer attached to the War Crimes Investigation, he entered films.

'I would play practically anything I was asked to play when I started, and I got involved in some very rough work; flung myself off horses and into cars, jumped off things and ran through windows, and did fights and knocked people about. I remember once jumping onto a three ton truck. The gap between the cabin of a three-tonner and the running board is quite large and my feet went straight through under the front axle of the cab. I could have lost both my legs but I was lucky. I managed to pull them back in time. In a film called *That Lady* [Terence Young, 1954] I played the Captain of the Guard "and other parts". I played grooms, masked assassins, I rode horses nobody had ever been on; I galloped up and down the river outside Madrid whirling a sword; flew backwards into the water and nearly drowned; I didn't care. The director was delighted. "This boy will do anything for me," he told everybody. "Anything at all." I don't think anybody would have minded much if I'd been killed.

'I never did anything like the big stunts, though I would have been prepared to, I suppose, at one time. Today, if it came to something like a sword fight I'd do most of it myself, though I wouldn't leap off any balconies. The fight I did in *The Dark Avenger* [Henry Levin, 1955] may not have looked very dangerous, but my God! That was four and a quarter minutes uncut, with Raymond Paul doubling Errol Flynn, and believe me I got smashed to bits in that thing. How do you think it feels getting a stool in the face? And then Flynn slipped while we were doing the close-ups and hacked right through my finger. I've never got hurt with the professionals; it was only the enthusiastic amateurs who caused the damage, and some of them went raving mad. They're terribly good in rehearsal, then somebody says "Action" and they're trying to prove they're some sort of Hercules. They forget everything you rehearsed and they go for you, with a sword or sometimes with their fists. I got a bit fed up with this one day with a certain actor. I said, "Will you stop hitting me, please. It *hurts*." He thought I was being yellow about it. "Oh," he said. "Can't take it, eh?" and he did it again. I managed to fall over in such a way that I grabbed the poker as I fell into the fireplace, and I whipped it over and fractured his thumb. He didn't hit me again.

'On *Beyond Mombasa* [1956] I was savaged by a mechanical crocodile. We'd shot the beginning of the scene in the river somewhere between Mombasa and Melindi. I had a temperature of 103 that day, I remember, but it was the last day of shooting.

We did this shot where I am supposedly attacked by a crocodile, and kill it. We did the intercut stuff in a tank at MGM with a mechanical crocodile, but the thing came so fast through the water it knocked me underneath. With all those wires and bolts and things I got quite hurt. I really got carved up on that film. There was a scene where I was supposed to fall down a mineshaft. There was no double, because they couldn't find anybody my height, and when they did he was a Kenyan policeman who flatly refused to do it. In the story I was shot in the back with a poison dart, and fell into this pit. It wasn't a sheer drop. It was a sloping thing, but I still went rocketing down forty or fifty feet, losing skin from all over my arm. The director was George Marshall, a very tough hombre; he'd been a boxer and God knows what. In the excitement, I'd forgotten to mime the blow of the poison dart, so George asked me to do it again. I did it again.

'A scene on *Pirates of Blood River* [John Gilling, 1961] *has* to be the worst thing I've ever had to do, but on the screen, of course, it doesn't look like anything at all. We were pirates attacking a settlement. I had to wade – and though I'm six feet four I was nearly out of my depth – through a swamp in Black Park near

*ight Christopher
ee leads his crew
rough the swamp in
irates of* Blood
iver. *Oliver Reed
ollows, third in line*

Pinewood. I don't think anybody had been in that water for a hundred years. It had about three or four feet of mud and filth and muck, the leftovers of years, and branches and snags and everything underneath. We had to walk through this for forty yards, and with the pulling of the mud and one's boots filling with water, adding an extra God knows what to one's weight, I couldn't walk upstairs for six months after that. Everything went in my legs and back. Some of those stunt men, who were the hardest cases you can imagine, flatly refused to do it again. For the smaller people, of course, it was tremendously dangerous. They were in danger of drowning. One of the shorter actors had to be supported through the whole thing, and poor Oliver Reed, who played one of my mates in the film – I remember his eyes were absolutely the colour of my socks when he came out of the water. He went under and came out dripping with this stuff. The director thought it was very funny.'

Lee also appeared in one of the few fifties' costume films to equal in style and flair the original from which it was remade. Fairbanks's 1926 *The Black Pirate* remains a classic, but *The Crimson Pirate*, Robert Siodmak's 1952 version, by re-doing the best gags, including the pirate's slide down a bellying sail held only by the traction of a knife blade, and inventing new ones where the imagination of Fairbanks's effects men had flagged, recalls much of its humour and excitement. A great deal of the credit goes to Burt Lancaster as the pirate. Although he began as a circus and vaudeville acrobat, Lancaster's first films were dramas, and it was not until the early fifties, when *Jim Thorpe – All American* (Michael Curtiz, 1952) gave him the role of the famous Indian sportsman, that he had the opportunity to show his athletic skill. 'On *The Crimson Pirate* he was at his peak,' Lee says. 'Not bulging with muscle but muscled all over. He was an expert tumbler and film fencer. He taught me a great deal of what I eventually knew about swordfighting for the screen. That was a dangerous film. Practically every stunt man in the world was on it.' The film was shot on Ischia in the Bay of Naples, and on another island off Spain. Lancaster did most of his own stunts, taking the occasional fall. Once, while making a hand-by-hand transfer on a rope between two ships, the boats swung together, dipping him into the water, then pulled apart again, throwing him high in the air and off the rope. His companion in most of his stunts on *The Crimson Pirate* and the earlier *The Flame and the Arrow* (Jacques Tourneur, 1950)

.bove *The Crimson Pirate:* 'Lang and Cravat'

was a five foot two Greek acrobat named Nick Cravat, one of Lancaster's oldest friends. They met in the New York settlement house where the star learned his gymnastics, and later formed a team, Lang and Cravat, with which they toured vaudeville houses. To cover up an unsuitable film voice, Cravat always played a mute, communicating with Lancaster by a mixture of sign talk (learned while visiting the star on location with *Jim Thorpe – All American*) and the wordless gesturing of Harpo Marx. A more violent counterpart to Fairbanks Snr's Snitz Edwards, Cravat was grinning, agile and pugnacious – the last characteristic, Lee recalls, being the most noticeable. 'Nick Cravat? Now there was a *tough* man. You couldn't hold him down. I remember one day he got involved in a fight and they couldn't hold him, none of them – and there were some pretty rough characters on that film. He was like a steel ball. They say even Lancaster wouldn't take him on.'

As the film progressed, stunt men like Paul Baxley, Allan Pomeroy and Charlie 'Moose' Horvath came to regard Lancaster not only as the star but as a fellow stunter, whose feats were meant to be emulated and, if possible, topped. Understandably, there were occasional slips. English stunt man Paddy Hayes was to fall

Left. The Crimson
Pirate: *stunt men
Allan Pomeroy (far
left) and Paddy
Hayes (behind Burt
Lancaster) with crew
members*

from a ship's yardarm as Nick Cravat cut a rope, but as the rope
parted the ship swung and Hayes hit the deck, though without
serious injury. The less fortunate Jackie Cooper, throwing a
seventy-five foot fall in which he planned to strike the ship's
rigging to break his fall, then go on into the sea, missed the ropes
altogether and landed flat on the water. He was paralysed for
weeks, a state not entirely compensated for by the £1 a foot paid
for the fall.

   Lancaster continued doing most of his own stunts well into his
fifties, including some solid fighting on *The Kentuckian* (1955),
which he also directed, and convincing trapeze work on *Trapeze*
(Carol Reed, 1956) where, though artists of the Cirque d'Hiver did
the dangerous high work, Lancaster used no double for most
acrobatic tricks. Trapeze films, a small but consistently popular
sub-section of the swashbuckling field, offer more hazards than
costume romances; as in the case of swordplay, an already dangerous business becomes more risky still when cameras, lights and
untrained performers are involved. Film companies have usually
preferred to use doubles for all but close-ups, accepting the
obviousness of the method. The Flying Codonas, Europe's top

Above. The
Kentuckian (1955):
Burt Lancaster

Below. Trapeze: *Burt
Lancaster*

trapeze team of the pre-war period, consistently worked in films, doubling Emil Jannings and Lya de Putti in *Variety* (E. A. Dupont, 1925) and appearing in their own life story *The Three Codonas* (Arthur Maria Rabenalt, 1940). Alfred and Tony Cadotta of the Flying Cadottas did the vine swings for Johnny Weissmuller in his thirties Tarzan films. Like most forms of action film, the circus drama faced new problems in the fifties, when audiences demanded authentic thrills and shunned those films in which doubling was obvious. Planning his massive circus drama *The Greatest Show on Earth* in 1952, Cecil B. DeMille searched Paramount's contract players for a star agile enough to play his film's aerialist, the Great Sebastian, and finally called in Cornel Wilde. Wilde, who wanted the role, hid from DeMille that all his life he had suffered badly from acrophobia, a morbid fear of heights.

'DeMille first had a French actor for the role, but after three months the French actor still couldn't climb a rope without using his legs and DeMille got very upset. Betty Hutton had started on an eight foot ladder, worked her way up to thirty-five feet and was doing very well, but the Frenchman was still grounded. They called me in in a big hurry. DeMille inspected me and asked if I was in good condition. I said, "Yes, I think so." He said, "Can you go up a rope without using your legs?" "I haven't done it in years," I said, "but I think so." So immediately he got up, his whole entourage following, and we went over to the stage where the trapeze stuff was set up. There was a rope, and I went up without using my legs, so he was very happy. They signed me and I started learning how to be a trapeze artist.

'I hadn't told anybody how heights terrified me. Going up that rope ladder which sways every which way as you go and is very narrow was an ordeal. By the time I got thirty-five feet up, which took me quite a time, I was wringing wet. But the platform at the top was just the end. Horrible! I have size thirteen feet and that platform wasn't wide enough for my feet to be completely on it. It's guyed off with tension wires so every time someone makes a gesture or takes a deep breath it teeters. When the trainer, Billy Schneider, would point and say, "You reach out and grab the trapeze", it felt like it was turning upside down. Finally I said "Billy, don't point. Just *tell* me."' For five days Wilde tried to grab the trapeze but each time he leaned out at a 45-degree angle to catch it the black void below sent him clutching for the safety rope. 'After the fifth day I was called to DeMille's office. Henry

Wilcoxon, the associate producer, and the whole entourage was there. DeMille said, ''I hear you're afraid of the height''. I said, ''Well, yes, I'm not used to it. Betty started on an eight-foot ladder and I'm starting thirty-five feet up. If it could be lowered I could get used to it bit by bit.'' CB turned to the production manager and asked, ''What would it cost to have that lowered?'' ''We can't do it!'' the production man said. ''It'd cost $5000 or $10,000''. ''I don't care,'' DeMille said. ''Lower it. I want the man to have a chance''. Next day I came back and they'd lowered it – five feet.

'But it did help. And Tuffy Schneider, the ground boss, put burlap bags on the net so I could see where it was. That day I finally reached the trapeze, swung off and felt fine. I started to enjoy it. The only thing was, I couldn't let go.' A sweating Wilde hung onto the bar until he stopped swinging and remained there until exhaustion and the imprecations of his coach forced him to let go. Gradually he got used to the sensation of falling. 'By the time we went to Sarasota, Florida, to shoot in the circus's winter quarters I'd lost an incredible amount of my fear of heights. Many times DeMille would say, ''Will it bother you if I take the net away? It's in the way of my boom.'' I'd say, ''No sir. It's ok''. If I'd said ''Yes'' he'd have done it anyway.

'DeMille was a kind man in many ways but he could also be cruel. We had a scene where I'm hanging by my legs and I catch Betty Hutton, have some dialogue with her and then pull her up, give her a kiss and let her drop. I'd worked with the double to prepare for this scene but it wasn't easy. On the day we were to do it DeMille set up the shot on the high trapeze, shooting from a crane and with the net higher than usual. He tried it with our doubles and realized that two arms length between the two heads made an impossible shot, one head at the bottom of the frame and one at the top, with a lot of distance between. He started raging, then told the double to pull her up *before* the dialogue, do the lines, then kiss her and let her drop.' When the double was unable to hold the girl for the three minutes needed to say the lines, Wilde tried and succeeded. Wilcoxon reported this to DeMille, who demanded that Wilde repeat the feat for his benefit. The actor's arms were already tired when shooting began. 'So now we start to shoot. The first take, something was wrong. Drop her in the net, start again. Second take – some camera thing he wasn't happy with. Take three, going very well until, about a minute in, one of us stumbles on a word. ''Don't cut the cameras!'' DeMille shouts.

"Lower her and start the scene again." I lowered her, pulled her up and started the scene over without a cut. It went perfectly that time. "Print," DeMille said. He called somebody, and handed me one of his commemorative half dollars. But my arms ached terribly. I had torn ligaments and strained joints in both arms and was in dreadful pain for the rest of the picture. At the end of the day I couldn't lift a cocktail – and believe me I needed one!'

Above *Errol Flynn (right) with Basil Rathbone in* The Adventures of Robir Hood

13 The Driver

For filmgoers of the fifties, Universal's 'American City' set, a wide street lined with cafés, shops and a marqueed cinema, has a reality conferred by the thrillers of Phil Karlson, Sam Fuller, Don Siegel and Budd Boetticher. Legs Diamond climbed up on that awning to rob the jewellery store; over in that alley Tolly Devlin died untidily in a clatter of dustbins. Yet as I see it for the first time in hot spring sunshine, it seems more lifeless than can be accounted for by the lack of actors, lights or props. The hearse-like studio limousine that cruises me to the backlot is the only car in sight, and merely emphasizes the nakedness of the pavements without their parking meters, the disturbing absence of traffic signs, and of the haze and smell of exhaust. More than people, cars are the life blood of the United States; without them, the American city street is a corpse.

Carey Loftin has made cars his life. For more than forty years he has driven them to their limits and beyond, accumulating a skill that has made him the cinema's top automobile expert. Like a remarkable number of stunt men, Loftin is a southerner. Tall, white-haired and soft spoken, his voice retains the drawl of Mississippi where he was raised. Yet his stories lack rural lassitude. They evoke the hot, dusty south of travelling shows and county fairs, of men in stripped-down Mercs and Caddys racing moonshine through the forests of Tennessee, and the same 'good old boys' re-building cars to compete in the clashing stock-car races of the small-town speedways. Loquacious about his craft and the technical sophistication he has brought to screen stunting – his wide, spatulate hands divide space as he talks, chopping, marking: hands sensitive enough minutely to adjust a screw, strong enough to tear a section from a steering wheel in a crash – he is more reticent about his own eminence. It is only later and from other sources that one discovers the respect in which he is held, and the fact that his driving on *It's a Mad, Mad, Mad, Mad World* in 1963 earned him $100,000 for a year's stunting, still the record. Refusing screen credit throughout his thirty-six years in Hollywood – his first credit was on *Vanishing Point* in 1971, and even then against his wishes; he disapproved of the script's bad language – he has anonymously engineered car stunts for countless films, and only the popularity of *Bullitt*, whose spectacular car chase around San Francisco he planned and supervised, brought long-delayed recognition.

'I started movies in 1936, but I'd been doing road show stunt work since 1933. It doesn't seem that long ago. My speciality was motor-cycle trick work; throwing them down at sixty miles an hour, then just riding the bike to a halt. I did a lot of ramp jumps too; driving cars on two wheels, and crashes – lots of those. Road show work didn't make much money, and I thought those were wasted years in my life, but it sure was useful on many stunts I've done since. Experience always comes in handy, very handy. Like most people in this business I came to California on a visit, in January 1935. I saw this motor-cycle show called "The Globe of Death"; an eighteen foot lattice ball that you drove on the inside of doing up-and-down loops and cross-overs. It was the first I'd seen or heard of. That was my first job in California, driving on that.

'I thought picture work was a lark. "God," I thought. "How long has *this* been going on?" I did mostly motor-cycle work when I first started, but it isn't an easy business to break into. One of the first films I did was at Paramount in 1937. I was hired for some straight cycle riding. They had a gag where a motor cycle and a taxi cab almost hit. The cab blocks the bike, so he does a complete 360 degree spin. They did this in cuts, which I didn't understand then; first a point of view shot of the bike, then of the car; they put down a turntable, anchored the cycle to it with the driver and a girl on the back, then they spun this thing, to get the close-up. When I finally understood what they were doing, I told the assistant director, "I can do that. You don't have to build all this stuff." "Go away," he told me. I had an Indian Chief in those days – it would really run – so when they broke for lunch I came up to this intersection on the cycle, laid it over and made about three circles and just screamed out to lunch. The guy who had worked out the turntable stunt got mad at me for showing off that way. Looking back, that's just what I did – showed off. But it sure helped me at Paramount.'

Word of Loftin's expert knowledge and obvious flair for driving spread among the assistant directors responsible for hiring stunt men. He was delighted, though on occasion his enjoyment worked against him. Throwing a motor-cycle stunt on *Nick Carter, Master Detective* in 1938 for director Jacques Tourneur after an assistant claimed it was impossible, he had to repeat the last part of the scene when the camera revealed on Loftin's face the broad grin of a man who has proved his point. For the finale of *The Bank Dick* (Eddie Cline, 1940), a comic chase in which W. C. Fields is pursued by a motor-cycle cop and a car, the car taking hair-raising chances and the cycle disappearing into a ditch to plough out the labourers working there, Loftin excelled himself. 'The second unit director, Ralph Seeder, was a friend of mine. I learned more from him than anyone. In the chase Bud Wolfe drove for Fields, but I'm driving the Buick police car following him. I'm also on the motor cycle that ploughs the guys out of the ditch, and I'm in the ditch too, digging. That could happen when the assistant director was a friend of yours and they did it in cuts. I've chased myself through more films than I care to remember.' Loftin's car stunts on forties films are easy to recognize, unique in their imagination and minute calculation of the chances. Many are for Universal, including some Abbott and Costello farces. In *Abbott and Costello in Society* (Jean Yarborough, 1944) a car weaves through crowded Los Angeles roped to the ladder of an articulated fire engine while a pursuing motor cyclist (Loftin) takes hair's breadth chances around it. Close-ups briefly reveal heavy hemp ropes barely holding down the car as it swings with smoking tyres through an intersection. Loftin remembers these films with nostalgia and the stunt man's brand of sardonic amusement.

'The one that had most action on it was *Abbott and Costello Meet the Keystone Kops* [Charles Lamont, 1954]. I'm doubling Bud Abbott, and me and a whole gang of stunt men are Keystone Kops on this old Model A. The driver was an Indianapolis guy, Louis Tomei, that I worked with many years. Everybody's skinned and bruised up but we're flying out and making all kinds of money. Now we have a little gag on the Universal backlot. We're sailing along in this Model A with the windshield down and we come to a railroad crossing. The arm drops and we come to a screeching halt. Then a little hand-car goes by. That's the whole gag. Louis checked the height of this barrier that dropped down, and since he wanted an exciting stop he told the director, "I'll just run

right up to it and slide under it. The windshield will just clear it, and I'll protect myself with my arms." Props like that are usually made of balsa wood, and unless you seal it you don't get a true white; it's more a yellow. Louis looked at the wood but he didn't dig his thumbnail into it. "I'm going to make some money on this one," he said to us. We raced up to the crossing, slid in under the barrier, Louis put his arm up to protect himself – and the barrier was made of real wood! He dislocated his shoulder. He yelled, "Who's the son of a bitch who painted a real board with breakaway paint?" We laughed till we cried. Everyone kept working; Louis drove with one hand for the rest of the film.'

Car stunting in the late thirties was primitive even by comparison with the reckless methods of the travelling shows, and like most top stunters Loftin set to work improving it. 'When I first came to Hollywood nobody had ever really heard of a roll bar' (the welded metal reinforcing stunters put in their cars to keep them rigid in a crash). 'I thought I was brave years ago rolling these old cars where I put wire or rope, and later spot-welded the doors together, for a little strength, but old time stunt men would just roll stock models and be damned.' Early stunt men used techniques so primitive as to be suicidal. William Duncan's only preparation for a fifty-five m.p.h. ramp jump in a 1922 serial was to put his rolled-up overcoat between chest and steering column. In an emergency he was ready to squeeze under the dashboard – directly in the path of the engine should it be pushed back in a crash. Cliff Bergere, a veteran stunter of the twenties, had a more complex but equally risky method.

I remove the driving seat and saw off both gear and brake handles, having already put the car in second gear. To minimize the risk of fire, all but half a gallon of petrol is removed from the tank and with a strip of angle iron fastened around the outside of the car to prevent the body from being smashed up, all is ready for the crash.[70]

Some near-disasters forced Loftin to work out new techniques of stunt driving. In 1949 he did location shooting in New York for Anthony Mann's *Side Street*; the *New York Times* covered it.

The action called for the taxi, chased by three police cars and with others (real ones from the First, Second, Third and Eighth Precincts) closing in from two other directions, to crash against the curb and overturn in front of the J. P. Morgan Building in Wall and Broad. Two of Hollywood's more foolhardy actors, Frank McGrath and Carey Loftin, were brought in to double for Granger and Craig in this scene. McGrath, who has wrecked many a car during his hazardous career, was thoroughly disgusted by having to go through twelve takes before he got the cab to do its flip-flop. On the first attempt it skidded within a few feet of the cameras, manned by Edward Hyland lying prone on the street. Ropes were then tied about both Hyland and his equipment so that they could be jerked to safety if necessary. Another camera mounted on a platform and facing the direction from which the chase would come was manned by Herb Fisher. Time after time the cab, with Loftin as the uneasy passenger, would career down the street followed by police cars with screaming sirens. For ten attempts before lunch it would crash over the high curb, and then roll off, still on all four wheels. On each run the stubborn cab developed more knocks and rattles, to say nothing of three flat tyres, one so battered that it had to be replaced. Then, on the second try after lunch, McGrath finally made it by succeeding in locking a rear wheel against the highest point of the curb. Over the cab went – but even then it wouldn't give up. It stayed on its back for a scant two seconds and, carried by momentum, slowly rolled back to land on all four wheels.[71]

Heavy cars with two-wheel brakes made such incidents common, and increased the risk in even the simplest stunt. With his regular partner, Max Balchowski, Loftin rebuilt his cars to perform almost to order any stunt he wanted. His growing expertise led, paradoxically, to his worst accident, on the violent road race at the climax of George Sidney's Elvis Presley vehicle *Viva Las Vegas* in 1963.

'They wanted a blow-out with a Ferrari. As we didn't want to wreck the Ferrari we had an old Jaguar coupe that the studio spent a lot of time on to make it look like a Ferrari, but even at that you don't want to see too much of it. There was a long straight road and a sweeping corner. I checked the ground with my heel, and decided, as I didn't want to hurt the car, I could do a blow-out and spin off so that the car would be hidden in a cloud of dust. I dug my toe in at another point just at the turn; the bank was bigger over there and the asphalt had more bank to it. So I thought: What I'll do is come down, get my speed – the other cars would be following me, but quite a way back – come down on the shoulder and throw it sideways. If it didn't turn over when it hit the pavement, it *had* to turn over when it hit the bank on the other side.

'I'd had the car set up to my satisfaction. When they started working on this car at the studio I was sitting inside and telling the men how to do the roll bars. "You start in the right-hand front corner, come up the post to the windshield line – not too high, just above the window – and across behind. And take another and run it across in back of me, leaving it as low as you can." I stopped, and the guy said, "Right. And I'll do the same thing on the other side and tie them together." I said, "No. I have to have room for my cushion; my elbow and knee pads. If the car caves in, I don't have to take that impact." He reached in and patted me on the back and said, "By God, you're smart." I said, "I've cheated on that a long time. It all helps."

'So I came into this turn, but I must have struck a pothole I missed, because the second I hit it the car started to roll. I never did get my memory back of what happened. The car wound up in the middle of the road, and what caused me to get hurt was a simple tail wind, blowing straight down the road. The Fuller's Earth from this explosion drifted in a ball across the road, and Max Balchowski, coming up behind me in the lead car, thought, "There's Carey across the road." Thank goodness he did check down though to where I *was*, in the middle of the road, even though there was still so much dust that he couldn't see me until he was just on me. The car was on its left side so as Max hit me he did a sort of ramp jump over me. He just buried me in that car. I broke my jaw in two places, had a collapsed lung, broke a shoulder and five ribs. No breaks in my hands but it cut them up. In my mind I thought the car rolled for, say, a minute – end over: sideways: knocked the wind out of me: can't see: that's what I thought happened. When we measured later the windshield was two inches high. No roll bar, you see.'

Undeterred, Loftin went back to work. Stanley Kramer's *It's a Mad, Mad, Mad, Mad World* – he drove for most of the principals, including Spencer Tracy, in rubber masks that made it seem they were at the wheel – earned him the all-time record stunt fee of $100,000, and he worked for Howard Hawks on *Hatari!* (1962) and *Red Line 7000* (1965). In 1965, John Frankenheimer hired him for *Grand Prix*, shot on location at the European racing circuits. 'At the pre-production meeting Frankenheimer lectured lectured *lectured* about what sort of picture he was going to have. "In other words we're not going to have a lousy racing picture like *Red Line 7000*. Anybody here work on that?" I held my hand up and he looked at me like he was going to fire me. "What did you do?" I said, "I engineered the car in the crash where the car went over the wall. It went 113 yards before it hit." "Oh", he said. "Well, that's all right."

'I only did three gags on that film. One was the bump at Monte Carlo coming into the chicane involving Brian Bedford, who I was doubling, and Tom Bamford, doubling Jim Garner. I wanted this car to spin, but it was twenty-six feet from rail to rail; twenty-eight from kerb to kerb and the guard rails are a foot in on either side. We had to simulate a bump and then spin. I go down the escape road and Bamford goes through the chicane and they cut to the car going into the water. I think this was the neatest set-up I ever had for spinning a car – hydraulic controls. I disconnected the front brake, put a T in the line and hooked the rear brakes onto the clutch master cylinder. As soon as I disengaged the clutch, the brakes went full on, but I could still drive it; to stop, I'd just disengage enough to pull up without bending everything out of shape. The tyres are quite wide, so I shaved the rubber until I had just two and a half inches on each tyre, just enough to get traction at low speeds. Frankenheimer didn't understand. I said, "If you did you probably wouldn't have me over here. I'm not going to explain, John." But

I talked to Phil Hill about it, as to whether I should cut the rubber off the outside of the tyre, or cut the inside off and leave a little on the outside. He plugged his ears. "I don't think that way, you crazy sonofabitch! I don't even want to hear any more", and he walked away.

'Tom Bamford and I took the car up to Nice, because doing something like this I like to test it first. It's a one-shot deal. I'm going to rub the car out, I know that. They're designed that way, to come apart. It's a safety feature. What I had to do was keep my foot on flat throttle and then, when I wanted to spin, do two things at once – whichever way I wanted to spin, jerk my wheel, and just stab the clutch and let it off. With no traction on the tyres, no front brakes, the engine disengaged and full rear brakes, it would really spin. The car, a Formula Three dressed up as a Formula One, ran at about 120 miles an hour, and it wouldn't lose more than ten miles an hour turning round. I did quite a few of them. Left spins, right spins; all fine. Tom was watching and he said, "You know, I think you're nuts. You don't need the money that bad to do this goddam thing." I said, "Let me put it this way, Tom. I'm happy with the way this thing is set up. And don't forget, you're in this stunt too. You've got to come into the bump, go right out of your groove and straighten up to go through the chicane. You want to go practise?" You know where *he* was for the rest of the day. He thought I was going to hit him, like for real, but I'd planned it like a picture fight. I hit the rail, not him, and then made the car spin. He had to fake it as if he'd been hit, go right out of the groove and still get back into shape to go through the chicane. He was practising all day but it went all right.

'When we planned the stunts I was worried John would want to do "main line" crashes in these cars, but Milt Rice, the special effects man, dreamed up something new. "Old Blue" or "Big Blue" they called it. He showed me this thing when I first went over there. He said, "Now, Carey, you're probably not going to like this. It's kind of dipping into your business." It was like a big cannon with about 450 pounds of air in it, and a quick-release valve, to shoot car carcases with. Get a pair of double O rings, thread the car on there and thump it off at . . . well, Milt said a hundred miles an hour but I'd say more like eighty. I said, "What do you mean 'dipping into my business'? I know the size of these cars, and you don't have much room to goof. I'll help you carry the thing, load it, put it into position and everything else. There's

no way you could get me to do a main line wreck in one of these cars.''

'The fire gag at Brands Hatch I worked out up at Downham Market. Jim Russell, an old-time racing driver, has a school there. At Snetterton there's a turn called the Jim Russell Turn and we decided to do the shot there. We had the car fitted up with butane tanks, fine as long as you're going forward; the fire streams out behind you. I should have done one lap without the fire. I came into this Jim Russell turn, which is a right, then a left, but with ripples in it. To cut a story short, I lost it. I spun, the car stopped backwards and I was in a ball of fire. I had my helmet and goggles but even then I held my breath and bailed out of there. Skinned my shins a little bit getting out.'

After *Grand Prix*, Loftin was stunt ramrod on most of the Matt Helm spy thrillers with Dean Martin, including *The Silencers* and *The Wrecking Crew*. He was in his fifties, and to some younger film-makers may have seemed too old for the work. 'On *The Wrecking Crew* we had a gag where Dean Martin has a bomb that he throws over and blows these guys up. We had ramps and air rams' (small platforms fitted with compressed air that boost a man

Left *Air rams boost three stunt men, including Harvey Parry and Carey Loftin, on* It's a Mad Mad, Mad, Mad World

or load into the air) 'and Phil Karlson, the director, asks have I seen them. I went over and looked at them. Paul Stewart, the effects man, had just finished them. I tried one, but didn't give it full pressure. You've got to build up to it, you know. You can black out going up. I told Phil I'd seen them and I said, "I'll get two guys my height or maybe a little higher". Phil said, "It's a pretty tough gag, Carey. I don't think you ought to do it." I said, "I know the secret of doing that. You've got to be locked stiff as a board. You won't hurt yourself if you lock your knees back and lean in the beginning whichever way you want to go, and you'll go in that direction." But Phil said, "We did a thing with air rams on a W. C. Fields picture years ago that I was assistant on. A couple of boys got hurt." I said, "Don't you remember me, Phil? I was there. I was in the ditch." "That's right. I forgot." "I also drove the car." "That's right!" "I also rode the motor cycle in it." "Yes," he said, and he came over serious "That's thirty years ago, Carey, and you're too old to do it." He would *not* let me do it, so I got in two guys who were older than I am, just to prove a point. I like experience.'

Despite Loftin's confidence in his personal stamina, he had

become too expert to waste his efforts on personal stunting, and like most top men involved himself mainly in the management of stunt routines. This led to his most famous job, the car chase in Peter Yates's *Bullitt* (1968). Steve McQueen, a skilled motor-cycle and automobile driver himself, played the San Francisco cop Frank Bullitt, involved in a complex gangland plot which leaves a dead grand jury witness on his hands and only a few days to sort out the details before a politically ambitious district attorney demotes him. Driving his Mustang through the city, he spots a Dodge containing the gunmen imported to commit the murder, and gives chase. Leaping, bouncing, spinning with shrieking tyres around the hills of San Francisco, the two cars crash and cannon off the road, other cars and each other until, after a gun duel on the freeway, the killers' car crashes into a gas station and explodes. English director Peter Yates, unknown in America at the time, had been signed by Warner Brothers on the strength of a slick and exciting film called *Robbery* (1967) recreating the Great Train Robbery, and the superbly planned and shot car chase which is the climax of its first half. Today, Yates, a Grand Prix driver *manqué* and, before getting into films, racing manager for Stirling

Moss, Peter Collins and other top competitors, realizes he was just a pawn in the studio's elaborate moves to shed the difficult Steve McQueen and a story in which they had little interest. 'They thought that if they could get an English director to go over and screw it up,' Yates said, 'the job would be done for them. I hated the script and Warners thought it was going to be such a flop anyway they let me do as I liked.'[72] Knowing and appreciating movie driving, Yates, in addition to restructuring the story and replacing Robert L. Pike's crushed middle-aged cop with a potent playboy detective with sophisticated tastes in cars and women, wrote in the car chase that was to give the film much of its lift. Carey Loftin was suggested to lay it out, and there was instant accord between the two men, particularly when Yates, describing the chase in *Robbery* and the Hollywood films from which he had cribbed some of its routines, found that most were stunts planned and executed by Loftin.

'I laid the whole chase out. Peter told me, "We want a chase to top all chases." I've worked in San Francisco a lot but after a few minutes I'm always lost, so I grabbed my Polaroid, got into the car, made sure I had a lot of gasoline, and just drove. When I found an interesting place I'd take a picture and make notes on the back. All the time I was figuring the continuity of the whole thing. We *were* heading towards the Golden Gate Bridge but they wouldn't give permission to go over it at speed. If you know the town, you'll recognize a couple of shots where we're heading towards the bridge, but now we wind up in Brisbane, way south of the town. I was going to double Steve McQueen, but I was under contract to Walt Disney at the time for *The Love Bug* so I didn't want to be piggish. When I got Steve out, I put another boy in there, Bud Ekins. Steve knows Bud as a good motor-cycle driver; "But he's not worth a damn in a car," Steve said. He didn't know I'd just used Bud driving my car on a Presley picture at MGM. So once I got Steve out of the car I put Bud in. I thought: A lot of this stuff I can do better watching than I can do in the car.

'We had two Mustangs for Bullitt's car, and the number one car cost nearly $3,000 just for work on it. We changed the suspension completely, Max Balchowski and I. The Mustang has a very weak frame. You do a little jump with them and the whole top end will collapse. So Max made two templates to fit the whole side of the fender where the spring is mounted, so that part wouldn't cave in, and tied the two together; a bolt-in section, like a bridge. We put on Koni shocks. To my mind they're the best. You can set those anyway you like, and adjust each one of them according to what you're doing. We set that up for the jumps. We still didn't want to raise the car too much because Steve wanted it to handle good. Naturally we had the big wide rubber and the mag wheels. In the case of the Dodge, we changed the rear spring for a stiffer spring with a bigger arch, put on Koni shocks, and twisted up the torsion bars to get a little more clearance. So many times now producers will refer to *Bullitt*. "We want a *Bullitt*-type chase" or "We want to do better than *Bullitt*." I say, "God, what a budget!" '

For the spectacular crash and explosion, although stunter Bill Hickman was in the scene and played a small role in the film, Loftin used an automatic technique developed for the car-race smashes in Stanley Kramer's *On the Beach* in 1958, and which has become his standard system for violent car stunts. The crashing car is a driverless drone fitted with impact switches to make it explode on cue. To control it, Loftin links his own car and the dummy side by side with a bar which he can release from his own seat. With the car frames locked together the car can be towed to speed and then released with perfect accuracy into shot. 'I've had a couple stick on me,' Loftin says. 'It makes your hair stand straight up when you drive waaaay deep at a point, pull the hydraulic pin and it doesn't come apart. I'm still pretty strong, especially when I get scared, and once, when this happened, I pulled the whole works out, and it *still* didn't release. Since then, I put a mirror wherever it is. I want to *see* that release. And I paint it all white too.' Loftin's system, varied to make the car brake, turn, spin or explode, depending on additional switches he operates with wires from his own car, has made the old methods superfluous.

His techniques allowed him to create incomparable stunts for *Vanishing Point* (Richard Sarafian, 1970). The film's anti-hero, Kowalski, is a speed-freak who ferries fast cars across America, high on amphetamines and the hard rock of the non-stop radio programmes. Bet that he can't get a Dodge Challenger from Denver to San Francisco in a few hours, he takes off, forcing other cars off the road, evading the police by ploughing out into the desert, a symbol of man asserting himself in a technological environment. Finally the police erect the ultimate road block, two bulldozers set blades foremost across the road. Contemptuously Kowalski accelerates into them and is killed. 'We tore up a lot of cars. I had five and never used the fifth, but I was down to number four several times, from busted frames and engine trouble. The engines took a beating from this riding across the desert. For the last shot, they wanted a car to come down the road at speed and crash into two bulldozers set across the road. It was only a narrow little road with a crown on it so I couldn't use a dummy and drive it in, but I know a rig you can use to tow a car in, and I used that. Max Balchowski tested this beforehand. With my rig, as long as I have pressure on it, the car will follow me. It steers the car. On a shorter cable, the car can even be towed around mountain roads, and as long as I don't put on the brakes and just keep the pressure on, it'll follow me, even if I'm in a slide. I've done car chases with just myself towing an empty car.

'After I decided on this system, I set up two little ramps just in

Below. Vanishing Point: *Carey Loftin*

Below. Vanishing
Point: *the road block*

front of the bulldozer blades. I was hoping that, if the car got up high enough when it hit, it would go end over end, over the blades. But I'd taken the motor and transmission out, and without that there wasn't much strength in the car. It just folded and stuck, which the director said he preferred anyway. He asked me, just before we got ready to go, "What's the point of no return on this?" I said, "When you yell 'Action'. On 'Action' I start towing the car with a charger. The dummy doesn't have brakes and it's loaded with explosive triggered by impact switches. That car's virtually a bomb." I put a sawhorse at the point where the charger would be when the car hit, and told the effects man riding with me to release the cable when we got there, otherwise I would have pulled the whole ass-end out of the car. It would happen if that cable had gone tight at the speed we were doing, which got up to eighty or

Below. Vanishing
Point: *the road block*

eighty-five miles an hour. I had some fun out of that effects man. "Is that all I have to do?" he said. "Yes," I said, "but it's very important. If you release the cable too early, the dummy car will veer off. If you pull it too late, you'll just roll the shit out of this car." Then I pulled my safety belt a bit tighter. He hadn't been going to put his belt on, but suddenly he decided perhaps he should. Every time I'd tighten my belt – putting him on – he'd tighten his. We came racing up to this sawhorse and he pulled the release at the right time all right, and it worked. But I threw the car sideways into a spin and said, "My God, we've lost the whole ass end of the car!" He got sort of excited.' Loftin laughs. 'I tell you, I won't do *anything* in this business unless I can have some fun with it.'

Below. Vanishing Point: *the end*

14 The Honoured Society

A disaster for many branches of the American film industry, which it robbed of staff, material and finance, the Second World War left the stunt field almost untouched. Since most stunt men were middle-aged in 1941, and even the most successful had enough breaks and lesions to make them unfit for military service, they were free to work in an industry booming on combat films and knockabout escapism. By common consent all stunt men worked on official government films for the minimum $35 a day, but it was a luxury they could afford. In 1944, a fall downstairs paid $75, a car skid the same. To crash a car at speed cost between $300 and $400, though an expert who offered something special demanded and usually got $500. In the same year, Richard Talmadge estimated there were a hundred Hollywood stunt men, of whom twenty were top men, able to name their own fees. Of these twenty, most were over fifty, and had annual incomes of more than $20,000.

After a long and acrimonious campaign, the Actors', Directors' and Screenwriters' Guilds had forced Hollywood studios to accept union organization – their trump card was to threaten calling off the 1939 Oscar ceremony if their demands were not met – and from 1936 members of the Actors' Guild, including stunt men, became eligible for a basic daily wage of $35, with adequate overtime and workers' compensation provisions. An injured stunt man drew $26·83 a week while he was out of work, plus payment of all medical expenses, and if he died on a stunt was eligible for insurance. Perhaps most important for ageing stunt men subsisting on occasional jobs, there was a pension plan. The new law offered many minor stunters of the thirties their first financial security, and they accepted it with gratitude. Restrictions on membership of the Actors' Guild, the stunt men's natural clannishness and most of all the growth of teams led by a top man in which membership was confined to intimates further reduced the number

of working stunters, and even today it seldom rises above 150,   Below *Cliff Lyons*
most of whom work irregularly. Another stabilizing factor was
the use of 'star doubles'. Action stars prefer the same stunt
stand-in on all their films, particularly if there is a strong resem-
blance. John Epper stunted for Gary Cooper for many years,
Don Turner stunted for Errol Flynn, Gil Perkins for William
'Hopalong Cassidy' Boyd and Red Skelton, Dave Sharpe for
Douglas Fairbanks Jnr and later Tony Curtis, Paul Baxley for
Alan Ladd. A stunt man like Baxley, a credible double for the five
foot six Ladd, but husky and imaginative enough to carry off

hectic scenes like the famous bar-room fight in *Shane* (George Stevens, 1953), could be vital to an actor's success.

Such doubles were in a privileged position, close to the star and able to nominate other stunters to work on their films. This association offered a stunt man the only real promotion he could hope for, and the one all modern stunt men seek – graduation into second-unit direction. Gil Perkins said:

In the forties, Yak [Canutt] got out of doing action. He started directing. Cliff [Lyons] did in the fifties. Because of their close association with stars like Wayne, they were given special opportunities. Had Red [Skelton] stayed in pictures, appearing in two or three a year, all of them jammed with action, I don't doubt that by now I would have been directing. Actually, the director who made most of Skelton's shows, or a hell of a lot of them, had arranged to take me into the production department. He said, 'You'll have to remain as an assistant director for a year. Then I can let you direct all my second units.' At forty-three years of age, three months after that discussion, he died of a heart attack . . .[73]

Not all were so unlucky. Talmadge, Lyons, Yakima and Joe Canutt, Paul Stader and Ricou Browning (who specialized in underwater work), Hal Needham and Paul Baxley, as well as other ex-stunt men, have graduated to second-unit work. A few stunt men or doubles of the forties and fifties have even made the difficult transition to character acting or leads, notably Jock Mahoney, Rod Cameron, Robert Fuller and Burt Reynolds. John Ford's top horse man, Ben Johnson, the hard-riding Trooper Tyree of *She Wore a Yellow Ribbon* who had been a rodeo star and is still a top horse-breeder, demonstrated acting as well as riding skill, and had character parts in countless Westerns, a career culminating in an Oscar for his Sam the Lion in *The Last Picture Show* (Peter Bogdanovich, 1972).

For those who remained stunters, there was the consolation of a spiralling scale of fees. In 1940, the record for one day's work was the $2,350 paid by Fox to Cliff Lyons for his seventy-five foot horse jump in *Jesse James* in 1939. A new record was set in 1950, with Paul Mantz's $6,000 for crashing a B17 on *Twelve O'Clock High* (Henry King) in which he skidded the plane a quarter mile on its belly. By 1969, the record had risen to $19,500 for twenty-six consecutive plane crashes by Jerry Summers on *Darling Lili* (Blake Edwards) at $750 a time, and rates in general rose with it.

The high prices paid for air stunts show the increased use made

Left *Don C. Stevens
sprained an ankle
when the leading edge
of this reconstructed
1883 glider peeled
back in* Gallant
Journey (1946)

of aircraft in Hollywood. During the fifties, the perfection of a
vibration-proof mount for helicopter shooting started a fashion
for vertiginous aerial shots. Enterprising pilots converted ex-war
planes to movie use, either in front of or behind the cameras.
Paul Mantz cajoled his drinking crony Darryl Zanuck into obtain-
ing from Howard Hughes a B25 with its wartime markings intact
and, re-naming it 'The Smasher', allegedly because most of his flying was done while intoxicated, used it as a flying camera platform.
In 1957 Mantz, Zanuck and some cronies took 'The Smasher' on a
ramshackle round-the-world flight; highlights included Mantz
'beating up' the beach at Cannes from zero feet and some near-
fatal emergency landings. 'We decided to keep our trips very
short,' Richard Zanuck said. 'On extended flights [Mantz] would
be completely drunk by the time we landed.'[74] By now almost
incapable of effective flying, Mantz teamed up with Frank
Tallman, a younger and more able pilot who did most of the work
for their Tallmantz Aviation Company. In 1963, Tallman flew one
of Hollywood's most daring air stunts for Stanley Kramer's *It's a
Mad, Mad, Mad, Mad World,* punching a two-engined Beechcraft
through a billboard. He emerged with styrofoam and balsa wood

clogging the starboard engine and dents in the nose and wings, but even with only three feet of clearance between his wing-tips and the steel framework they never touched.

Tallman had been set to do the flying on Robert Aldrich's 1965 *The Flight of the Phoenix*, about a group of men stranded in the desert after a plane crash who cobble together another plane from the wreck and fly it back to civilization, but a few days earlier he had broken his leg pushing his son on a go-kart, a freak accident which led sadly to amputation. At short notice, Mantz, then sixty-two, agreed to fly the awkward 'Phoenix', made from a boom and one engine of a Flying Boxcar, in the desert at Buttercup Valley, near Yuma, Arizona. In the second cockpit was Bob Rose, the stunt man who flew with him on his first movie, Breezy Eason's 1931 *The Galloping Ghost*. Mantz tested the plane successfully, but as its improvised ski undercarriage touched down after the second flight, the skis dug in and the fuselage started to fold. Rose jumped, and survived with a few broken bones, but Mantz was decapitated when the engine broke loose as the plane crashed.

Pilots like Mantz had been replaced by a new, cooler breed: John Hawke, ex-RAF 'Red Devils' exhibition pilot who rebuilt

two B25s as flying camera platforms from which most of *The Battle of Britain* (Guy Hamilton, 1970) was filmed (ironically, John Fulton, pioneer special effects expert whose helicopter shots for *The Bridges of Toko-Ri* (Mark Robson, 1955) won him an Oscar, died during preparations for this film, of natural causes); 'Skeets' Kelly, who shot *The Battle of Britain*'s dogfights from Hawke's psychedelically-decorated number one plane; Gilbert Chomat, French helicopter virtuoso, whose piloting for *Alfred the Great* (Clive Donner, 1968) and *Figures in a Landscape* (Joseph Losey, 1971) earned the highest praise; Ken Tyler, veteran of 144 successful movie crashes. But Tyler was killed on his 145th crash in 1962, and Kelly and Chomat, along with two other men, died shooting Etienne Perier's *Zeppelin* in Ireland in 1970 – more recruits for Dick Grace's Squadron of Death.

Westerns remained the most dangerous action features. More common, and often more cheaply and quickly made than other films, they encouraged the use of stunt men but offered only minimal safeguards. Edward Dmytryk directed *Broken Lance* in 1954. 'Richard Widmark is chasing Bob Wagner. They come to the edge of a cliff over a lake, and Widmark is just about to shoot Bob when an Indian on a higher cliff shoots him. It was a long drop into the water and Russ Saunders was doubling Widmark. There was a huge rock in the water, the top just sticking out above the surface, and the rest sloping away. Since there was a risk of hitting the exposed rock, which was as large across as a room, I told Russ to push off as he fell so he'd land well out, but he insisted on doing it like a real dead man would, just falling straight. We set it up, and as soon as he started to fall I knew he had gone too close. I couldn't look. I turned away and called out "Cut" – luckily the cameraman didn't take any notice – then we ran down to the water. Russ hadn't hit the rock above the surface, but he'd landed just where it shelved off. As we got there, the water was already red with blood and as he slowly came out, blood and water were pouring from his left sleeve. He'd broken his elbow in three places, which is worse than breaking just the arm. He was in traction for months, and very rashly he took on another job before the elbow was fully healed. It was damaged again and after that he could never use it properly.'

Twenties stunt man Fred Kennedy was killed doing a simple horse fall for *The Horse Soldiers* in 1959. Director John Ford, on many of whose films Kennedy had worked, wanted, in the words

*ight Bob Morgan in
ne sequence that cost
im a leg:* How the
West Was Won

*right Bob Morgan in
the sequence that cost
him a leg:* How the
West Was Won

of another stunt man, 'to give the old guy a Christmas present'.
On *The Hallelujah Trail* (John Sturges, 1965) Billy Williams, one
of three stunt men playing drunken Indians who steal a wagon
and drive it off a cliff, misjudged his first jump and could not get
off the wagon before it went over. He was killed in the fall. In
perhaps the most highly publicized stunt accident, Bob Morgan,
stunt-man husband of actress Yvonne de Carlo, lost a leg, bones
from his spine and had his face disfigured in a climactic runaway
train sequence directed by second-unit director Richard Talmadge for *How the West Was Won* (1963). The scene, one of the
most hair-raising for any modern Western, included a running
gunfight between Eli Wallach's bandit gang and sheriff George
Peppard, with a variety of dramatic falls, including one in which
Loren Jones threw himself on top of a tall saguro cactus, and a
battle on a flat truck covered with wildly pivoting logs which
ended with the train's derailment and crash. Morgan, doubling
Peppard, had completed his shots and was resting on the edge of
the flat car when the 150 pound fibreglass logs suddenly shifted,
nudging him onto the track. He was terribly injured as the axles
rolled him under, but survived when his strength and leverage

pushed the truck bodily off the rails.

It is a measure of the unique quality of American action film and stunting that neither has worked well in other countries. Overseas location shooting in the fifties, as studios sent units to make more ambitious adventure films free of union interference and high Hollywood costs, forced the European and American cinemas together, but the marriage never worked. English studios supported a few stunt men before the war, but the US actors who arrived in the late forties surprised European stunt men with their athletic ability and enterprise. Their stunt men were correspondingly more professional. With little work to keep them occupied, English stunt men quickly drifted out of the business, and most American directors had to train men from scratch for their films. Arriving in England in 1951 to shoot the battles on *Ivanhoe* (Richard Thorpe), Yakima Canutt found that professional methods astonished the few stunt men still working. 'I couldn't get any sand for falls, so I brought in peat moss. We put that down and covered it up with greenery to blend in with the other ground. They were pretty impressed. "Nobody ever did anything like that before," they said.

'During the making of *Ivanhoe* I took fifteen or sixteen new men out of the extra group that had good athletic backgrounds – some of them had been commandos – and put them through a sort of training course. They did some very fine work. In fact, several of those men got to be the top stunt men in England: Ken Buckle, John Sullivan, Jackie Cooper and fellows like that. I had a group of these boys over in Spanish Morocco on *Zarak* [Terence Young, 1957]. We got ready to do some falls, and I'd had a bunch of open L stirrups copied for the boys to use. I put them on the horses but Buckle didn't like them. "You might get caught and hung up in those." I said, "What are you talking about? They're a safety thing. There's no way in the world you can hang up in them." Well, Ken showed me a way. He's kind of big, and when he made a fall down the side of the horse his belt hooked in it. We kidded the hell out of him about that – the only man in the world who can get caught in an L stirrup.'

This nucleus grew into a small stunt community. With television, a precarious living was possible, and there were always a few men with athletic training who preferred the transient glamour of movies to more conventional work. Bob Simmons had been an Army Physical Training instructor and Senior P.T.

Instructor at Sandhurst military academy before Canutt picked him from the *Ivanhoe* extras to do stunts. He has since worked his way up to become stunt coordinator on many features – Peter Yates's *Murphy's War*, Etienne Perier's *When Eight Bells Toll,* and on the James Bond films, which on occasion he has shared with Peter Diamond and Paul Baxley. Gerry Crampton was recruited by Simmons, who works with him, as does Alf Joint, the senior British stunt man, credited with the highest stunt jump, 158 feet from a Malta cliff for a chocolate commercial. He did it twice, knocked himself insensible and was concussed for weeks. Except those like Simmons lucky enough to be regularly employed on a series, work is thin and the film establishment difficult. European film-makers seldom appreciate the experience and professionalism behind even the simplest action film, and assume a Western can be shot merely by imitating the American model, an assumption generally dispelled after a few actors have been maimed or killed.

Derek Ware, one of the most ambitious of English stunt men, an amateur military historian as well as founder of his own team and a stunt men's agency, collided with this ignorance when he was approached to handle the battles for Tony Richardson's remake of *The Charge of the Light Brigade* in 1968. 'They were going to hire the Shah of Persia's imperial bodyguard because they'd got "falling horses". I told the man who interviewed me, "They haven't got falling horses at all." He said, "I saw forty of them fall in unison." "You didn't see them *fall*," I said. "You saw them pull up sharply. The riders dismounted and pulled them round. They laid on their sides and the riders lay down behind them and fired off their guns. When you saw it, coming most unexpectedly, it looked like the horses fell, but it won't look like that in the film." I also pointed out that the Persians were a lancer regiment. He said, "What difference does that make?" I explained that there was only one detachment of lancers at the Charge of the Light Brigade, the Seventeenth/Twenty-First Cavalry on the left. The other four detachments were light dragoons and hussars. They would only use the sabre. "Unless the horsemen have been trained in the sabre," I said, "you're going to have a lot of horses without any ears." This precisely came true. They were clouting those horses around the head something awful.' Bob Simmons eventually coordinated the film's stunts – by most accounts a less than happy experience.

At the other end of the scale, American stunt men trained for decades in the rigid Hollywood environment are baffled by directors to whom style and historical accuracy are all-important. Making *Alfred the Great* in Ireland in 1968, English director Clive Donner found unexpected problems with his stunt coordinator in achieving the battles he wanted. 'I started planning the battles in *Alfred the Great* one year to the day before I turned film on the first battle. During that year we wrote the battle scenes, found locations, built models of the location, worked out the footage a given hundred, five hundred or thousand men would take. Two sketch artists were engaged, one for each battle, to design all the set-ups in constant consultation with me working out the exact measurements of the space a man would take up on the model. The sketches were then photostatted and made up into two volumes; copies of these books were then issued to the people concerned; production department, camera department, art department.

'We then engaged the stunt master; Bernard Smith, who produced *How the West Was Won*, was very anxious I should have a stunt master who was very, very experienced. He naturally wanted Yakima Canutt, but Yak wasn't available. We did have

Below *Gilbert Chomat shooting Pau Stader's battle for Alfred the Great*

long talks with him, however; he was very helpful and did suggest the man we finally got, Paul Stader. Paul came over and I gave him the script to read of the two battles. I explained to him the kind of fighting I wanted. The Vikings fought in a very soldierly way with swords and shields, a trained and disciplined fighting force. But the Saxons were not soldiers. They were farmers, and their weapons were farm implements or bits of wood. They fought like animals. I said, "One of the ways I want them to succeed in the first battle is to as it were get in under the armour." While the Dane was slashing away with his sword the Saxon could get in and throttle him.

'We discussed various details about the way I wanted the fights to go. I said I didn't want any obvious Hollywood tumbles and falls. I wanted it all to have as ferocious and unchoreographed a look as possible. Two things happened after that. One was that the Irish Army contingent we engaged began their training. Paul and I got together with their commander, a sergeant major who was in charge of the one thousand of them. He then selected from those soldiers twenty-five who were mostly junior subalterns and NCOs and taught them how to be stunt men. Intelligence I think he went for, willingness and a certain kind of physical adaptability. Then he started recruiting his force of stunt men. At one time we had about thirty, all English. What would happen was that in the big battle scenes he put the professional stunt men in the foreground and the less well-trained people in the rear. We had a lot of trouble, especially in the second battle, with people not acting. I shot the second battle from about three or four hundred yards away with narrow angled lenses. We had five cameras and so if there was some idiot who wasn't trying or his wig fell off and he started grinning, it showed up. That's why we needed so many stunt men. We placed them all round the battle to keep it alive.

'Stader was in the thick of the battle, fighting. He's a marvellous man, but a bit of a maniac. He would never stop. He would "die", then crawl out of the battle, pop up somewhere else and keep fighting. He reckoned that by staying in there he could keep up their personal enthusiasm. We had these giant aero engines for the wind and you couldn't hear a thing. Paul was right in there screaming, "Come on, you motherfuckers! Get on with it!" They tended to respond more. Paul is great, and will go on and on for you, but I would have been happier with somebody using his loaf beside me who could have spotted things that had gone wrong and known how to put them right. Quite frankly, he was a bit old-fashioned. He didn't really understand this concept of Danes against Saxons at first. He only understood it when I explained that it wasn't all Bang Bang, but *one* side Bang Bang, the *other* side Grab Grab. It had to be spelled out.'

This impasse seems unlikely to be resolved in a fragmented international film industry. English stunt men frequently express the hope that the European stunt community will organize itself to bring coordinators in closer contact with the directors who use their services, but the looked-for consolidation has not come nor, if the experience of Hollywood is any guide, is it likely to. Europe's few good stunt men are already surrounding themselves with reliable teams as Talmadge, Canutt and Lyons did in the fifties, and a decline into compartmentalization seems unavoidable. One of the most striking is that formed around the French racing and stunt driver Remy Julienne, whose spectacular driving on films

Below. The Italian Job: *L'Equipe Remy Julienne*

like *The Italian Job* (Peter Collinson, 1968) and *Stuntman* (Marcello Baldi, 1968) rivals in polish and daring anything achieved by American stunters. The remarkable sequences of *The Italian Job* where, after stealing a gold shipment from a crowded Italian street (in a violent snatch, directed by Derek Ware, with hooded thieves, water cannons and masses of police), the thieves escape in Mini Minors by racing through sewer pipes, over rooftops and even through a cathedral, have no equal anywhere. Julienne was paid £2,000 a day for the driving, but unfortunately its odder sections – the cars whizz through a society wedding, and pair off to 'waltz' as they crash a rehearsal of the Blue Danube by a symphony orchestra – were cut. A worthy successor to Gil Delamare, top French stunt man who died in a sixties car crash, Julienne is a remarkable throwback to more piratical days. In addition to managing his own stunt driving team for shows and fairs, his recreations include wild-boar hunting with a hand pistol and other risky sports. Though Hollywood will always be the centre of stunting, men like Simmons and Julienne could be the nucleus at least of a European resurgence.

In America, the stunt field has passed almost totally into the hands of those experts who specialize only in the big stunts that bring instant, large rewards. Few hire out for simple falls and jumps; like musicians, they work in regular groups under a known coordinator who expects his men to be thoroughly trained in all disciplines. 'To say somebody's a specialist,' one top double told me, 'is like saying he's a bad stunt man.' Producers who pay for location shooting on action films demand a yield in thrills, and arguments of risk or complexity no longer apply. If you can't do it, somebody else will. Among the most highly respected of the pan-adept stunt men is Mickey Gilbert, whom Andrew Marton regards as the greatest of the modern stunters. 'I met Mickey and his father-in-law Joe Yrigoyen on *Ben-Hur*, and they were with me on TV series like *Man and the Challenge* and *Cowboy in Africa*, so when we did the feature version of *Cowboy in Africa*, *Africa Texas Style* in 1967, Joe was the stunt coordinator and Mickey doubled the star, Hugh O'Brian. When we went to Nairobi, Joe and Mickey took with them four educated American cowboy horses, two to ride and two as back-ups. We'd trained these horses to be with elephants and to stand the African weather. I remember that the air fare from here to Nairobi for the four horses plus Mickey and Joe was $21,000. We spent it gladly because it paid off.

'Mickey is a unique person. First of all, physically he's a magnificent specimen, and he's absolutely without fear. He took the chance of having turned loose on him a rhino we had caught three days before, a completely wild rhino, so wild it demolished the hard teakwood box in which we brought him from the jungle to the holding pen. Mickey said, "I'm not going to run. I'm going to side-step him, and as he goes after me I'll cut down the margin on the side-stepping." This is incredible cold-blooded thinking. We chose a location where every fifteen feet there was a little tree, not enough to block the view but enough to stop the rhino and let Mickey spin around. He was as good as his word. We had three cameras on it and in five minutes we had enough for two reels of the most incredible "bull fight" between intelligence and brute strength.'

Such bravado is rare in a field where animal-training has become a sophisticated branch of special effects. Since studios no longer use animals merely for thrills, and expect them to perform with almost the same precision as human actors, modern animal-trainers have adopted radically new techniques. These date from the fifties, when Hollywood's lion farms metamorphosed into centres like Ivan Tors's Africa USA – show-places at which trainers worked full-time on accustoming even the most savage creatures to work with them. Old Charlie and Friday have been replaced by young animals raised in captivity to trust men, and take direction. When the director of *Vampire Circus* (Robert Young, 1972) wanted animals that behaved savagely, English trainer Mary Chipperfield had to show them how, teaching a tiger to play with a toy human arm so that he would attack the real thing when told. On *Living Free* (Jack Couffer, 1972), one of the popular films based on Joy Adamson and her friendship with a pride of African lions, actress Susan Hampshire worked safely with five wild lionesses. The lead lioness, used for close-ups, was two years old and weighed three hundred pounds. 'I knew she was totally wild,' the actress said, 'and I had total respect for her.' This respect was shared by the handlers. 'They never used guns or whips, only a rope and leather gloves. They didn't drink or smoke, slept a lot, and never for an instant dropped their guard. They *never* let the animals get behind them. She learned that a blow on the nose of a lion was like stroking the animal, and could persuade her when playing became too robust. 'When they jump on your back it's terribly frightening, and I nearly panicked when she fastened her mouth on my wrist. If you pull it away, they want it. I had to leave it there until she got tired of it.'[75]

Every creature has been trained for the movies at one time or another, from rhinoceroses and giraffes to turkeys and cockroaches. Hollywood expert Moe DiSesso specializes in the bizarre. His triumph was educating five hundred rats for *Willard* (Daniel Mann, 1971) in which a psychopathic teenager (Bruce Davison) makes friends with rats and sets them on a world he despises. 'After twenty-one years in the business and having trained everything from owls to racoons to turkeys, I never had a call for rats, much less five hundred rats,' DiSesso says. He decided to start from scratch. 'Since it only takes twenty-one days for a rat to have a litter of ten or twelve little rats, we bought a dozen and left it up to them. The real problem came with training the animals to do the many different things called for in the script – climbing furniture, running in and out of a suitcase, climbing stairs, baring their teeth, squeaking on cue, and most important of all getting used to being handled by humans.' DiSesso trained baby rats to associate the sound of an electric buzzer with food, rewarding them with daubs of peanut butter. By the time they had grown, the rats, trained in

Right. Willard: *the rats*

groups of twenty-five, would take direction admirably, and had become used to being handled by humans through DiSesso's son lying down in their pen fifteen times a day 'to help them associate humans with security and food'.[76]

Actors who have worked with animals accept rats with equanimity, but all of them reserve their dislike for two kinds of creature. One is the chimpanzee, a staple of the jungle film. Jock Mahoney, who was Tarzan for some years, said of *Tarzan Goes to India*, 'I'm luckier than Lex [Barker] was. He had to work with a chimp. There's not going to be a Jane or Cheeta in this one. I'm glad the chimp's gone. They're the dirtiest, meanest animals to work with.' A later Tarzan, Mike Henry, agreed. His lovable pet chimp bit him savagely on the face, necessitating a number of stitches in his chin. Actors are equally uncomfortable working with birds, which are too stupid to be trained. On *The Birds* (1963), Alfred Hitchcock gave in and relied on photographic process work for most of his shots, though three thousand miscellaneous birds were used. After having hundreds of finches dumped down a chimney into a room, Rod Taylor complained of the regularity and precision with which they defecated into his hair. John Frankenheimer's *Birdman of Alcatraz* (1962) took a stricter line. Frankenheimer said:

It was a terribly difficult film to make. Because there's no such thing as a trained bird. You've got to use a hungry bird. We used canaries in some scenes, but you can't train *them* at all. At other times we used sparrows – about fifty for one bird. Ray Berwick is a bird-trainer and he would work with a bird, but once you got the lights and the camera and the crew around, the bird would be petrified, and we had to sit there until it felt like doing it. It was torture, it really was. And it was like being in prison because we had a netting, a wire-mesh constructed over the set, so the bird couldn't fly out. We were all trapped; it was a very claustrophobic movie.[77]

With actors producing their own films, the star, both financally and physically, now expects to take his own risks. Steve McQueen does a proportion of his own stunt driving (though Loren Jones is his regular double) and in Don Siegel's *Dirty Harry* (1972) Clint Eastwood refused to be replaced by his usual stand-in Buddy Van Horn and did a dangerous bridge-to-bus roof jump himself, adding substantially to the scene. But the most agile of action stars is Charlton Heston, who declines the assistance of stunt men in all but the most hazardous situations. On *Number One* (Tom Gries, 1970) he broke two ribs in a hectic professional football game,

Stars who take their own risks. Above *Glenn Ford in* Cowboy; below *Clint Eastwood in* Dirty Harry; overleaf *Jean-Paul Belmondo in* The Burglars

though not all stunts have been so painful, due to the guidance of Joe Canutt, his regular double for some years and his personal stunt coordinator. Joe did the chariot leap on *Ben-Hur* and jousted with his own brother Tap on *El Cid* while doubling Heston, but Yakima Canutt remembers it was Basil Dearden's *Khartoum* (1966) that really forged the team. 'Heston isn't only a good actor, but one of the most astute birds I've ever worked with. If he's got something to do that he's never done, he'll come out and work at it. We had a thing in *Khartoum* where General Gordon has to lay down his horse at the run. I was going to do this on a Monday (the first-unit director would just send out the principals and let me get on with it, which is the best way). Heston came out to do this thing. Of course I had Joe to do the horse fall, but while we got ready to do it Heston said, "Yak, I believe I can do this fall." I said, "I don't want to gamble or take any chance, Chuck." "Well," he said, "Joe had me out Sunday and he taught me how to throw him." I looked for Joe but of course he was very carefully going the other way. So Heston rode in, put the horse down, got up and rode him off. Beautiful.'

The pressure on people like Heston to do their own stunts – because it looks better and involves less expense – has also changed the attitude to women stunters. For years, most doubling of female stars had been done by men, but improved photography and finally wide screen made this impossible, as it did the practice of using white actors to double black and Indian stars. Directors turned to stunt girls, who for the first time achieved their proper recognition.

Stunt women work under disadvantages which few male stunters face. In the serials, Helen Holmes and Helen Gibson held their own against men, fighting, jumping and piloting trains and planes with the best of them, but the beginning of conventional film drama ended this. The twenties and thirties were decades of 'leading men', and women were reduced to the status of passengers or victims, unable to defend themselves or act to save their lives. If a woman stunter did a motor-cycle gag, it was usually as a passenger, clinging to the male driver and hoping he knew his job. Their natural dexterity and resilience, greater than that of men, was never exploited, with the result that the greater risks, the corresponding lack of reward – female stunters have seldom received the same fees as stunt men – and the triviality of their work drove them out. It was one thing to risk your life in a good stunt, another to chance burns by posing on the bonnet of a car in skimpy clothing while it leapt through a barrier of flame, as Audrey Scott had to do for a thirties car commercial. Few stunt women stayed even the usual five years in the business, but retired, often into marriage with stunt men, a disappointing end for women whose skill has earned praise in a field where it is meagre.

Dick Grace acknowledged respectfully the courage of Opal Boswell, who doubled for Colleen Moore in *Lilac Time,* standing unflinchingly in a field as Grace crash-landed his plane only a few yards from her, and twenties stunt girls like Winnie Brown and Janet Ford were acknowledged as equals by most male stunters. Few men would have taken on the jobs they accepted, not only because of their risks, but because of the ridiculous action. Mary Fuller, the first serial star, described in a 1916 article a stunt so absurd that nobody should have bothered to chance her life on it.

I was taking the part of a mermaid seated on a lonely rock that projected thirty feet in the air from an angry sea beneath. The tail of the mermaid suit was a wonderful fit, and was sure to stay in place. On my breast I had placed water lilies, and around my neck were strings of coral. Suddenly, I noticed, with fear, that the tide was rapidly rising. I called out, in alarm, to my director and cameraman, but nobody heard me. The

Left. Tarzan and the Amazons: *Betty Frazee encourages a six foot alligator during shooting at Silver Springs, Florida*

creeping tides were threatening to cover me. I couldn't get up and run –
the tail wouldn't permit me. I couldn't find anyone to save me; the
cameraman was fascinated with the picture, and continued to turn the
cranks. The spray from the sea swept over me; splashes of water over my
face and body. My coral and lilies were swept away. I began to move, but
not towards the shore. My direction was out to sea. I was gasping with
fear when finally the men saw my danger and carried me back to terra
firma, but the cameras were caught in the tide and never returned.[78]

Loretta Rush took more risks in thirties' films than many men,
until a car crash forced her retirement; ironic, since she had
survived the car smash on which stunt girl Marcella Arnold,
doubling Ann Rutherford, had been thrown out and killed. For
Flowing Gold (Joseph de Grasse, 1924), doubling Anna Q. Nilsson,
she did a fall into burning oil which few male stunters would have
cared for. The effects department divided the tank in half with a
partition which had an underwater escape hatch. Miss Rush dived
through the layer of burning gasoline, found the hatch and strug-
gled through to safety on the other side with nothing more than
singed eyebrows. Work of this standard brought on a boom in the
early thirties, but by 1938 there were only thirty-seven Hollywood

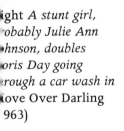

*ight A stunt girl,
probably Julie Ann
Johnson, doubles
Doris Day going
through a car wash in
Move Over Darling
(1963)*

stunt girls, most of whom worked casually. The best of them, like Frances Miles, or expert horsewoman Audrey Scott, could earn $2,500 a year, the rest got by on occasional jobs, spending most of their time as extras. By the late fifties, stunt girls were getting a basic $138 a stunt, with some work paying as much as $1500, but they still lagged behind male stunters. Rodeo rider Polly Burson probably received less for doubling Betty Hutton in *The Perils of Pauline*, Paramount's simple-minded 1947 fantasy on the Pearl White serials, than the original star did in 1914.

One of the top modern Hollywood stunt girls is Stephanie Epper, daughter of John Epper, Gary Cooper's regular double; her sister and three brothers are also stunt people. Along with Patty Elder, Julie Ann Johnson, Regina Parton (daughter of Reggie Parton, one of the founders of the American Stuntmen's Association) and black stunt girl Peaches Jones she has cut a place for herself in a competitive industry. The central problem for any stunt girl remains that of protecting herself in conventional film situations, often riskier than those stunt men face. As English stunt girl Connie Tilton has pointed out, these often come down to saving oneself from the shoddy work of male colleagues. Doubling

Right (and continued overleaf) *A stunt goes wrong on* The Train (1964): *the crash . . .*

. . . the engine, having demolished one camera, lands dangerously close to another

. . director John
*Frankenheimer, Burt
Lancaster and the
engine driver
exchange views as to
responsibility

Sophia Loren in *The Millionairess* (Anthony Asquith, 1960) she
leaped into the icy Thames from London Bridge, only to find the
man hired to pick her up in a rowboat had misjudged the current
and was yards downstream, while in *Tiger Bay* (J. Lee Thompson,
1959) where she replaced Hayley Mills in a dangerous leap from a
ship into the choppy sea, the stunt man diving in to rescue her
panicked at the waves and almost drowned both of them. She
knocked him out and towed him back to the ship. Connie is
critical of directors who habitually demand that girl stunters
perform in brief clothing – not on moral grounds but because
padding becomes impossible. (In Charlton Heston's 1972 *Antony
and Cleopatra* Joe Canutt's lively second unit spectacles include a
high dive into the sea by a courageously nude stunt girl.) On
occasion she has been cut by 'toffee' safety glass, notably when,
doubling Dawn Adams in *The Two Faces of Dr Jekyll* (Terence
Fisher, 1960), she plummetted through a glass ceiling wearing only
flimsy Edwardian underwear. Perhaps there is an element of
revenge in her revelation that stunt girls always know when a
woman is standing in for a man in some dangerous scene; females
instinctively protect their breasts in a fall while the male stunter

shows an understandable solicitude for his lower abdomen.

If anyone should doubt the degree of danger in the stunt woman's work, a film like *The Rare Breed* (Andrew V. McLaglen, 1965) will persuade him. Stephanie Epper and Patty Elder were hired to double Deborah Kerr and Juliet Mills in a fall from an overturning wagon driven by Hal Needham. The wagon was rigged with a cable to cramp and turn over, throwing the girls into a sand pit while Needham, holding a cable attached to the part of the wagon still being pulled by the team, was to be yanked off and dragged behind it. Everything went wrong at once. The wagon failed to separate on cue so that the three were still on it and well beyond the prepared landing places when it turned over. 'It should have killed them both,' Needham said. 'It was pure accident that they hit a sand pit where we'd buried a camera. I was supposed to go out one side, but the wheel hit me and knocked me out the other side. I separated my collar-bone, and they didn't even get hurt.' He sounded almost resentful, and one recalled the classic story of the bruised stunt girl who, after a particularly punishing week, approached the assistant director and wearily asked, 'Who do I have to sleep with to get *off* this picture?'

Above. The Rare Breed: *Patty Elder and Stephanie Epper are thrown off while Hal Needham is dragged forward with the team*

15 A New Breed

Organization has never come easily to stunt men. In the twenties, fanciful newsmen filled the gap by periodically 'revealing' the existence of fraternal groups which swore blood oaths or – shades of First World War flying romances – met ritually at the death of a member to toast his empty chair. Barnstormers were particularly vulnerable to such speculation. Gladys Ingle was touted as the leader of an all-girl group called the Thirteen Black Cats, apparently an invention of (or for) the newsreels; while a 1934 article said confusingly: 'There used to be in Hollywood a company of a dozen first-class stunt men known as the Black Cats. Some people called them the Suicide Club, and it is on record that no member ever refused a stunt, no matter how difficult or dangerous it was . . .' A later writer was more specific. 'Richard Grace . . . was one of the founders of the Suicides' Club. This club was started by stunt men in 1928 to provide insurance and help in sickness to its members. Everyone contributed twenty per cent of his earnings to a fund.' Elsewhere, Grace was quoted as saying: 'Some years ago twenty-three men formed a Squadron of Death in Hollywood. . . . I alone remain of that original band. Eighteen of my twenty-two colleagues have died on duty, and the other four are hopelessly crippled.' Yet in their autobiographies both Grace and Joe Bonomo directly contradict all these claims, castigating journalists for nominating an arbitrary elite of 'Black Cats' or 'Suicides' who very soon after ran out of luck. Because of their superstitions, to which one must add the natural clannishness and competitiveness of the stunt men, one doubts all these stories, and since Grace used 'Squadron of Death' to describe *dead* comrades rather than live ones, this quotation at least is obviously a fiction.

No effective organization of any kind existed among stunt men until 1962, when a group of established stunters formed the Stuntmens' Association of Motion Pictures (SAMP), a fraternal organization within the Screen Actors' Guild to represent the interests of stunt men. (Stunt women had already set up their own guild in 1958, and had formed similar groups as far back as the thirties.) The move was a symptom of the expansive industrial situation in which stunt men found themselves. The number of registered stunt men had shrunk to 150 as the pension plan siphoned off older members, and though, as usual, a large proportion (sometimes fifty per cent) of those registered were inactive or semi-retired, the hard core of working stunters were seldom out of work. The association had reason to be proud of its safety record. Bad accidents, like that on a *Man From UNCLE* episode where Marv Willens telescoped two vertebrae and was paralysed, were relatively rare. Perhaps because for the first time in its history the stunt men seemed to have found a place in Hollywood, the events of 1969 came as a particular shock. A National Commission on Causes and Prevention of Violence under Dr Milton S. Eisenhower sat for some months, and in September issued a report blaming the gratuitous violence of television for much of the deterioration in law and order.

Public reaction was predictably extreme. Middle-class America greeted the report as a long-overdue diagnosis of the cultural malaise, and the media, sensitive to a dangerous ground-swell of opinion, purged the 1970 schedules of violence. From boom, the stunt field went overnight to bust. For the stunt man, proud of his new status, it was a body blow. Not only were they labelled as pornographers of violence, but their living was whisked away as the networks dropped most of the series on which they had worked. They gloomily contemplated programmes in which fights were more ballets than battles, or were replaced by 'noises off' and the occasional flight into frame of a breakaway chair. Few stunt men worked more than fifteen days throughout the whole of 1970, according to SAMP figures, and many didn't work at all.

The association responded in a way many people believe to have been both inept and immoral. A fitful attempt was made to sanitize the stunt man's image, and its council sent a letter to President Nixon, on whose orders the commission had been set up, attempting to justify the mayhem on TV and the stunt man's involvement in it. 'Violence is nature's plan,' it said in part, 'and no one can legislate against or purge reality.' This letter and the events of 1970 crushed all chance of a cohesive stunt community in Hollywood. The fumbling attempt at postulating a stunt man's morality, though containing much with which the stunters privately agreed, looked

in cold print both morbid and offensive. Most stunt men, emotionally immature, work in the business for personal motives in-
extricably involved with their vision of themselves. It is an
introspective calling, as remote from normal society as that of the
torero or the mercenary soldier, and though there are apologists
for both these trades, the act of justification is basically absurd for
all three; they would do it whether there was a reason or not. But
faced with these statements, the more perceptive recoiled into
their shells, and the concept of a stunt union quietly faded away.

Forced into alternative employment, stunt men found new jobs
or returned to old ones. Bar-tending was popular. Both Paul
Stader and Gene Lebell opened fight gyms. Everett Creech designed
a compact head camera for sky divers and racing drivers. Reg
Parton, a co-founder of the SAMP, built dune buggies, and later
formed a stunt troupe to tour Vietnam bases giving exhibitions, a
grotesque confrontation between the alleged villains of the breakdown of moral order and the true authors of its decline. The truth
gained strength during 1970 as, like all fads, the abhorrence of
violence faded, and 1971 TV schedules were as bloody as ever. But
though stunt men were now back in work, the confidence of many
had been shaken. Splits occurred within the organization as
younger men, wary of what the SAMP stood for, broke away to
form smaller groups, often based on the personal and emotional
associations common in the thirties. In this they were following
the example of one of the best new Hollywood stunt men, Hal
Needham, who had left the SAMP with other young stunters in
March 1970 to form his own Stunts Unlimited. Stunts Unlimited
broke many basic laws of the business. It was represented by a
talent agency, something the Actors' Guild had always opposed.
It operated partly as a cooperative, unique in this competitive
field. It set codes of conduct and discipline, which older stunters
found a threat to their piratical style. And it trained new men in
stunt technique, by common consent a dangerous and repre-
hensible activity when skill was directly negotiable.

Stunts Unlimited reflects the personality of its founder. Still
remarkably youthful at forty-one, and, with his actor's profile and
spring-heeled walk, one of the few stunt men who fits the conventional image, Hal Needham has fought harder than most to
penetrate the stunt business. 'Before I got into movies I was a tree-
topper; a forester and logger. But I broke my ankle while I was in
the tree business in 1955. I was in a restaurant and I met a guy who

Hal Needham

Left and right *From Hal Needham's personal stunt brochure*

was a paratrooper with me when I was in the services. He and I got talking, and he was trying to get into the picture industry. As we talked and became better friends he said, "You've got the background. You should be a stunt man." I thought, "Hell, I'd like that." So I sold my tree business and became a stunt man. The first job I did was on *The Spirit of St Louis* [Billy Wilder, 1957]. I did a parachute jump in that where the guy jumps out, cuts away his parachute, pulls another, cuts that away and so on. I also did some wing rides and a plane exchange where they were barnstormers. But after *The Spirit of St Louis* I spent nine months looking for a

job, because I had no reputation. Nobody knew who I was. I sold all my vehicles and used up all my money. I started tending bar at night to see myself through. Then I did a couple of shows with Art Baker and Jack Smith called *You Asked For It.'*

You Asked For It, a grisly phenomenon of a TV industry that produced programmes like *Candid Camera* and quiz shows in which contestants got a booby prize or pie in the face as often as any reward, featured professional escapologists, contortionists and tumblers, as well as stunt men who performed death-defying routines suggested by viewers who vied with each other to invent new and dangerous stunts. Many new stunt men agreed to work for the show, which paid a meagre $250 a time, and remember it as a terrifying experience. Jack Wilson was hired to make a fifteen foot jump on roller skates through a sheet of flame. In order to get up enough speed to leap the gap, the show's engineers built Wilson a forty foot ramp twisted up at the end; when he took off into the flames he was still fifteen feet in the air. Even then the stunt might have gone well had the prop men not set the fire with shredded cardboard and gasoline, far too hot a combination, and heaped the material up so that it blazed hottest at the point where Wilson passed through. The first take scorched him, and on the second face, hands and arms were badly burned. Undeterred, the show called up a few weeks later and asked Wilson if he could stand on top of a tall building at Long Beach and twirl a girl in a circle while wearing roller skates. 'I can't twirl a girl on a skating rink,' Wilson protested. 'How am I going to do it ten storeys high? Get another stunt man.'[79]

'I did two or three pretty phenomenal gags on there,' Needham says. 'One of them was probably the most outstanding stunt I did in my life. I was in an aircraft, flying. I got out onto the wheel of the aircraft and a friend of mine was on horseback and as we flew over I dived and knocked him off the horse. We were indicating fifty-seven miles an hour when I left and we were about eighteen feet in the air. As a matter of fact we had to do it twice that day. Those gags kind of helped. It at least got the stunt men talking about me, even if it was only to say, "Well, *that* son of a bitch ain't going to be around long enough to be any kind of threat to us."

'Then I had a big break. I was working as an extra on an episode of *Have Gun Will Travel* called "The Haunted Forest" up at Big Bear, and they had to have some tree climbers. I watched them a while and I said, "Those guys don't know how to climb." A production man heard me and said, "I suppose *you* do." "That I do," I said. So they put the spurs and the belt on me and I did the climbing sequences. It was my chance to show off. About two or three days later, the star of the show, Richard Boone, and the guy who was doubling him had a little disagreement, and so I approached him on the fact that I thought I was a hell of a good stunt man; why not give me a chance? And he did. I doubled him for five and a half years on *Have Gun Will Travel*. It took six months for them to get any confidence in me. They took me on because Boone said "Hire him", but after a while they began to see I knew what I was doing and they allowed me to suggest people to hire. Boone always had to have four or five opponents, and so I would suggest people, and in doing so I built a rapport with the other stunt men so that when they had jobs they'd think about hiring me.'

Needham's second break also came about through *Have Gun Will Travel*. Andrew V. McLaglen, son of actor Victor McLaglen and director of many episodes in which Needham had stunted, graduated to feature production and took Needham along as his stunt coordinator. He has arranged the stunts for all McLaglen's action and Western films, *McLintock* (1963), *The Rare Breed* (1965), *Shenandoah* (1965), *The Way West* (1967) among others, and established himself in the process as one of Hollywood's top stunt ramrods. His methods, notably the use of younger stunt men, brought him into conflict with the establishment, of whom he is critical. 'I thought when I first came into the business I had leprosy. Nobody would even *talk* to me. They don't want to risk losing their jobs. I'm competitive and I like competition, but the older guys . . . they're looking for the pay day, they're looking for the easy way out. They're tired of abusing their bodies, tired of getting up in the morning and being sore.' When the SAMP was formed, Needham joined, later became a member of its council but, when he tried to bring in newer stunt men to the board and institute changes, the established members, he claims, squeezed him out. Taking the best younger men with them, Needham, Ronnie Rondell and Glen Wilder started Stunts Unlimited.

There is a good deal of oppsstition to Stunts Unlimited within the stunt field, and many men allied neither to the new nor old groups are sceptical of its ability to survive. Nevertheless, it represents an inevitable development. Except for the top technicians, most of whom specialize in second-unit direction or co-ordination, many Hollywood stunt men are too old for an industry that, even in the last decade, has become noticeably more danger-ous. The field also suffers, like most sections of the cinema, from a backward recruitment policy and a lack of responsiveness to new ideas. In common with many other stunt men, Needham is critical of the specialization that forty years of stunting has imposed on the business. In the modern cinema, with its variety of action, the specialist limits himself out of business. Singly or as a team, the Stunts Unlimited men tackle anything, and bring to it a freshness and imagination not always in the work of a man who has done a gag so often that its movements are as preconceived as a ballet. Needham, who shares Andrew Marton's admiration of Mickey Gilbert and his adaptability, regards his own colleague Ronnie Rondell (son of veteran assistant director Ronnie Rondell Snr) as one of the finest modern stunt men because, like Dave Sharpe, his personal ideal, he is willing to try anything.

'Rondell's an athlete. He can work on bars. He's a surfer, a tumbler. He's never been known as a horseman, but I took him out and put him on horses I've seen good horsemen miss. His natural athletic ability enables him to do things a cowboy can't do. For instance, if a cowboy is going to do a transfer from his horse to, say, a coach, he'll ride that horse right in there, reach over, get hold of the coach and pull himself on. That's not very spectacular. Rondell doesn't ride that way. He may wind up ten feet away from the coach and have to dive for it, but it looks better.' Occasionally this flexibility can encourage a director to ask more of a stunt man than he has a right to expect, and Needham has had his share of this. 'I've met two or three directors who would have killed me if I'd let them. I don't know whether they're being malicious when they do it or whether they just don't realize the risks of what they want. A lot of people look on a stunt man and think you're a super-man.

'A director said to me one time, "I want you to fall backwards into this pot that's got a pound of flash powder in it." I said, "Wait a minute! I can't fall into that and let them set if off. I'd burn to death." And he said, "Well, you're supposed to be a stunt man, aren't you?" I was playing a German, so I took off my helmet and put it on his head. I said, "You're too Western for me, pard. *You* do it. But," I said, "there's a way to do it and get a better shot than you're talking about." I'd put him on the spot. "What do you

Right *Ronnie Rondell*
in a sixty-five foot
fall on Kings of the
Sun

suggest?'' So I told him. The camera has no depth perception, so a
man doesn't have to be right on top of the pot when it blows to be
thrown by it. He can be just at the edge of it. So we put a spot
trampoline just between the pot and the camera, and got one of
the young kids – I couldn't do it myself – to come in, hit the
trampoline, jump over the pot and, as he did, do a 'Branny' – a
front flip with a twist to it so that you land going backwards. If
you do it loose, without your toes pointed or anything like that, it
looks like it's just thrown you up in the air and twisted you around.
The timing of the explosion, setting it off just as the guy hits the

trampoline, has to be right on. The first time I saw this stunt done was on *Shenandoah*, where I was stunt coordinator. Ronnie Rondell did it for me. George Kennedy was one of the actors on the film and he'd just got out of his car and walked up onto the set as we called "Action". Rondell came running down to this cannon with a box of ammunition on his shoulder and as he hit the trampoline we blew the cannon all to hell. The wheels fell off, and Ronnie went right up through the explosion. George thought it was real. "Oh, My God!" he said, and ran down to pick up Rondell. Bill Clothier, the cameraman, who's been on dozens of Westerns, including almost all of John Wayne's, said it was the best individual stunt he'd ever seen.'

To encourage Rondell's sort of flexibility, Stunts Unlimited instituted monthly classes in which new stunt men, not necessarily part of their group, get a grounding in all aspects of some technique: the use of air rams, rapelling from cliffs, karate and judo, horse falls and fights. All functioning members of Stunts Unlimited – there are more than twenty – contract for their own jobs and keep the proceeds, but the group also maintains a stock of stunt equipment, some of it highly sophisticated and developed to its specification, which is rented out to studios. The rentals finance an office and the training programme. Inside the group there is collective control and discipline. 'We police our group,' Needham says. 'If we get a bad report we go right to the production office and ask, "What happened to this man? Was he just being obnoxious? Was he drunk? Did he not show up?" And we have what we call a "slamfest" for guys that get out of shape, who do something they shouldn't. We usually meet at somebody's house, because it's very private. Nobody's allowed there but the members. They read you the rules and regulations, which are: you are on the carpet, and nobody is allowed to say anything good about you. They go right round the room, and if a man has any grievance at all about your conduct or the way you handle yourself, he brings it out. You're not allowed to say one word while all this is going on. Then, when they're through, you tell them what *you* think. The guy on the carpet gets as long as he wants; they can't shut him up. When it's all over, they ask you to leave the room. They then take a vote on whether everything is ironed out between you. It can be pretty rough. I've been in there a few times, and it's been touch and go whether they'd let me stay in the group.'

Despite the difficulties of leading a rationalizing element in a fluid field, Needham is confident about the future of Stunts Unlimited and similar groups. They offer the only hope for a trade that many directors feel has priced itself out of the financially depressed film industry. 'These boys won't put on their pads for less than $500,' one European stunt man commented, 'and they want the road ploughed up before they'll take a fall. They're killing the business.' Needham justifies his high prices. 'A young kid will sometimes come in and do a job under the usual rate, but I personally feel it usually ends up costing the company more money. I can talk to directors and production men and show them my side of the coin. I can say, "This will be best for you. It'll look good on film and it'll give me a safety factor." I've had to do things over – everybody has – but generally you'll get a gag the first shot. But you take a kid or an inexperienced person. They get in there and they goof. Say they're turning over a car. He misses his spot, doesn't get the car over, rolls out of shot – anything can happen. So he has to re-rig the whole thing; get the car back in shape, maybe repair it, plan the thing over. For a big company, it's costing them $5,000 an hour to keep a full unit on the set. Say they blow it twice, and spend an hour and a half re-rigging – you're talking about $10,000 or $12,000. So it pays them to bring me in for $1,250 and get it the first time. A smart company will hire an experienced, knowledgeable guy with a track record to go in and at least set it up. When I work as a stunt coordinator on a job, I don't do any stunts. My place is behind the camera to make sure everybody's in his spot, to make sure they're on time and it looks good. I know some coordinators who will go in and steal all the easy money, picking up a few hundred extra dollars by doing some easy stunts in the gag he's set up. But he causes dissension among his men, and usually ends up with a bad job.'

Today, Needham stunts mainly for a special job, like his second-unit direction on Arthur Penn's *Little Big Man* (1970) in which the action was meant to out-do any previous Western. Among the stunts was a new version of the historic *Stagecoach* gag. The details were different, but in a sense nothing had changed. Canutt's bravado has survived even into this automated new industry because, like death and skill, it is the stunt field's only constant, just as a pursuit of personal fulfilment is its only acceptable motive. 'Penn wanted a man on either horse, and instead of jumping between the horses where you have a board to catch you, we had to jump from horse to horse hooked to a coach and running

ight. Little Big Man:
Ial Needham and
Alan Gibbs

flat out. Myself and Alan Gibbs spent six months perfecting it, working with the horses, getting it set up and everything. After I'd set it up I was going to get in a man to do the job, but then I thought, "What the hell. If somebody's going to be killed, it might as well be me." '

Needham's attitude fits precisely into the new, energetic action cinema of the seventies, one which, in its belief that thrill must be piled on thrill in order to keep the audience's attention, has revived the cliff-hanging tradition of silent serials. As both Hal Needham and Carey Loftin point out, the modern stunt man is more often required to repeat and improve on a stunt of the past than invent new routines. Determined to have a better car chase than *Bullitt* but deprived of Carey Loftin's services by Peter Yates, who hired him to create the varied and dangerous stunts of *The Hot Rock* (1971), including a lurching helicopter trip among Manhattan's skyscrapers, *Bullitt's* producer Philip d'Antoni engaged Bill Hickman, Loftin's 'gunman' driver on *Bullitt*, to handle stunts for *The French Connection* (William Friedkin, 1971), notably a race between an elevated train and a car, with Gene Hackman's car cannoning off stanchions and astonished fellow motorists, which some critics felt outdid its model. (Hickman, as in the previous film, also acted; he is Mulderig, the antagonistic FBI man accidentally shot by Hackman in the final scene.) Everett Creech also had a unique opportunity to outdo the work of a master when he co-ordinated the stunts for *Evel Kneivel* (Marvin Chomsky, 1972), a remarkable examination of the stunt mystique with George Hamilton (who also produced) playing the real-life motor-cycle stunter Bobby 'Evel' Kneivel whose barnstorming leaps over lines of parked cars have made him famous. Chomsky intercuts dramatized incidents with grainy 16mm footage of Kneivel's real exploits, including a terrifying crash in which he broke most of the bones in his body, while the script by Alan Caillou and John Milius gives Kneivel some perceptive comments on the role of public daredevils in American society. Modern life has been robbed of individuality, he reasons, and it is only in death – whether vicarious or real – that we can assert ourselves. 'The only choice left to us is about our death,' he proclaims, 'and mine will be glorious!' In the last shot, the man who calls himself 'the last gladiator of the new Rome' plunges across the desert on his cycle; the camera leaps before him to show the Grand Canyon yawning across his path.

Above *The climax of What's Up, Doc?*

The past also laid a heavy hand on *What's Up, Doc?* (1972), a popular exercise in nostalgia at the expense of Howard Hawks, whose abrasive comedy style is captured only fitfully by director Peter Bogdanovich. Deciding to revive the forties' practice of using action comedy to enliven a flagging finale, Bogdanovich shrewdly hired Paul Baxley to coordinate a precisely violent comic car chase around San Francisco, involving vehicles ranging from a delivery boy's tricycle to a series of cars, and recalling the Abbott and Costello farces on which Loftin and Talmadge worked. (In a rare but commendable departure, all stunt men receive a screen credit.) Gil Perkins has a small role as a driver, while Gil Casper managed the dangerous multiple car chase which, after demolishing other cars, the tall ladder of a sign-painter, a huge sheet of plate glass, garbage cans, a newly cemented drive and a Chinese parade, complete with dragon, ends when all four cars plunge off a wharf into the bay. For the connoisseur of stunt work it was a delightful if melancholy reminder of the days when such things were as essential a component of Saturday afternoon at the movies as one's bag of jaw-breakers, and a kind of epitaph to the great days of the stunt man's trade.

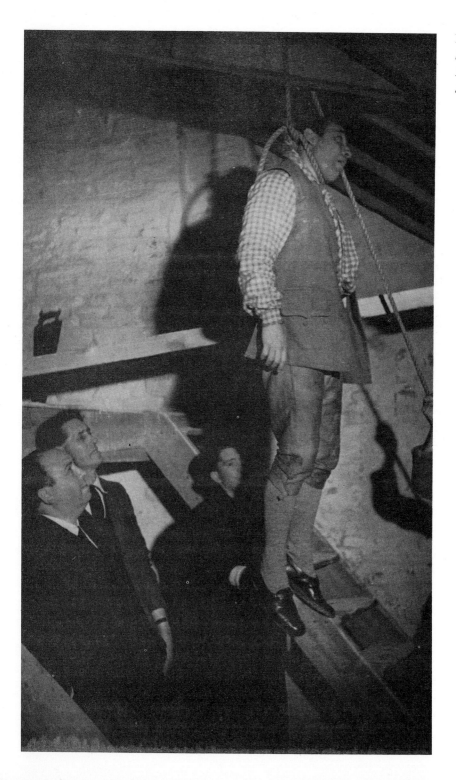

Left *Sam Lee is hung for Alfred Hitchcock (left) on* Jamaica Inn (1939)

Towards a Bibliography

The footnotes below list many of the books and magazines used in researching this book, but a few comments on these and others from which I haven't quoted may be useful to people interested in learning more about the stunt business.

Any cinema bibliography is bound to be as much *caveat* as guide, and this more so than most. All writing about the stunt business – and there isn't much – has to be approached with some scepticism. The secrecy that has always surrounded stunting, a natural unwillingness on the part of stunters to particularize about technique, and the lack of education that prompts most action stars and stunters to employ ghost writers for their memoirs have produced a muddy picture. As I write, the only general book in English about the stunt business is *Stunting in the Cinema* by Derek Ware and Arthur Wise (Constable, 1973). *Les Cascadeurs* by Odilon Cabat and Jacques Levy (Jerome Martineau, Paris, 1966) is an agreeable short study of French stunt men, with the emphasis on Remy Julienne, Jean Sunny and the late Gilles Delamare. Among the few memoirs of stunt men the liveliest, if not most accurate, are those of Joe Bonomo, which he published himself in 1968. *The Strong Man*, with its tabloid presentation and masses of pictures, is as good an introduction as any to the stunt business and, by implication, to the stunter's way of thinking. Of Dick Grace's books, *The Squadron of Death* is a typical ghosted autobiography, muddled in chronology and generally suspect, but *I Am Still Alive*, with its sketches of safety set-ups and undramatically accurate descriptions of stunts, is arresting and informative. One naturally dislikes ghosted books, but Audrey Scott's *I Was a Hollywood Stunt Girl* (Philadelphia, Donovan and Co, 1969) shows the problems of doing it yourself. Miss Scott has not supplemented her memory with research, nor has she the writing skill to extract drama from the events she discusses; the result is dull and reiterative. Though both are spotted with errors (often simple ones, of spelling or chronology) Clyde Beatty's *Jungle Performers* (ghosted by Earl Wilson) and Mack Sennett's *King of Comedy* (by Cameron Shipp) at least evoke the atmosphere of the careers about which they are written. The genuine superiority of reminiscence to false dramatisation makes one look forward to the publication of Yakima Canutt's memoirs, the manuscript of which he kindly allowed me to examine.

I sympathize as much as anyone with John Ford's dictum 'If history and legend conflict, print the legend', but it has taken rather too firm a hold on writing about the action film. Terry Ramsaye's lively *A Million and One Nights* is a fountainhead of falsehood about action stars like Tom Mix, and even otherwise unimpeachable works on early Hollywood are uncritical of doubtful statements by and about Dick Grace and Ormer Locklear, while lesser books contain errors so often retailed that they read like the basic heresies. In his *Movie Horses* (Bobbs, Merrill, 1967), a brief but useful guide to film horse work, Anthony Amaral credits Cliff Lyons with never having hurt a horse or man during his whole career, an assertion which even a cursory glance at the record would disprove, and in *The Fifty Year Decline and Fall of Hollywood* Ezra Goodman makes a similar fallacious claim on behalf of Breezy Eason. A disposition to whitewash can be found in most official histories or prestige biographies; Bosley Crowther's *The Lion's Share* (Dutton, 1957) falsifies the bloodier facts of *Ben-Hur* and *Trader Horn*, Cecil B. DeMille's risible autobiography (W. H. Allen, 1959) elevates him to the level of the lesser saints and ignores in the process the risky or suggestive aspects of his films and private life, and George Carpozi Jnr's *The Gary Cooper Story* (Arlington House, 1970) manages to cover Cooper's entire career without one mention of John Epper or any other double, a far-from-uncommon omission.

The best source of fact on the stunting film, aside from specialist magazines like *Films in Review* and *Classic Movie Collector*, and the news sheets issued by Californian stunt enthusiast John Hagner, are those where it is offered in passing, and therefore thought not worth the effort of falsification. General books on Hollywood like Landery's *Hollywood Is the Place* and Rob Wagner's historic *Film Folk* (The Century, NY, 1918), have brief sections on stunt men sandwiched in between pieces on cameramen, editors and directors. Since the editors of Errol Flynn's *My Wicked, Wicked Ways* (Heinemann, 1960) were more concerned to exploit his sexual athleticism than his exertions on the set, the book has some generous tributes to the stunters with whom Flynn worked, and there is a similar honesty in Brian Connell's *Knight Errant* (Hodder and Stoughton, 1955) about Douglas Fairbanks Jnr. Magazines and newspapers, preferably not those devoted exclusively to film, also provide reliable material, perhaps the best of all outside personal contact. *Photoplay*, that least impressionable of fan magazines, carried many articles on stunt and action stars in its heyday, as did its sad British counterpart *Picturegoer*, though the latter's howler quotient is discouragingly high. My own personal preference runs mainly to back files of American newspapers, particularly the *New York Times* : authoritative, detailed, well-researched and, most important for the student, fully indexed, the *Times* is an invaluable source of material for any film historian.

Notes

1. Kevin Brownlow, *The Parade's Gone By*, Secker & Warburg, 1968.
2. Charlie Chaplin, *My Autobiography*, The Bodley Head, 1964.
3. ibid.
4. *The Silent Picture*, spring 1970.
5. *Photoplay*, November 1929.
6. Harold Lloyd and Wesley Stout, *An American Comedy*, Longmans Green, 1928.
7. Mack Sennett and Cameron Shipp, *King of Comedy*, Doubleday, 1954.
8. *Sight and Sound*, winter 1965/6.
9. ibid.
10. *An American Comedy*.
11. ibid.
12. *The Listener*, 15 April 1971.
13. *New York Times*, 14 June 1914.
14. *Pictures*, undated, 1915.
15. *Films In Review*, January 1968.
16. *Films In Review*, December 1959.
17. ibid.
18. *Photoplay*, February 1922.
19. *The Moving Picture Weekly*, undated, prob. 1921.
20. Terry Ramsaye, *A Million and One Nights*, Simon & Schuster, 1926.
21. *Motion Picture Classic*, September 1932.
22. Unattributed clipping, BFI Library.
23. Anita Loos, *A Girl Like I*, Hamish Hamilton, 1967.
24. *The Listener*, 15 April 1971.
25. *The Parade's Gone By*.
26. *A Girl Like I*.
27. *Films In Review*, March 1963.
28. Charles Landery, *Hollywood Is The Place*, Dent, 1940.
29. Dick Grace, *The Squadron Of Death*, Constable, 1930.
30. *Photoplay*, November 1927.
31. *Picturegoer*, April 1922.
32. *Picturegoer*, April 1924.
33. *New York Times*, 3 September 1944.
34. *The Leader*, 15 September 1945.
35. Dick Grace, *I Am Still Alive*, Rand McNally, 1931.
36. *Photoplay*, November 1927.
37. *Action*, September/October 1971.
38. ibid.
39. *The Silent Picture*, summer 1971.
40. *I Am Still Alive*.
41. *Photoplay*, March 1930.
42. *Films In Review*, March 1960.
43. *Photoplay*, April 1930.
44. *Films In Review*, March 1960.
45. *New York Times*, 3 January 1930.
46. *New York Times*, 17 May 1931.
47. Commentary for documentary *The Pictures That Moved* (Commonwealth Film Unit, 1968).
48. *Classic Movie Collector*, no 20, spring 1968.
49. Joe Bonomo, *The Strongman*, Bonomo Studios, 1968.
50. *Motion Picture World*, 7 August 1920.
51. Robert C. Cannom, *Van Dyke and the Mythical City Hollywood*, Murray and Gee, 1948.
52. ibid.

53. *Photoplay*, November 1929.
54. Clyde Beatty and Earl Wilson, *Jungle Performers*, Robert Hale, 1946.
55. ibid.
56. Charles Higham and Joel Greenberg, *The Celluloid Muse*, Angus and Robertson, 1969.
57. Private letters held by the Lincoln Centre Library of Performing Arts, New York.
58. *Photoplay*, August 1925.
59. BBC radio interview, March 1972.
60. *Photoplay*, February 1928.
61. *New York Times*, 6 July 1930.
62. *Photoplay*, February 1928.
63. Pressbook, *The Hunchback of Notre Dame*.
64. *The Celluloid Muse*.
65. *Popular Mechanics*, January 1935.
66. *Hollywood Is the Place*.
67. Ezra Goodman, *The Fifty Year Decline and Fall of Hollywood*, Simon & Schuster, 1961.
68. *Jungle Performers*.
69. *Films In Review*, October 1955.
70. *The Leader*, 15 September 1945.
71. *New York Times*, 8 May 1949.
72. *Manchester Guardian*, 27 April 1972.
73. Bernard Rosenberg and Harry Silverstein, *The Real Tinsel*, Macmillan, 1970.
74. Mel Gussow, *Don't Say Yes Until I Finish Talking*, Doubleday, 1971.
75. BBC radio interview, April 1972.
76. *Films and Filming*, September 1971.
77. *The Celluloid Muse*.
78. *Picture Play*, May 1916.
79. *Hollywood Studio*, March 1972.

Index of Film Titles

Index of People